USDA

United States Department of Agriculture

Reforestation Systems Compared on Coastal Clearcuts: 10-Year Results

William I. Stein

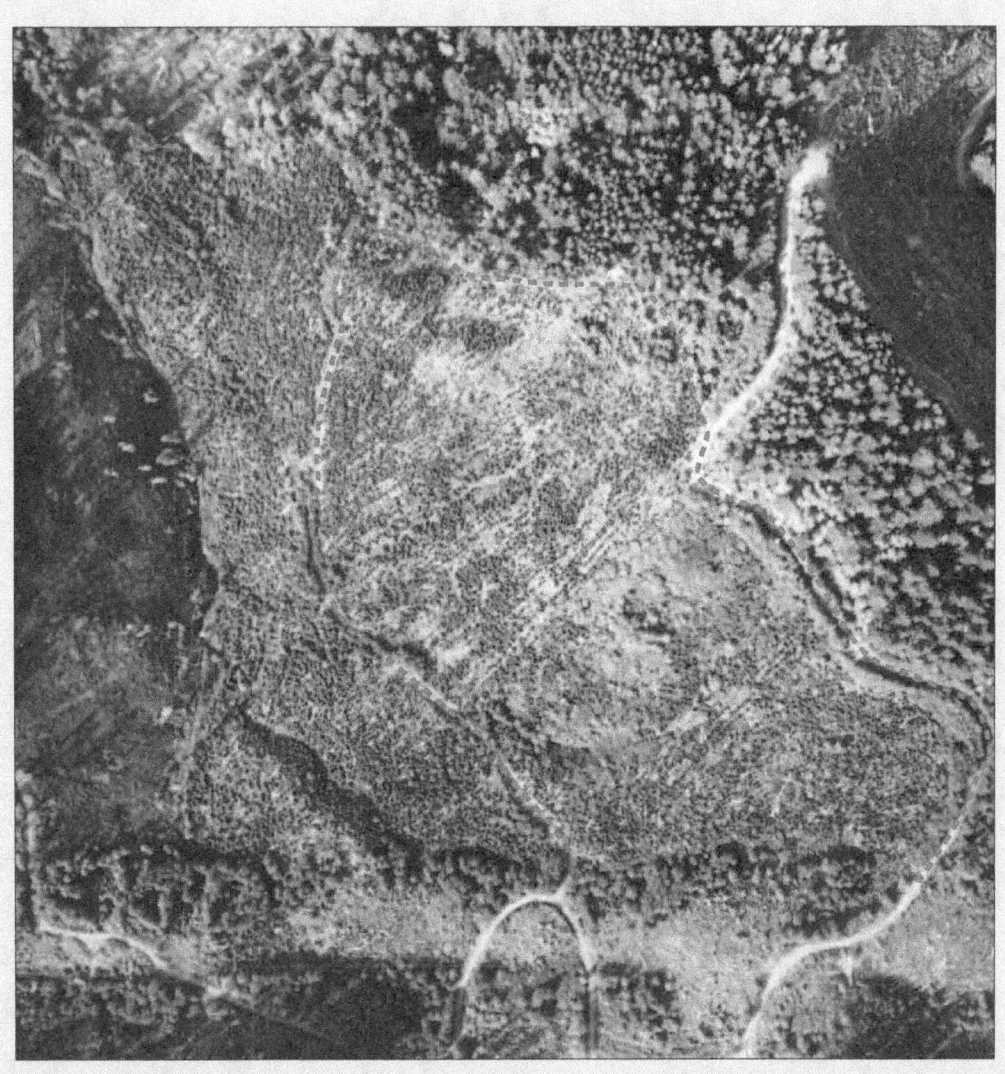

Forest Service

Pacific Northwest Research Station

Research Paper PNW-RP-601

September 2014

Author

William I. Stein is a scientist emeritus, Forestry Sciences Laboratory, 3200 SW Jefferson Way, Corvallis, OR 97331. Most photographs are by the author; exceptions are noted.

Pesticide Precautionary Statement

This publication reports research involving pesticides. It does not contain recommendations for their use, nor does it imply that the uses discussed here have been registered. All uses of pesticides must be registered by appropriate state or federal agencies, or both, before they can be recommended.

CAUTION: Pesticides can be injurious to humans, domestic animals, desirable plants, and fish or other wildlife—if they are not handled or applied properly. Use all pesticides selectively and carefully. Follow recommended practices for the disposal of surplus pesticides and pesticide containers.

Cover:

Aerial view of 10-year-old stands on the Upperten study site (dotted line) that averaged the lowest tree survival and growth. Rows of live trees are clearly visible in the burn and spray-and-burn treatment areas (upper left), and less so in the spray area (lower right), but no rows are visible in the control area (center) covered by dense and tall competing vegetation. (Photo courtesy of USDA Forest Service, Siuslaw National Forest.)

Abstract

Stein, William I. 2014. Reforestation systems compared on coastal clearcuts: 10-year results. Res. Pap. PNW-RP-601. Portland, OR: U.S. Department of Agriculture, Forest Service, Pacific Northwest Research Station. 123 p.

In a large factorial study replicated in six locations, responses of five Douglas-fir (*Pseudotsuga menziesii* (Mirb.) Franco) and two western hemlock (*Tsuga heterophylla* (Raf.) Sarg.) stock types, tubed and untubed, were observed when planted after each of four site preparation treatments with and without later release. In 10 years, more Douglas-fir seedlings survived than did western hemlock seedlings, 69.6 vs. 57.7 percent, averaged much taller, 543.7 vs. 416.6 cm, and larger in diameter, 8.2 vs. 5.2 cm. Survival of tubed seedlings averaged 82.2 percent, untubed 50.5 percent. Seedling survival, height, and diameter averaged highest in areas prepared by preburn spraying followed by broadcast burning and later release. Large Douglas-fir stock (2+1 and large 2+0) outgrew medium or small stock. Stems clipped near ground line in the first 3 years, largely by mountain beavers (*Aplodontia rufa*), comprised two-thirds of all mortality.

In repeated examinations, vegetative cover was measured along linear transects, stem density and height on milacre plots, and live biomass by destructive sampling. Live vegetative cover averaged 52 percent before site preparation. Rapid establishment of pioneering herbaceous species after site preparation soon erased temporary reductions in total cover. The woody shrub component of total cover was reduced from 23.7 to 9.8 percent by broadcast burning and from 28.0 to 2.5 percent by preburn spraying and broadcast burning. By the third examination, woody shrub cover was double as much in control areas as in the spray-and-burn treatments, 42.0 vs. 20.4 percent. Spraying herbicide for release caused only a minor reduction in woody shrub cover. By the 10th year, woody shrub cover averaged 47.9 percent in the control but only 32.1 percent in the spray-and-burn treatment. More tree cover after spray-and-burn than for other site preparation treatments appears attributable to lower competition of woody shrubs throughout the decade. Red alder (*Alnus rubra* Bong.) and salmonberry (*Rubus spectabilis* Pursh) were the most abundant competitors.

Keywords: Reforestation, Pacific Northwest, Coast Range, clearcutting, Douglas-fir, western hemlock, red alder, salmonberry, site preparation, broadcast burning, herbicide spraying, planting, stock types, seedling survival and growth, mesh tubes, natural regeneration, mountain beaver, vegetative competition, release spraying.

Summary

From the late 1940s onward, much effort has been expended on improving the reforestation of clearcuts in the Pacific Northwest. By 1975, the need for a comprehensive side-by-side quantitative comparison of reforestation techniques then in use was clearly evident. Which combinations of site preparation, stock type, protection, and release were most effective, and how great were the differences in stand development over time?

Thus, a very large effort to compare reforestation techniques was jointly undertaken by the Pacific Northwest Research Station and the Siuslaw National Forest. Over 4 years, replications of a factorial study were installed on six large clearcuts located along a north-south distance of about 100 miles, 5 to 16 miles inland from the Pacific coast. This report provides a comprehensive summary of what was produced by different combinations of reforestation techniques, during their first decade, in terms of tree survival and growth under varying amounts of vegetative competition.

The study was designed to solve salient problems encountered in coastal forests of the Pacific Northwest. These forests thrive in a long growing season at low to mid elevations in a generally cool and moist climate. Such conditions are excellent for fostering tree growth as well as fast and dense development of competing vegetation. In clearcutting operations, steep slopes are cable-yarded and much slash remains when older stands are harvested, leaving wildfire hazards, fast growth of pioneering and residual vegetation, and limited access for planting. Many areas have resident mountain beaver (*Aplodontia rufa*) populations; hares, deer, and elk also feed on fast-developing, lush vegetation as well as on any tree seedlings present. The most common harvesting sequence is to clearcut, broadcast burn, plant protected nursery stock, and later, if necessary, apply a release treatment. Was this entire reforestation sequence necessary or even desirable?

The replicated factorial design included comparison of five Douglas-fir (*Pseudotsuga menziesii* (Mirb.) Franco) and two western hemlock (*Tsuga heterophylla* (Raf.) Sarg.) stock types, tubed and untubed, planted in each of four site preparation choices—control, burn only, spray only, and spray and burn.

The six clearcuts used in the study had formerly supported mixed stands primarily of Douglas-fir and red alder (*Alnus rubra* Bong.). All six sites were judged to be brush-threat areas, as indicated by the understory vegetation present. The clearcuts represented topographic and vegetative conditions commonly found in the

Coast Ranges of Oregon and Washington. One quarter of each clearcut received one of the site preparation treatments. Six plots, each containing seven rows of tubed trees and seven rows not tubed, were planted in each quarter and arranged so that three plots could be given an herbicide release treatment later.

Nursery stock of seed sources appropriate to the site were planted on each area. This involved designating a year or more ahead which year-old stocks then growing in the nursery were suitable, then growing container stock from seed of the same sources. Three sizes of 2+0 Douglas-fir were sorted from bundles of stock after these had been routinely processed in the packing shed. Sites were planted in February or March along pre-staked rows, and generally tubed the same day. A single planter planted all 14 rows in the plot.

Average shoot length, root length, stem diameter, oven-dry weight of shoots and roots, and shoot-root ratio were determined from samples of the nursery stock. Size of the nursery stock planted differed widely by site, among stock types and even within a stock type. Tree survival and growth were determined periodically and development of vegetative competition was measured by means of linear transects for percentage of cover, milacre plots for species height and stem density, and biomass samples for weight of dry matter produced.

Ten years after planting, two-thirds of the trees were still alive. Survival averaged 82.2 percent for tubed trees and 50.5 percent for untubed trees. Two-thirds of all seedling mortality was the result of clipping, mainly by mountain beavers. Most clipping occurred in the first 3 years after planting. Large tubed Douglas-fir stock planted after spray-and-burn site preparation and later released survived best and gained the most height and diameter growth. All types of Douglas-fir stock substantially outgrew western hemlock stock. Figure 1 illustrates the gain and cubic volume produced when tree survival, height, and diameter data are combined and expressed as a percentage of the control treatment.

Before site preparation, total live vegetative cover averaged 52 percent on the study sites. The reduction caused by site preparation proved temporary as pioneering herbaceous species soon brought total cover to high levels in all treatments. But marked reductions in the woody shrub component from 23.7 to 9.8 percent by broadcast burning and from 28.0 to 2.5 percent by preburn spraying and broadcast burning had a lasting effect. By the 10th year, woody shrub cover averaged 47.9 percent in the control, only 32.1 percent in the spray-and-burn treatment. Conifer cover at 10 years was highest where woody shrub cover was lowest, and where site preparation had been most intense—the spray-and-burn treatment.

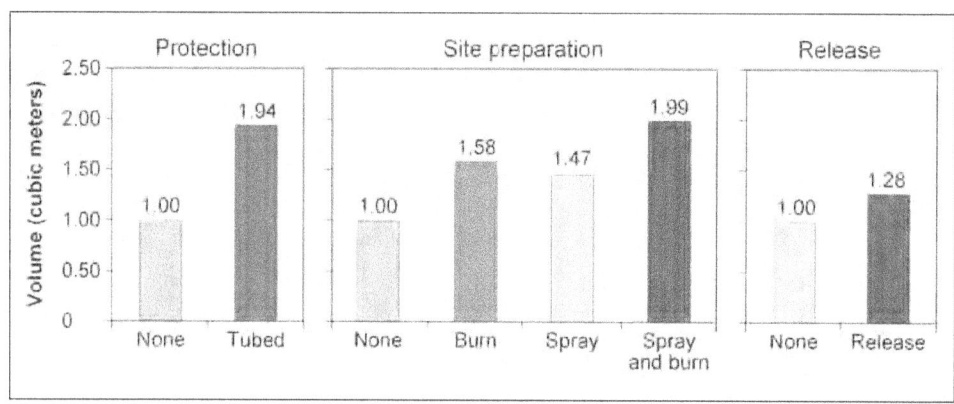

Figure 1—Relative volume per acre at 10 years, control vs. treatment.

Study results amply demonstrate that different reforestation combinations yield different densities and heights in the resulting conifer stands. Information from the study quantitatively supplements what reforestation practitioners had already known from observing results of many field plantings. Results also confirm that the effects of initial stock size carry forward at least a decade.

Every reforestation technique tested has applicability somewhere. What technique combinations to apply in a given situation, depends on management objectives and the conditions on a specific area. Statistically significant differences have been demonstrated for several practices tested, but some gains are small and as a practical matter might not be worth the effort required or cost involved. Study results add to the guidelines available; what choices to use still rest with the informed practitioner prescribing for individual sites.

Contents

1   **Introduction**

2   **Methods**

2   Factorial Design

3   Area Descriptions

7   Site Preparation

9   Planting

10   Seedling Protection

12   Plantation Release

12   Data Collection

14   Data Summaries and Analyses

15   **Conifer Development**

15   Initial Seedling Size

20   Survival

24   Tree Mortality and Damage

31   Tubing for Seedling Protection

32   Height Growth

39   Damage Effects

43   Tree Diameter

49   Stand Analysis

51   Stocking

54   **Vegetation Dynamics**

54   Cover

61   Species Found

68   Live Biomass

72   Vegetation Density and Height

80   **Discussion and Application**

82   Statistical Comparisons

82   Seedling Protection

84   Size of Nursery Stock

87   Site Preparation

90   Release

91   Choosing Treatment Combinations

93   **Acknowledgments**

95   **Units of Measure**

96   **Literature Cited**

101   **Appendix**

List of Tables

6   Table 1—Location and description of Coastal Reforestation Systems Study sites, Siuslaw National Forest

8   Table 2—Treatment history of each study site

9   Table 3—Spray formulation and rate used for site preparation on each site

17   Table 4—Average shoot length, root length, and stem diameter of the nursery stock planted

18   Table 5—Average dry weight of shoots and roots and shoot:root ratio of the nursery stock planted

21   Table 6—Average 10-year survival of untubed and tubed trees by site

21   Table 7—Average 10-year survival of trees by site preparation and site

22   Table 8—Average 10-year survival of trees by species, protection, stock type, and site

24   Table 9—Average 10-year survival of trees not released and released by site

25   Table 10—Causes of seedling mortality by species and year

28   Table 11—Causes of seedling mortality by site, protection, site preparation, and stock type

32   Table 12—Third- and fifth-year position and condition of plastic mesh tubes on live trees

34   Table 13—Average height of untubed and tubed 10-year-old trees by site

35   Table 14—Average height of 10-year-old trees by site and site preparation

36   Table 15—Average height of 10-year-old trees by site, species, protection, and stock type

38   Table 16—Average height of 10-year-old trees by site and release treatment

40   Table 17—Count and average height of undamaged and damaged 10-year-old trees by site and species

43   Table 18—Average tree height at year 0 and 10 by site and slope location

44   Table 19—Growth deformities observed on live 10-year-old trees

44   Table 20—Average diameter at breast height of 10-year-old trees by protection and site

46   Table 21—Average diameter at breast height of 10-year-old trees by site and site preparation

47   Table 22—Average diameter at breast height of 10-year-old trees by site, species, protection, and stock type

48   Table 23—Average diameter at breast height of 10-year-old trees by site and release treatment

50   Table 24—Volume per acre at age 10 for stands resulting from different treatments

52   Table 25—Average height and diameter of the largest 90, 75, and 50 percent of 10-year-old trees in site preparation and release treatments

53 Table 26—Average stocking of planted and naturally established trees by site preparation and release treatments

58 Table 27—Average surface cover over 10 years by site and examination

62 Table 28—Species and groups tallied along line transects

64 Table 29—Species comprising major fractions of vegetative cover during the decade by site preparation and release treatments

70 Table 30—Average dry weight of live vegetation at each examination by site preparation and release treatments

74 Table 31—Number of stems and average height for species found on milacre plots in pre- and post-release examinations

75 Table 32—Stems per species group by examination, site preparation, and release treatments

76 Table 33—Number and average height of main species on milacre plots by examination, site preparation, and release treatments

86 Table 34—Average initial height and rank of stock types and 10th-year status

Appendix

101 Table 35—Seed origin, production nursery, and lifting date for planting stock used in the study

102 Table 36—Damages observed on 10-year-old trees by site, species, and stock type

104 Table 37—Average height of 10-year-old trees by site, site preparation, stock type, and release

107 Table 38—Percentage of total cover for species found on line transects by site, examination, site preparation, and release treatments

Introduction

From the late 1940s onward, much effort has been expended on improving reforestation of clearcuts in the Pacific Northwest. Research by public agencies and private sources led to upgrades in the quality of nursery stock, while many trials of varying scope and intensity widened the array of proven field techniques. Most information resulted from short-term studies of limited scope. By 1975, the need was clearly evident for a comprehensive side-by-side quantitative comparison of the various techniques being used. Which combinations of site preparation, stock type, protection, and release were most effective, and how great were the differences in stand development over time?

Thus, a very large effort to compare reforestation techniques was jointly undertaken by the Pacific Northwest Research Station and the Siuslaw National Forest. Over four years, from 1975 to 1978, replications of a factorial study were installed on six large clearcuts located over a north-south distance of about 100 mi, from 5 to 16 mi inland from the Pacific coast. Limited information produced by the study has been available in several reports and publications (Stein 1984, 1990). This report provides more comprehensive insights on what different reforestation technique combinations produced during the first decade of reforestation in terms of tree survival and growth under varying amounts of vegetative competition.

The key study objective was to develop quantitative comparisons of the site preparation, planting stock, animal protection, and release options that might be used in combination to reforest sites in the Coast Ranges of Oregon and Washington. Many reforestation studies have dealt with one particular phase of reforestation or another; few have measured how site preparation method, planting stock size, and other controllable reforestation factors interrelate to influence tree establishment and early growth. This study aimed to measure such interrelationships. The array of data produced by the study provides a substantial basis for technical and economic guidelines on reforestation of clearcuts near the coast.

Early in the 1980s, a comparison study of site preparation methods as well as another study that compared release methods were installed on the Siuslaw National Forest as part of a nationwide endeavor to compare chemical and other methods of vegetation control. Those studies included several techniques already being compared in this study. Results of both the site preparation and release study have been published (Stein 1995, 1999), thus providing an opportunity to compare results gained from this study with those of similar, but less extensive studies.

A short, comprehensive description of climate, soil, and vegetative conditions in coastal forests was provided in an earlier publication (Stein 1995). Only a few highlights are repeated here to provide the reader some insights on coastal forest conditions that often hinder prompt and adequate reforestation.

In the Pacific Northwest, coastal forests thrive in a long growing season at low- to mid-elevations in a generally cool and moist climate. Soils derived from sandstone are relatively deep and productive for conifers, primarily Douglas-fir (*Pseudotsuga menziesii* (Mirb.) Franco) and western hemlock (*Tsuga heterophylla*) (Raf.) Sarg.). Several hardwoods and tall shrub species also thrive, particularly near streams and water channels. Cable yarding is the most common harvesting system where much of the terrain consists of short, steep slopes. Much slash remains when dense, older stands are harvested, posing an increased risk of wildfire, fast growth of pioneering and residual vegetation, and limited surface access for regeneration. Many areas have resident mountain beaver (*Aplodontia rufa*) populations and these rodents as well as Roosevelt elk (*Cervus elaphus roosevelti*) and black-tailed deer (*Odocoileus hemionus columbianus*) feed on fast-developing, lush vegetation as well as on any tree seedlings present. The most common regeneration sequence was to clearcut, broadcast burn, plant, and protect nursery stock initially and perhaps apply a release treatment several years later. Some foresters questioned whether the entire sequence in such a reforestation system was necessary or even desirable.

Methods

Factorial Design

One complete replication of the study was installed on each of six clearcuts. Each clearcut was divided into four nearly equal quarters, and one of four site preparation treatments—untreated control, herbicide spray only, broadcast burn only, or spray and burn—was applied to each quarter. Six plots, each containing 14 rows of planted nursery stock, were arranged in each quarter so that half the plots could later be given an aerial spray for release (fig. 2). In most instances, rows in each plot were laid out across the contour.

Buffer strips 20 to 30 ft wide across the contour separated adjacent plots. Buffers were 50 ft wide up and down hill between the bottom of one plot and the top of the next. Rows of nursery stock were planted at the usual field spacing (9×9 or 10×10 ft). At 10×10 spacing, each plot was about 140 ft wide and 200 ft long—nearly two-thirds of an acre in size. Buffers and areas not allocated to plots were planted with appropriate stock in the same season as the study trees.

Five types of Douglas-fir nursery stock and two of western hemlock were planted in each plot. Each type of nursery stock was allotted randomly to two rows—one row was tubed with tall plastic mesh tubing to protect trees from deer, elk, rabbits, and mountain beavers, and the other was not. Twenty trees

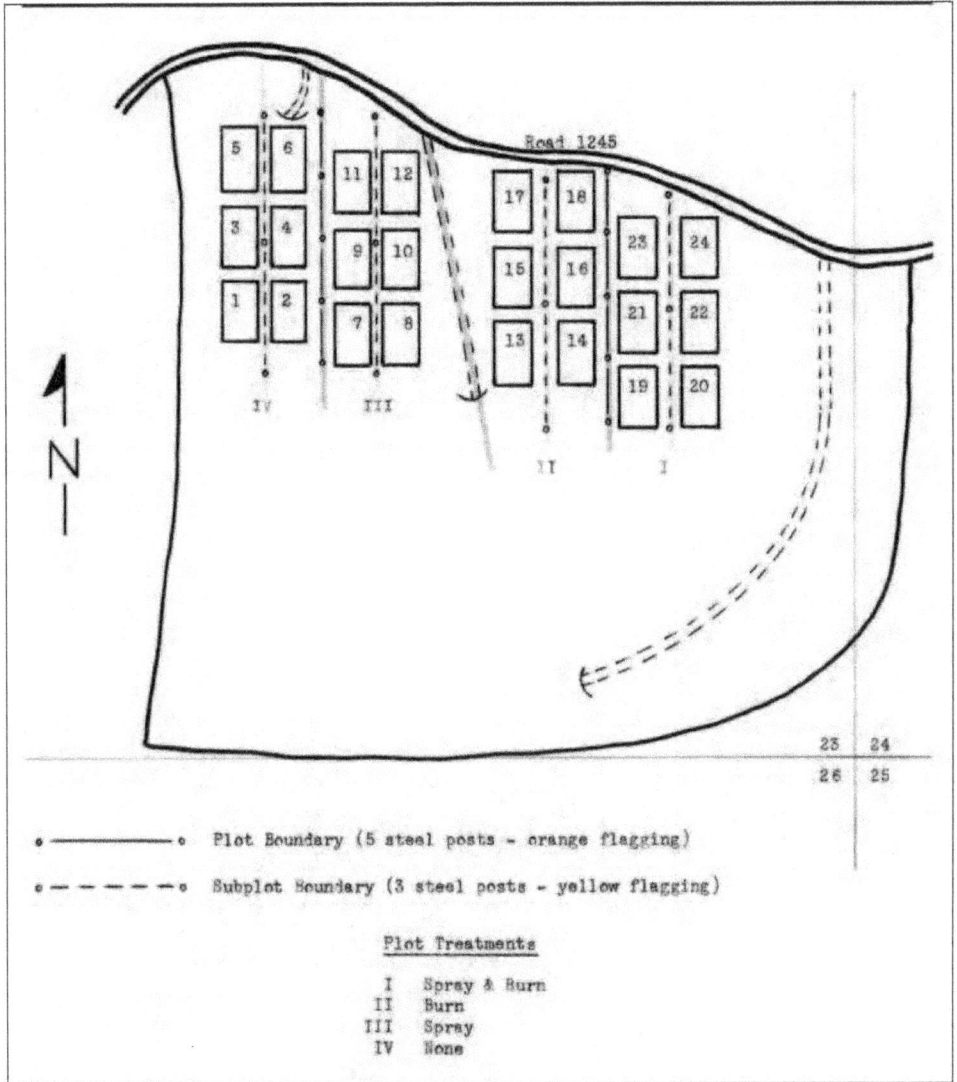

Figure 2—Typical site layout showing area divided for site preparation and release treatments with tree plots arranged in each subdivision.

were planted in each row; when non-plantable spots were encountered, rows were extended into the buffer strip below the plot sufficiently to accommodate 20 trees. A separate random row arrangement of stock and protection level was designated for each of the 24 plots located on one clearcut. The same random allocation was used on all study sites.

Area Descriptions

Six freshly logged clearcuts were chosen as study sites (fig. 3). These areas, widely distributed over the Siuslaw National Forest, represent the range of conditions commonly found in the Oregon Coast Range. The location and descriptive details

Figure 3—Topographic and surface appearance of study sites during installation phases: (A) Pitchfork, fall 1975: (left) sprayed in August; (right) control; (B) Beaver, spring 1977: unburned half, planted; (C) Upperten, August 1976: broadcast burning; unburned study area front and right; (D) Randall, July 1977: (left and center) burned; (right) unburned; (E) Poposchultz, summer 1980: distant view; lighter vegetation marks burned area; (F) Bay's Wolfe, July 1979: control, planted.

for each site are listed in table 1. A short narrative description of each site follows to record the variety of topographic surrounding that sheltered from or exposed study areas to strong coastal winds.

The Pitchfork site, located several miles southwest of Denzer Bridge, is deep within the Coast Range. The site stretches from the southwest to the east side of a finger ridge extending southeastward from a main ridge of Cannibal Mountain to the north. The area is sheltered from strong winds on the south and west by the ridges of Yachats Mountain (1,050 to 1,228 ft in elevation) and to the north by Cannibal Mountain (elevation 1,946 ft). Drainage down canyon is to the east. From the lower of two ridgetop landings in the clearcut, the ground drops steeply between several benches and then more gradually near the stream at the lower edge. Dissection across the contour is minor and gentle. Uppermost study plots are located below the first steep pitch from the landing. Deer and elk frequent the area; elk use appears predominant.

The Beaver site is located downslope from a main ridge (elevation 1,000 ft) trending northwestward that curves within the section to descend toward the southwest. Thus, the area, located on the upper, south side of a short, prominent southwest drainage, is open to strong storm winds. Severe blowdown has occurred on the ridgetop since the study started, and near gale winds were experienced several times on the area. The ocean is visible from upper parts of the site. The slope is steeper near the ridgetop than in the midsection of the clearcut. Dissection across the slope is gentle with the exception of one deep draw, and the south quarter of the area is basin-like. Study plots start near the ridge road and extend only part way down in the clearcut (fig. 2). Deer use on the area is common; elk infrequent.

The Upperten site is on the southeast slope of a side ridge that extends southwest from Klickitat Ridge, a main northwest-southeast oriented ridge to the north. The site is in the upper, sheltered basin of Tenmile Creek, surrounded by higher ridges in all directions except for the actual winding stream drainage to the south. Surrounding peaks include Klickitat Mountain to the northeast (elevation 2,307 ft), Cummins Peak to the west (2,475 ft), and Saddle Mountain to the south (2,297 ft). Moderate slopes on the area are reasonably uniform except for the drainage of a small stream on the north side. Dissection across the contour is moderate, with a pronounced draw and ridge within the area (see cover photo). Study plots span the area between upper and lower roads. The site is within a protected elk management area and adjacent to a power line right-of-way. Elk use is regular and heavy; grazing cattle have also been seen, and deer frequent the area.

The Randall site is the furthest inland of the six study sites. It is located almost entirely on a north to northwest slope, gentle at the top and very steep in

Table 1—Location and description of Coastal Reforestation Systems Study sites, Siuslaw National Forest

Descriptor	Study site					
	Pitchfork	Beaver	Upperten	Randall	Poposchultz	Bay's Wolfe
Ranger district	Alsea	Waldport	Waldport	Alsea	Mapleton	Hebo
Township and range	14S, 10W	12S, 11W	15S, 11W	12S, 9W	19S, 11W	3S, 9W
Section	27, N ½	23, SE ¼	25, SW ¼	14, SW ¼	14, NE ¼	22–23, N ½
Area (ac)	79	82	73	45	128	122
Elevation range (ft)	400–750	600–900	850–1,250	1,000–1,400	500–750	640–880
Distance to ocean (air miles)	11	5	8	16	9	10
Aspect (degrees of azimuth):						
Control	180	200–260	90–120	340–90	210–220	345
Spray	100–160	200–320	110–180	290–360	190–210	265–280
Burn	225	200–220	120–145	290–350	100–180	285
Spray and burn	205	200–340	170	10–320	140–200	115–340
Slope (percent):						
Control	35	10–60	45–65	15–50	25–30	25
Spray	25–45	30–60	0–45	50–55	20–35	10–55
Burn	35	15–60	35–50	60	20–50	20–25
Spray and burn	35	15–25	40–55	45–70	10–50	10–60
Topography	Alternately steep and gentle	Slope moderates downhill	Steep draws and ridges	One main draw to north	Moderate slopes with benches	Moderate slopes with draws
Soil type[a]	Slickrock	Tolovana-Reedsport	Hembre	Preacher-Bohannon-Slickrock	Slickrock	Klootchie, Lebam
Texture	Gravelly loam	Medial silt loam	Silt loam	Slickrock loam	Gravelly loam	Medial silt loam

[a] Source: National Resources Conservation Service, National Cooperative Soil Survey, Web Soil Survey, January 2012.

a short midsection. Higher ridges rise to 1,484 ft to the southwest, and elevation drops to less than 500 ft in a narrow valley within a mile to the northeast. Dissection across the contour is moderate except for one major draw. Study plots occupy most of the area except for the slopes leading into the central draw. Deer frequent the area regularly; elk infrequently.

The Poposchultz site is located primarily on the south side of a rounded ridge between forks of the Maple Creek drainage. Higher ridges occur within 1 to 4 mi to the south (Mount Popocatepetl, elevation 1,020 ft), east (Goodwin Peak, 1,826 ft), and north (1,130 ft). Stream bottoms less than one-half mile away to the south and west are under 100 ft in elevation. Because of its westward exposure within sight of the ocean, the higher parts of the area are exposed to frontal winds. The area is generally a mixture of short steep slopes, benches, and gentle terrain, with the steepest slopes facing toward the east. Dissection is variable and includes some slumps and concave terrain. Study plots are located from the ridgetop southward, but run on a bias across the contour. Deer use is common; elk use less frequent.

The Bay's Wolfe site slopes primarily westward toward Wolfe Creek which flows southwestward. An intervening ridge system to the southwest (Buzzard Butte, elevation 1,684 ft) blocks direct exposure to the ocean, and 1,000 ft or higher ridge systems are located to the west, north, and east. The southern part of the study area has a knoll and saddle topography; the rest slopes reasonably uniformly from the upper road westward. Dissection across the contour is moderate. Study plots are located from the road straight down slope except in the saddle and knoll where they are bounded by upper and lower roads. Deer use on the area is common, elk use more limited.

Site Preparation

Study replications were installed on one or two sites per year. Although the same site preparation treatments were applied on each area, some variation in techniques was inherent owing to the site and season, the administration of work, the crews or contractors involved, and many other factors. Research personnel assisted in site selection and study layout. All site treatments and contracts were carried out under the direction of ranger district personnel.

The most suitable clearcut of several available in each geographic location at the time was selected for the study. Suitability considerations included adequate size, uniformity of topography, high competitive shrub potential, possibility of limiting the slash burn, and logging completed recently or likely to be completed in time. All clearcuts selected had supported mixed stands of alder and conifers, and residuals of woody shrubs were common. Logs were removed from all study areas by cable systems.

The four site preparation treatments were applied to quarters of a clearcut or to quarters of the study area delineated within a very large clearcut. Site treatments were assigned at random as much as possible, but topographic position sometimes dictated which half of the area was to be slash-burned. Slash burning was limited successfully; less than an acre of slash was burned unintentionally (Upperten). The date treatments were applied in each study area are listed in table 2.

Table 2—Treatment history of each study site

| Study site | Treatment period | | | | |
	Logged	Sprayed	Burned	Planted	Released
Pitchfork	1974–75	8/1/75	9/18/75	3/9–18/76	10/7–8/78
Beaver	2/76–6/76	6/7/76	8/28/76	2/10–18/77	10/13/79
Upperten	1974–76	6/5/76	8/22/76	2/2–8/77	10/6/78
Randall	1976	5/29/77	7/15/77	2/22–24/78	10/9/80
Poposchultz	7/76–12/76	5/27–28/77	7/24/77	2/24–3/2/78	9/29/80
Bay's Wolfe	11/76–2/77	6/9/77 and 5/78	10/13/78	3/12–27/79	9/23/80

Descriptive information about each treatment includes:

Control—
Slash and live vegetation on control areas were not treated after logging. None of the study sites was YUM (yarded unmerchantable material) yarded; hence, unmerchantable logs and tops of alder and conifers were common, even abundant, on the areas. In at least one instance (Randall), unmerchantable live alders that had developed along an adjacent older road and skid road were slashed after logging had been completed. Such slashing was done where needed, not just in the quarter designated as the control.

Spray only—
A broad-spectrum herbicide spray was aerially applied in the growing season. Formulations involving trichlorophenoxyacetic acid (2,4,5-T) were state-of-the-art when the study started and were used on all six study areas, on the last three by specific authorization. Similar formulations were used on all study sites, but there were minor variations owing to time and local practice. Spray rate varied from 10 to 20 gallons per acre. The spray formulations are shown on a common basis in table 3.

Burn only—
Slash and live vegetation were broadcast-burned when conditions were dry enough for a good burn, and smoke management requirements could be met. Good clean

Table 3—Spray formulation and rate used for site preparation on each site

Study site	Acid equivalent per acre			Solution per acre[a]	
	Picloram	2,4-D	2,4,5-T	Wetting agent	Total
	- - - - - - - *Pounds* - - - - - - -			- - - - *Gallons* - - - -	
Pitchfork	0.5	—	3.0	0.15	20
Beaver	0.5	2.0	2.0	0.46	15
Upperten	0.5	2.0	2.0	0.75	15
Randall	0.5	2.0	2.0	0.05	15
Poposchultz	0.5	2.0	2.0	0.01	10
Bay's Wolfe	0.5	2.0	2.0	0.05	10
	1.0	4.0	—	0.10	20

[a] All chemicals were dissolved in water except at Pitchfork where 0.5 gallon of diesel was included.

burns were obtained on Pitchfork, Upperten, and Poposchultz. A good burn was also obtained on Beaver, but some dead carcasses of tall salmonberry remained. Burning did not kill some shrub clumps and grassy spots on the north slope at Randall. Slash burning was not accomplished the first season that Bay's Wolfe was available. Thus, vegetation developed an additional year at Bay's Wolfe before treatment. Results of burning in the second autumn were highly variable, and much rapidly developing salmonberry escaped unscathed.

Spray and burn—
One quarter of each study site was sprayed before it was burned. The same formulation and timing were used for the preburn spray as were used on the quarter that was only sprayed. Burning of slash followed spraying by 7 to 19 weeks (table 2). Both quarters to be burned on a study area were completed on the same day. Good burns were obtained on spray-and-burn quarters at Pitchfork, Upperten, and Poposchultz. At Beaver and Randall, spray-and-burn quarters received somewhat better burns than the quarters only burned. At Bay's Wolfe, the spray-and-burn quarter received a second preburn spray before it was slash-burned in the second year after logging. A clean burn resulted, in marked contrast to the result on the quarter that was only burned.

Planting

The trees planted on each study site were grown from seed of sources judged suitable for that site. In some instances, stock of the same origin was suitable for more than one of the sites. The seed origin and the nursery at which each lot of stock was produced are listed in the appendix (table 35).

Every effort was made to obtain stock of the same or of similar origin for the seven classes of stock used at an individual site, short of growing all stock specifically for the area. The general approach was to identify 1 year ahead of planting the production lots to be used. Plans were built around first-year Douglas-fir seedlings already being grown for use on the area. The 2+0 Douglas-fir stock would be obtained one season later from this lot. Whenever available, seed of the same source was also allocated for production of the container Douglas-fir. Douglas-fir 2+0 stock of the same or of a similar source was also identified for production of 2+1 stock. When possible, seed for production of western hemlock container seedlings was also matched with bare-root western hemlock already growing in production beds. The bare-root western hemlocks for all but one site were plug+1 stock—grown the first year in a container and the second year in a transplant bed.

Container stock was produced in several kinds of container. The container type in which the stock was grown is indicated in parentheses in table 35. There was no intent to directly compare container effects, but initial size of the container seedlings reflects the regime and container in which they were grown. Large, medium, and small bare-root Douglas-fir stock was obtained by sorting nursery-processed bundles of 2+0 Douglas-fir into size classes. Because the average size of the seedlings produced varied from year to year, the average size of each class of 2+0 Douglas-fir stock also varied from year to year. The actual and relative sizes of stock used at each study site are presented in the "Conifer Development" section.

At each site, trees were planted by either a Forest Service or contractor crew. The usual planting requirements were practiced such as care of planting stock, microsite clearing, and planting technique. Trees were planted at the usual spacing prescribed for the site—10×10 ft at Pitchfork and 9×9 ft on the other five sites. Row ends and planting spots in each row were prestaked, generally with color-coded stakes. Stock for each row was packaged and labeled in advance to avoid confusion in the field. Usually, a single planter planted all 14 rows in a plot to minimize planter effects (fig. 4). If the planter encountered non-plantable area at or near the staked point, he was instructed to pull the stake and extend the row at the downhill end enough to accommodate all 20 trees. Planting on all sites was completed in February or March of the scheduled year.

Seedling Protection

Half the rows of tree seedlings, as designated randomly before planting, were protected with tubing. Commercially produced mesh tubing was used for Douglas-fir, nominally 30 or 36 inches tall and two to three inches in diameter (fig. 5). Six-inch-diameter tubes were made up for western hemlock by each ranger district

Figure 4—All 14 rows in a prestaked plot were planted by the same planter.

Figure 5—Plastic mesh tubing was installed on trees given protection (left photo), usually on the day they were planted.

from rolls of mesh with the same diamond pattern as those purchased. Tubes were supported by 4-foot-long wooden stakes—some were lath and others were cut narrower and thicker. Twist ties were used to hold the tube to the stake. Whether tubes were supported by one or two stakes and by two or three ties differed according to district preferences.

Rows of trees designated for protection were to be tubed as soon as possible after planting. This meant the tree should be tubed on the same day it was planted. In some circumstances tubing was delayed for one or more days. In one recorded instance, trees in several rows at Bay's Wolfe required replanting because clipping damage was inflicted on trees where tubing was delayed to the third day.

Plantation Release

One-half the area subjected to each site preparation treatment was later aerially sprayed with glyphosate (fig. 6). The release spray was applied in early autumn when vegetation was nearing the end of its third growing season. This meant that on two study areas—Upperten and Bay's Wolfe—the release spray was applied when tree seedlings were completing their second growing season, not their third. From a study design standpoint, it appeared more important to apply the release spray to vegetation at the same stage of development at all locations rather than to trees of comparable age when both objectives could not be fulfilled simultaneously. Planting had to be delayed one year on Bay's Wolfe till slash was burned. On Upperten, logging over an extended period permitted vegetation development to be more advanced on the unburned part of the area than on the burned part.

Glyphosate was applied at a rate of 1 quart in 9.75 gallons of water per acre. It was applied to half the area of every treatment even though release was not necessarily needed after some site preparation treatments.

Data Collection

Periodic examinations were made to monitor the development and fate of tree seedlings. The first examination, an observation for appearance, initial height, apparent vigor, biotic damage, and microsite condition, was made by early summer of the first season. A key purpose of the initial examination was to determine if seedlings appeared healthy. Most seedlings on all sites were healthy. Heights of surviving seedlings were measured to the nearest centimeter after the first, third, fifth, seventh, and tenth growing seasons. Field crews were instructed to measure seedlings as they found them without changing tube position or vegetative competition. Damage of consequence observed on seedlings was recorded and attributed to cause where possible. The status of each seedling relative to competing vegetation was also rated at each examination.

Figure 6—Bands of browned vegetation in April after release spraying the previous autumn: (A) Beaver; (B) Bay's Wolfe.

An estimate of vegetative cover on each study area was obtained by examination of 40 vegetation transects—10 in each site treatment, thus five in each release treatment. Cover and composition were determined for the first time before site preparation and periodically afterward on all six sites. The initial sampling of vegetation occurred before tree plots were installed. Hence, vegetation transects and tree plots do not fully coincide as to area covered.

Vegetative cover was determined repeatedly along the same 50-ft-long line transects oriented downhill. All transects represent slope distances as measured by a tape stretched as horizontal as possible. Increments of vegetation were measured to the nearest 0.1 ft as they occurred within a half-inch band below and above the stretched-out tape. Slash increments not covered by vegetation were measured at each examination and also increments of bare ground from the third examination onward. Tree, shrub, and major herbaceous species were recorded by species or species groups. The rest of the herbaceous species were lumped as miscellaneous herbaceous.

Stem counts were made on three milacre plots located 10 ft from and at right angle to the 0-, 25-, and 50-ft points along each transect line. All woody vegetation and ferns whose main stems were rooted in the milacre were counted. Height was measured from ground line to where the top bulk of a species' crown occurred.

During vegetation measurements, biomass samples were also collected. Center stakes for biomass plots were located 5 ft to the left and at right angle to the 10-, 25-, and 40-ft point along each transect line. In consecutive examinations, destructive samples were taken in round-the-clock order starting with the two o'clock position 2 ft from the staked center point. Live vegetation encompassed by a circular hoop that enclosed an area of 2 ft^2 was cut and placed in separate bags for woody, herbaceous or tree material. When vegetation overhanging the sample column could not be reached, a comparable amount of the same species was collected nearby.

Data Summaries and Analyses

This study has spanned the era from manually recording data on field sheets to data entry entirely into electronic files. All tree and vegetation data were initially recorded manually on field sheets. Early on, a systematic protocol was devised for checking tree data. Individual field sheets were visually scanned line by line to remedy inconsistencies and omissions. After electronic entry, data were checked against field sheets again line by line, and needed corrections were made.

Statistical tests are focused on 10-year stand development. Did tree survival and growth differ among technique combinations tested, and if so, how much?

The study has a split-split-split-plot structured on a randomized complete block design. Sites are presumed to be random effects and all treatments are fixed effects. Analyses were made in SAS PROC MIXED with preplanned contrasts included. The dependent variables for 10th-year tree data—survival, height, and diameter— were individually subjected to analysis of variance, after data from the three tree plots in each eighth of a study site were combined.

Type 3 tests of fixed effects had this form and outcome:

Fixed effects	Degrees of freedom		Tree		
			Survival	Height	Diameter
	Numerator	*Denominator*	- - - - - - - - *Pr > F* - - - - - - - -		
Site preparation	3	15	0.066	0.195	0.293
Seedling protection	1	20	<.001	<.001	<.001
Site × protection	3	20	.975	.856	.807
Stock types	6	240	<.001	<.001	<.001
Site × stock types	18	240	.404	.999	.973
Protection × stock types	6	240	.874	.781	.893
Site × protection × stock types	18	240	.819	.999	.998
Release	1	280	.026	<.001	<.001
Site × release	3	280	.052	<.001	<.001
Protection × release	1	280	.056	.099	.247
Site × protection × release	3	280	.506	.128	.252
Stock × release	6	280	.864	.594	.487
Site × stock × release	18	280	.996	.821	1.000
Protection × stock × release	6	280	.563	.793	.905
Site × protection × stock × release	18	280	.839	.994	.997

An array of contrasts were also tested, each having 1 and 240 degrees of freedom.

Descriptive data observed on individual trees such as cause and timing of mortality, damage on live trees, and condition of cages were summed to identify factors that influenced 10-year stand development.

Similarly, data on vegetative cover, biomass, and height of species are indicative of the different levels of competition that trees were subjected to during the decade of stand development. Vegetation data are not tied to specific tree plots; they indicate the average vegetative competition within each eighth of every study site. Hence, correlation analyses do not appear germane or necessary.

P-values are included in text statements founded on statistical tests. P-values up to P = 0.3 are given, as readers may value any indication of trends in a very large study where only some of the many variables could be controlled and tested.

Conifer Development

Initial Seedling Size

Initial size of seedlings used in the study was determined by sampling trees from each type of stock planted. A representative sample was drawn from two or three bundles or bags of each lot when lots were subdivided into color-coded packages prior to planting or at completion of planting. Generally, a larger sample was taken than needed and later randomly reduced to the actual number measured and weighed.

After thorough washing in the laboratory, 25 trees from each stock type and site were measured individually for shoot length, root length, and stem diameter; then oven-dried at 70 °C for 48 hours for determination of shoot- and root-dry weight. Shoot:root ratios were later calculated from the shoot- and root-dry weights. Shoot length was measured in centimeters and tenths from the base of the terminal bud to the root collar. The root collar was defined as located 1 cm below the coty-ledonal scars. Stem diameter was measured to the nearest millimeter at the root collar. Lengths were determined on stretched out roots; enough tension was applied to reduce but not eliminate curves and kinks. Roots of some container seedlings were not measured; for these, the length of the container has been listed as the nominal root length.

Size of nursery stock planted varied among study sites as well as between stock types (tables 4 and 5; fig. 7). Considering averages for all stock types combined, differences were relatively minor among study sites in shoot length and stem diameter of the stock planted. Average shoot length ranged from 25.0 to 29.1 cm and stem diameter from 4.2 to 4.9 mm. Stock size differences were two-fold or greater between sites for average shoot dry weight, 3.3 to 8.2 g, and root dry weight, 1.5 to 3.7 g, and intermediate for shoot:root ratio, 1.6 to 2.6, and root length, 20.6 to 27.3 cm. Seedlings planted at Pitchfork averaged larger in all attributes except shoot:root ratio than seedlings planted at other study sites.

The range in average size between the largest and smallest type of stock was generally more than double—shoot length, 18.9 to 39.1 cm; root length, 17.8 to 29.5 cm; stem diameter, 2.4 to 7.0 mm; shoot dry weight, 0.9 to 11.3 g; root dry weight, 0.4 to 5.8 g; and shoot:root ratio, 1.6 to 3.3. Even small bare-root Douglas-fir stock averaged larger than container Douglas-fir or western hemlock stock, except in shoot length. The average shoot:root ratio was low even for large 2+0 Douglas-fir but somewhat high for bare-root hemlock.

On all sites, the averages for large, medium, and small 2+0 Douglas-fir stock reflect the shoot length differences that were the primary criterion on which they were sorted. The difference in shoot length between adjacent sizes averaged about 10 cm. Except for root length, the other attributes have the same downward grada-tion between the three sizes of 2+0 Douglas-fir stock. As roots were trimmed during packing, one could expect smaller and perhaps less consistent differences in root length among the three 2+0 Douglas-fir stock types.

On three of the six study sites (Pitchfork, Randall, and Bay's Wolfe), average shoot length of 2+1 Douglas-fir stock was shorter than for large 2+0 Douglas-fir

Table 4—Average shoot length, root length, and stem diameter of the nursery stock planted

Species and stock type	Study site						Average and standard error	Range of sizes	
	Pitchfork	Beaver	Upperten	Randall	Poposchultz	Bay's Wolfe		Minimum	Maximum
Shoot length:	*Centimeters*								
Douglas-fir:									
Transplant 2+1	41.2	41.5	37.6	31.6	39.0	31.3	37.0 ± 0.6	21.0	54.0
Large 2+0	47.0	35.7	37.2	38.3	35.9	40.5	39.1 ± 0.6	25.1	67.0
Medium 2+0	35.5	26.0	27.3	27.0	27.0	28.8	28.6 ± 0.4	20.0	46.0
Small 2+0	25.4	17.7	19.9	15.0	15.0	20.1	18.9 ± 0.4	8.9	31.0
Container	18.9	16.9	16.9	17.3	18.1	29.7	19.7 ± 0.5	10.2	38.2
Western hemlock:									
Bare root	22.5	20.9	30.9	—	—	32.3	26.6 ± 0.8	13.5	45.5
Container	12.4	19.0	25.3	20.6	21.7	21.3	20.1 ± 0.6	8.7	43.0
All types	29.0	25.4	27.9	25.0	26.1	29.1	27.2 ± 0.3	8.7	67.0
Root length:	*Centimeters*								
Douglas-fir:									
Transplant 2+1	33.7	32.8	23.4	33.8	30.4	23.1	29.5 ± 0.6	15.5	62.9
Large 2+0	38.6	31.6	35.1	24.3	20.1	20.3	28.3 ± 0.8	8.0	61.0
Medium 2+0	32.3	30.8	29.8	25.1	25.1	21.4	27.4 ± 0.5	13.5	49.0
Small 2+0	34.4	24.8	21.4	21.4	21.4	21.5	24.1 ± 0.5	11.6	57.0
Container	16.0	16.0	16.0	25.2	24.5	21.7	19.9 ± 0.4	16.0	42.5
Western hemlock:									
Bare root	25.3	23.1	24.7	—	—	20.5	23.4 ± 0.6	11.0	42.0
Container	11.0	25.0	16.0	21.5	17.9	15.6	17.8 ± 0.4	11.0	26.6
All types	27.3	26.3	23.8	25.2	23.2	20.6	24.4 ± 0.2	8.0	62.9
Stem diameter:	*Millimeters*								
Douglas-fir:									
Transplant 2+1	7.8	7.6	7.5	6.3	7.8	5.1	7.0 ± 0.15	3.0	11.8
Large 2+0	9.5	6.3	5.5	5.8	5.1	6.0	6.4 ± 0.16	3.1	12.2
Medium 2+0	6.0	4.6	4.4	4.3	4.3	5.0	4.8 ± 0.08	3.3	7.8
Small 2+0	5.3	3.4	3.9	3.7	3.7	3.7	4.0 ± 0.09	2.2	7.5
Container	1.8	2.7	2.7	2.5	2.9	3.0	2.6 ± 0.04	1.2	3.5
Western hemlock:									
Bare root	2.3	3.1	4.4	—	—	3.7	3.4 ± 0.11	1.2	6.9
Container	1.3	2.0	2.7	3.1	2.7	2.6	2.4 ± 0.06	1.1	4.6
All types	4.9	4.2	4.4	4.3	4.4	4.2	4.4 ± 0.07	1.1	12.2

Table 5—Average dry weight of shoots and roots and shoot:root ratio of the nursery stock planted

Species and stock type	Study site						Average and standard error	Range of sizes	
	Pitchfork	Beaver	Upperten	Randall	Poposchultz	Bay's Wolfe		Minimum	Maximum
Shoot dry weight:						Grams			
Douglas-fir:									
Transplant 2+1	15.0	12.3	12.7	8.0	14.4	5.3	11.3 ± 0.50	1.7	30.7
Large 2+0	24.2	7.4	5.9	5.3	5.1	7.4	9.2 ± 0.64	1.3	41.8
Medium 2+0	8.7	3.7	3.5	2.5	2.5	4.3	4.2 ± 0.21	1.4	14.2
Small 2+0	7.0	1.5	2.2	1.6	1.6	2.2	2.7 ± 0.20	0.5	14.0
Container	0.9	0.8	0.8	1.1	1.1	2.0	1.1 ± 0.04	0.2	2.9
Western hemlock:									
Bare root	1.4	1.4	3.4	—	—	2.6	2.2 ± 0.16	0.4	8.9
Container	0.4	0.6	1.3	1.4	0.8	1.0	0.9 ± 0.05	0.2	3.2
All types	8.2	4.0	4.3	3.3	4.3	3.5	4.6 ± 0.18	0.2	41.8
Root dry weight:						Grams			
Douglas-fir:									
Transplant 2+1	8.1	6.6	5.2	5.0	7.5	2.7	5.8 ± 0.25	1.1	14.4
Large 2+0	9.2	3.8	2.2	2.8	2.6	2.9	3.9 ± 0.24	1.0	14.0
Medium 2+0	3.8	2.3	1.6	1.6	1.6	1.9	2.1 ± 0.10	0.7	6.7
Small 2+0	3.3	1.1	1.1	1.5	1.5	1.3	1.6 ± 0.09	0.5	5.9
Container	0.5	0.5	0.5	0.8	0.6	0.9	0.6 ± 0.03	0.2	1.8
Western hemlock:									
Bare root	0.4	0.7	1.5	—	—	0.6	0.8 ± 0.08	0.1	6.2
Container	0.2	0.2	0.5	1.0	0.4	0.4	0.4 ± 0.03	0.1	2.0
All types	3.7	2.2	1.8	2.1	2.4	1.5	2.3 ± 0.08	0.1	14.4
Shoot:root ratio, dry weight basis:						Ratio			
Douglas-fir:									
Transplant 2+1	1.9	1.9	2.5	1.6	1.9	2.0	2.0 ± 0.04	1.0	3.9
Large 2+0	2.7	2.0	2.8	1.9	1.9	2.6	2.3 ± 0.05	0.9	5.1
Medium 2+0	2.3	1.6	2.3	1.7	1.7	2.3	2.0 ± 0.05	1.1	3.6
Small 2+0	2.1	1.4	2.1	1.1	1.1	1.7	1.6 ± 0.04	0.7	3.0
Container	1.9	1.7	1.7	1.5	2.0	2.3	1.9 ± 0.05	0.9	4.3
Western hemlock:									
Bare root	3.8	2.3	2.7	—	—	4.4	3.3 ± 0.13	1.3	8.5
Container	2.0	2.8	2.6	1.5	2.5	3.0	2.4 ± 0.07	0.4	4.5
All types	2.4	2.0	2.4	1.6	1.8	2.6	2.1 ± 0.03	0.4	8.5

Figure 7—Relative size of stock planted at Pitchfork (A) and Beaver (B): stock types from left—Douglas-fir bare-root 2+1; 2+0 large, medium, small; container; western hemlock bare-root 1+1, and container seedling.

stock. Douglas-fir 2+1 stock was also smaller than large 2+0 stock in several other size attributes at Pitchfork and Bay's Wolfe. On five of the six sites, shoot:root ratio was slightly lower for 2+1 Douglas-firs than for large 2+0 Douglas-firs.

These generalizations about stock characteristics need to be kept in mind as seedling survival and growth results are evaluated:

1. In general, stock used on the six study sites differed in size, but least in shoot length and stem diameter, the attributes most commonly observed.
2. There was a large range in average size among stock types. The stock types ranked in the same order reasonably consistently with Douglas-fir 2+1 and large 2+0 stock largest, and container Douglas-fir and all western hemlock stock substantially smaller.
3. The difference between the minimum and maximum value for each size attribute indicates that each stock type had a wide range of individual tree sizes within it.

Survival

Two-thirds of the 40,263 trees[1] planted in the study were alive 10 years later (table 6). Tree survival differed greatly between sites, however. At Poposchultz, 82.5 percent of the trees were alive at 10 years, but only 51.2 percent at Upperten.

Protection provided by mesh tubing significantly aided tree survival, 82.2 vs. 50.5 percent (P < 0.001). Among sites, the range in average survival was much less for protected trees, 91.7 to 70.8 percent than for unprotected trees, 75.2 to 32.5 percent (table 6).

For the entire study, the three site preparation treatments strongly tended to aid tree survival (P = 0.066), but results were not consistent at individual sites (table 7). For example, at Randall, tree survival was practically the same in all treatments, 67.7 percent in the control and 68.4, 68.4, and 71.6 in the other three. At Pitchfork, Poposchultz, and Bay's Wolfe, tree survival in the control equaled or exceeded survival in one of the site preparation treatments.

Ten-year survival of Douglas-fir stock averaged significantly greater (P < 0.001) than for western hemlock stock, 69.6 vs. 57.7 percent. Western hemlock survival averaged consistently lower than Douglas-fir on all sites (table 8).

---

[1] The balanced design totaled 40,320 trees. At the first examination in midsummer after planting, 57 trees were missing. The vacant spots and vicinity provided no evidence that they had been planted or if seedlings had already been removed. The number of seedlings missing ranged from 0 to 14 per site. These 57 doubtful cases have been excluded from mortality summaries. Thus, trees planted totaled 40,263—there were 28,762 Douglas-firs and 11, 501 western hemlocks; 20,272 uncaged trees, 19,991 caged; 10,069 site preparation—control, 10,063 burn, 10,080 spray, and 10,071 spray and burn. The differences in trees per treatment are minuscule relative to the total number involved.

Table 6—Average 10-year survival of untubed and tubed trees by site

Site	Untubed		Tubed		Total and average	
	Number	*Percent*	*Number*	*Percent*	*Number*	*Percent*
Pitchfork	1,856	55.3	2,932	87.3	4,788	71.3
Beaver	1,758	51.8	2,707	81.9	4,465	66.6
Upperten	1,120	32.5	2,312	71.1	3,432	51.2
Randall	1,552	46.3	3,080	91.7	4,632	69.0
Poposchultz	2,527	75.2	3,018	89.8	5,545	82.5
Bay's Wolfe	1,419	42.3	2,376	70.8	3,795	56.5
Total and average	10,232	50.5	16,425	82.2	26,657	66.2

Table 7—Average 10-year survival of trees by site preparation and site

Site	Control		Burn		Spray		Spray and burn		Total and average	
	Number	*Percent*	*Number*	*Percent*	*Number*	*Percent*	*Number*	*Percent*	*Number*	*Percent*
Pitchfork	1,116	66.4	1,318	78.6	1,063	63.3	1,291	76.9	4,788	71.3
Beaver	934	55.6	1,059	63.4	1,271	75.7	1,201	71.7	4,465	66.6
Upperten	617	36.9	1,015	60.4	880	52.7	920	54.9	3,432	51.2
Randall	1,137	67.7	1,149	68.4	1,144	68.4	1,202	71.6	4,632	69.0
Poposchultz	1,396	83.1	1,483	88.3	1,244	74.1	1,422	84.6	5,545	82.5
Bay's Wolfe	693	41.3	666	39.7	1,110	66.1	1,326	78.9	3,795	56.5
Total and average	5,893	58.5	6,690	66.5	6,712	66.7	7,362	73.1	26,657	66.2

Table 8—Average 10-year survival of trees by species, protection, stock type, and site

Species and stock type		Site						
		Pitchfork	Beaver	Upperten	Randall	Poposchultz	Bay's Wolfe	All sites
Douglas-fir:								
Transplant 2+1	*Number*	777	780	542	753	854	584	4,290
	Percent	80.9	81.6	56.7	78.4	89.0	60.9	74.6
	Untubed	327	329	182	292	411	227	1,768
	Tubed	450	451	360	461	443	357	2,522
Large 2+0	*Number*	753	734	598	680	835	633	4,233
	Percent	78.6	76.5	62.4	70.9	87.0	65.9	73.6
	Untubed	301	294	220	226	392	255	1,688
	Tubed	452	440	378	454	443	378	2,545
Medium 2+0	*Number*	736	680	572	678	823	566	4,055
	Percent	76.7	70.9	59.6	70.6	85.7	59.0	70.4
	Untubed	291	264	201	234	380	217	1,587
	Tubed	445	416	371	444	443	349	2,468
Small 2+0	*Number*	736	612	484	633	779	542	3,786
	Percent	76.7	64.0	50.4	65.9	81.1	56.5	65.8
	Untubed	318	217	173	191	366	197	1,462
	Tubed	418	395	311	442	413	345	2,324
Container	*Number*	637	561	466	638	803	553	3,658
	Percent	66.4	58.7	48.8	67.0	83.6	57.6	63.7
	Untubed	240	227	128	194	376	209	1,374
	Tubed	397	334	338	444	427	344	2,284
Total	*Number*	3,639	3,367	2,662	3,382	4,094	2,878	20,022
	Percent	75.9	70.4	55.6	70.6	85.3	60.0	69.6
	Untubed	1,477	1,331	904	1,137	1,925	1,105	7,879
	Tubed	2,162	2,036	1,758	2,245	2,169	1,773	12,143
Western hemlock:								
Bare root	*Number*	568	530	436	606	732	527	3,399
	Percent	59.2	55.3	45.6	63.1	76.3	55.0	59.1
	Untubed	182	192	147	204	315	189	1,229
	Tubed	386	338	289	402	417	338	2,170
Container	*Number*	581	568	334	644	719	390	3,236
	Percent	60.5	59.3	35.0	67.2	74.9	40.8	56.3
	Untubed	197	235	69	211	287	125	1,124
	Tubed	384	333	265	433	432	265	2,112
Total	*Number*	1,149	1,098	770	1,250	1,451	917	6,635
	Percent	59.8	57.3	40.3	65.1	75.6	47.9	57.7
	Untubed	379	427	216	415	602	314	2,353
	Tubed	770	671	554	835	849	603	4,282

Overall, survival of Douglas-fir container stock averaged significantly lower (P < 0.001) than for the four bare-root stock types combined 63.7 vs. 71.1 percent (table 8). However, on four of the six sites, survival of Douglas-fir container stock differed little from small-size bare-root stock. Survival of small and medium-size 2+0 Douglas-firs was significantly lower than for large 2+0 stock, 68.1 vs. 73.6 percent (P < 0.001). Western hemlock bare-root stock tended to survive a bit better than hemlock container stock (P = 0.105). Without exception, survival of tubed trees of every stock type was higher on all sites—averaging 21.3 percent higher for Douglas-fir and 29.1 percent higher for western hemlock. For both species, mortality was highest in the first three years, and declined by smaller increments in subsequent years (fig. 8).

Survival trends were consistent among treatments as indicated by non-significant differences in interaction tests between protection and site preparation, site preparation and stock types, and between protection, site preparation, and stock types (see "Data Summaries and Analyses" section).

Spraying vegetation the second or third year after planting significantly aided tree survival although the actual averages were close, 66.9 vs. 65.5 percent (P = 0.026) (table 9). After release, survival of Douglas-firs continued to be higher than for western hemlocks on all sites, but species response to release varied among sites (fig. 9). There were also significant interactions between protection and release (P = 0.056) and between site preparation and release (P = 0.052). This seems almost

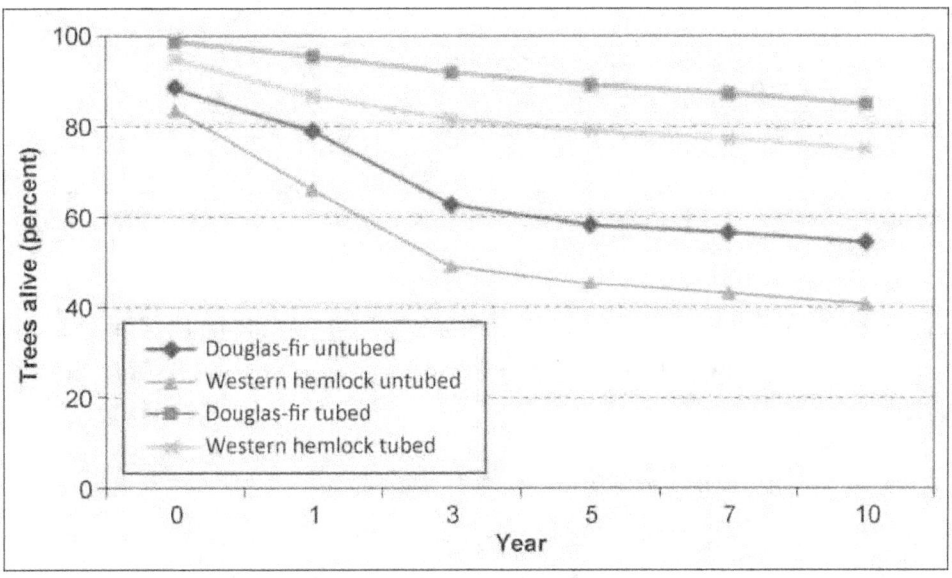

Figure 8—Survival trend for Douglas-firs and western hemlocks, untubed and tubed, years 0 to 10.

Table 9—Average 10-year survival of trees not released and released by site

Site	No release		Release		Total and average	
	Number	Percent	Number	Percent	Number	Percent
Pitchfork	2,386	71.1	2,402	71.5	4,788	71.3
Beaver	2,317	69.2	2,148	64.0	4,465	66.6
Upperten	1,670	49.8	1,762	52.6	3,432	51.2
Randall	2,266	67.5	2,366	70.6	4,632	69.0
Poposchultz	2,782	82.8	2,763	82.2	5,545	82.5
Bay's Wolfe	1,766	52.6	2,029	60.5	3,795	56.5
Total and average	13,187	65.5	13,470	66.9	26,657	66.2

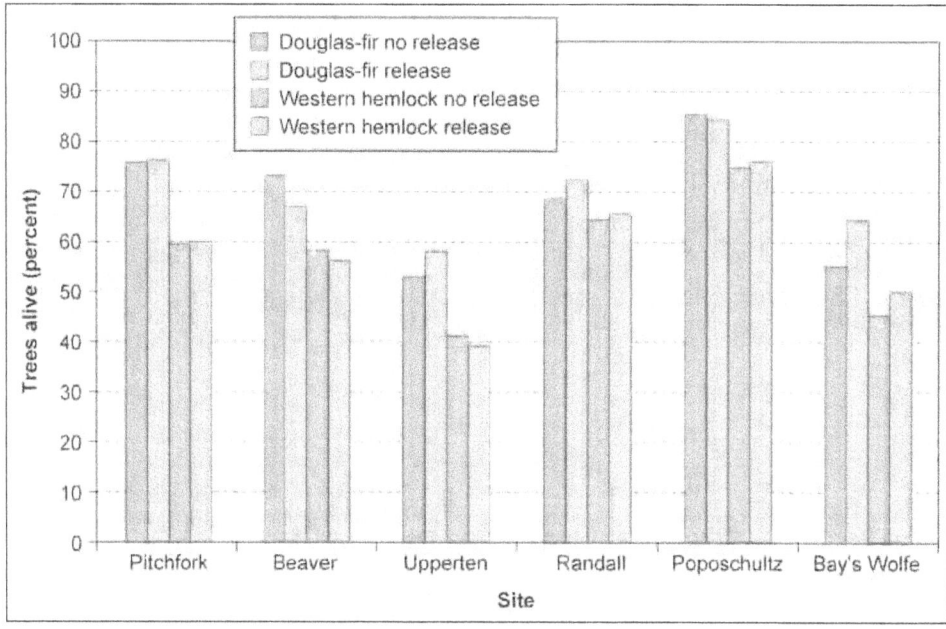

Figure 9—Trees alive at 10 years by site, species, and release treatment.

inevitable as one site preparation treatment reduced varying amounts of residual vegetation more than another, thus fostering unequal vegetative cover for release to affect.

Tree Mortality and Damage

One third of all trees planted died over the 10-year period (33.8 percent). In periodic examinations, observers recorded a cause of death for nearly three-fourths of all dead seedlings, 9,915 of 13,606 (table 10). Stem clipping near ground line was the main cause of mortality, 8,927 seedlings, comprising 65.6 percent of all mortality.

Table 10—Causes of seedling mortality by species and year

Number of seedlings

Species	Year	No damage	Clipped, unknown	Clipped, mountain beaver	Pulled up	Browsed	Trampled	Bark chewed	Gopher	Foliage disease	Insects, terminal bud	Insects, foliage	Unknown	Tube injury	Chain sawed	All causes[a]
Douglas-fir:	0	146	172	1,307	187	24	12				1		20			1,869
	1	315	279	1,013	26	129	1						64	1		1,829
	3	271	194	2,111		133	1	2		1		1	128	4		2,845
	5	318	161	385		24	2	7	2				141	10		1,051
	7	296	35	102	1	17	3	2					18	30		503
	10	369	13	49		4	2	4		1		1	6	15	50	514
Subtotal		1,715	854	4,967	214	331	21	15	2	2	1	2	377	60	50	8,611
Western hemlock:	0	363	92	714	21	15	7				1		26			1,239
	1	372	299	593	9	121	4	1		1			88	1		1,488
	3	67	151	924		33	1					1	90	1		1,268
	5	101	70	148		10						1	52	4		386
	7	115	32	49		7	1	4					13	7		228
	10	135	7	27		4	1	7						7	21	209
Subtotal		1,153	651	2,455	30	190	14	12	0	1	1	2	269	19	21	4,818
Total		2,868	1,505	7,422	244	521	35	27	2	3	2	4	646	79	71	13,429
Percent		21.1	11.1	54.5	1.8	3.8	0.3	0.2	0.2	0.2	0.2	0.2	4.7	0.6	0.5	100.0[b]

[a] 177 dead seedlings not included owing to insufficient identity in database.

[b] Percentage of mortality based on total number dead, 13,429 plus 177 = 13,606.

Of this total, observers attributed mortality of 4,967 Douglas-firs and 2,455 western hemlocks directly to clipping by mountain beavers. An additional 854 Douglas-firs and 651 western hemlocks were allotted to the clipped unknown column; most likely many of these were also clipped by mountain beavers, but rabbits or other agents could have contributed. Nearly ninety-percent (87.9 percent) of all clipping damage occurred by the third examination. Sufficient time had elapsed by then to indicate if a stem clipped earlier near ground line was dead or had grown a new shoot. Of course, such tender new regrowth could again be clipped.

Mortality and damage from clipping by mountain beavers and other agents continued even as the stand became older and taller. In fact, 12.1 percent of all mortality from clipping occurred after the third year, 745 Douglas-firs and 313 western hemlocks. In addition to stem severance, some seedlings did not survive partial or total burial by mountain beaver and others were undermined enough to cause growth impairment or mortality (fig 10).

Douglas-fir seedlings sustained less mortality from clipping than western hemlock 20.2 vs. 27.0 percent of the total number planted (see footnote 1) for each species (table 10).

Both untubed and tubed seedlings sustained mortality from clipping. Of course, tubed trees sustained much less such mortality than untubed trees, but the number that died was substantial, 1,243 vs. 7,684 (table 11). Clipping of tubed trees occurred when the tube was undermined, when the tube was tipped or knocked off, especially where elk were active, or when large tubes on western hemlocks opened up. Terminal shoots were also clipped when they extended out of the side or top of the tube. Few tubed trees were pulled up, 17 vs. 227 untubed; trampled, 9 vs. 26; and mortality from browsing was less for tubed trees, 149 vs. 372.

Seedling mortality from clipping was highest on three sites—Upperten 2,400; Randall 1,789; Bay's Wolfe 1,713—and markedly lower on Poposchultz, 566 (table 11). Pulled-up seedlings were found in quantity only on Pitchfork, 151, and Upperten, 75, where elk herds hung out nearby. Trampling occurred almost exclusively on Pitchfork, 27 seedlings, and mortality from browsing was greater on Upperten than on the other five units combined, 389 vs. 132 seedlings.

Regarding site preparation, more seedling mortality from clipping occurred in control areas (2,691) than in areas given a site preparation treatment, with lowest incidences in the spray-and-burn areas, 1,653 (table 11). But seedling mortality from pulling was highest in the spray-and-burn areas, 95, as was trampling, 17. Mortality from browsing occurred nearly three times as often in burned areas than in the other two treatments, 382 vs. 139.

US Forest Service, Pacific Northwest Region

Figure 10—Mountain beavers, common foragers in coastal forests, inflict multiple forms of damage on conifer seedlings: (A) mountain beaver; (B) clipped near ground line; (C) fully buried; (D) undermined; (E) foliage clipped repeatedly.

Table 11—Causes of seedling mortality by site, protection, site preparation, and stock type

Site treatment	No damage	Clipped unknown	Clipped, mountain beaver	Pulled up	Browsed	Trampled	Bark chewed	Gopher	Foliage disease	Insects, terminal bud	Insects, foliage	Unknown	Tube injury	Chain sawed	All causes[a]
							Number of seedlings								
Site:															
Pitchfork	323	76	992	151	19	27	13	0	0	0	0	310	17	0	1,928
Beaver	626	504	887	10	55	1	2	0	1	0	1	116	8	0	2,211
Upperten	361	496	1,904	75	389	2	5	0	0	1	1	29	7	0	3,270
Randall	225	235	1,554	5	5	1	1	0	1	1	0	14	3	0	2,045
Poposchultz	426	156	410	2	34	2	3	0	0	0	1	13	4	71	1,122
Bay's Wolfe	907	38	1,675	1	19	2	3	2	1	0	1	164	40	0	2,853
Total	2,868	1,505	7,422	244	521	35	27	2	3	2	4	646	79	71	13,429
Protection:															
Untubed	1,242	1,091	6,593	227	372	26	15	1	2	2	0	340	3	38	9,952
Tubed	1,626	414	829	17	149	9	12	1	1	0	4	306	76	33	3,477
Total	2,868	1,505	7,422	244	521	35	27	2	3	2	4	646	79	71	13,429
Site preparation:															
Control	965	537	2,154	60	86	4	4	0	0	1	2	238	33	47	4,131
Burn	696	253	1,970	50	187	6	8	0	0	0	2	147	24	24	3,367
Spray	641	502	1,858	39	53	8	6	2	2	1	0	171	14	0	3,297
Spray and burn	566	213	1,440	95	195	17	9	0	1	0	0	90	8	0	2,634
Total	2,868	1,505	7,422	244	521	35	27	2	3	2	4	646	79	71	13,429
Stock type:															
DF Transplant2+1	281	109	865	54	58	3	4	0	0	0	0	48	7	8	1,437
DF Large 2+0	352	146	843	41	54	5	4	1	0	0	0	47	11	8	1,512
DF Medium 2+0	341	157	939	50	73	4	2	1	0	1	0	73	13	8	1,662
DF Small2+0	341	221	1,140	42	72	3	3	0	0	0	1	90	13	17	1,943
DF Container	400	221	1,180	27	74	6	2	0	2	0	1	119	16	9	2,057
WH Bare root	590	351	1,100	18	92	3	6	0	0	0	2	151	7	8	2,328
WH Container	563	300	1,355	12	98	11	6	0	1	1	0	118	12	13	2,490
Total	2,868	1,505	7,422	244	521	35	27	2	3	2	4	646	79	71	13,429

[a]177 dead seedlings not included owing to insufficient identity in database.

DF = Douglas-fir; WH = western hemlock.

Seedlings of all sizes died from clipping, with mortality among smaller seedlings tending to be greater:

Stock type	Clipped	Pulled
	Number of seedlings	
2+1 Douglas-fir	974	54
2+0 large Douglas-fir	989	41
2+0 medium Douglas-fir	1,096	50
2+0 small Douglas-fir	1,361	42
Container Douglas-fir	1,401	27
Bare-root western hemlock	1,451	18
Container western hemlock	1,655	12

Compared to mortality by clipping, other identified causes of seedling mortality among stock types were minor. In limited areas, elk pulled up, trampled, or laid on seedlings soon after they were planted (fig. 11). More large seedlings than small died from elk damage, range among stock types 57 to 21. Pulling most likely resulted during feeding, when roots were not yet anchored sufficiently to withstand an upward yank. More western hemlocks than Douglas-firs died from browsing, but totals ranged from only 54 to 98 among the seven stock types. Comparing damage as a proportion of seedlings planted, more Douglas-fir than western hemlock seedlings were pulled or trampled 0.82 vs. 0.38 percent, but the reverse was true for browsing, 1.15 vs. 1.65 percent (table 10). Both species sustained some mortality owing to entanglement in or tipping of the protective tube; the proportion was not markedly different for Douglas-fir 0.21 vs. 0.17 percent for western hemlock.

Many seedlings alive at 10 years overcame damage some time during the decade. An attempt to sum cumulative damage sustained by live seedlings resulted in much greater numbers than the total of 26,657 live seedlings. That summation reflected the way observations were made and recorded. At each of the six examinations, an entry for cause of damage was entered for every damaged live seedling. Although only recent damage was to be recorded, the same damage might be recorded at successive examinations. Then, the same damage might be continuing—browsing, for example. Another complication: if a different kind of damage appeared on the seedling in successive examinations, the young tree might get another entry in the damage column. These three possibilities, and perhaps others, assured that many damaged seedlings accumulated multiple damage entries. The summation for the decade showed that browsing became the foremost cause of damage, clipping was second, tube injury third, and bark chewing followed.

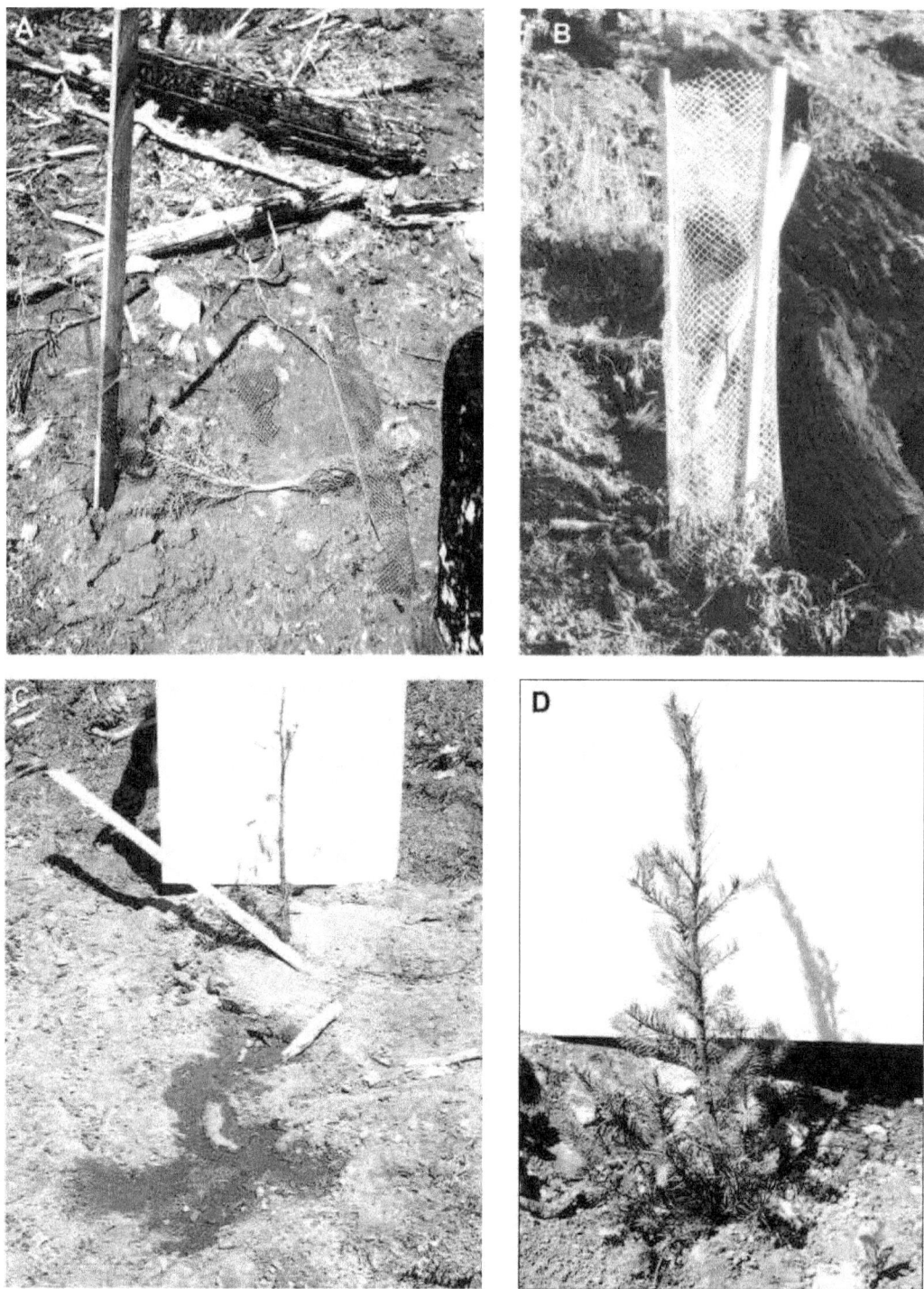

Figure 11—Damage by elk appears more destructive to newly planted trees than later browsing: (A) trees pulled up; (B) tubes knocked down or damaged; (C) multiple damages in bedding area; (D) moderate browsing.

Any one of the examinations provides a snapshot in time on the damages observed at that examination. At the 10th-year examination, the main damage categories on 26,657 live trees were:

Damage	Trees
	Number
None	23,681
Tube injury	922
Browsed	670
Bark chewed	600
Clipped	429
Whipped	236
Porcupine	39
All others	80
Total	26,657

A scattering of stems, some 5 ft tall or more, were used as "feeding stations." The terminal shoot and side limbs were severed, and later regrowth was clipped again. Such "feeding stations" appeared more often to be western hemlocks then Douglas-firs, but these limited instances were not separately identified within the damage categories.

Obviously, by the 10th year, most live trees were no longer subject to mortality agents most common to young seedlings (app. table 36).

Tubing for Seedling Protection

Stiff mesh tubing is often used to protect newly planted conifer seedlings from for-aging animals. Its use to protect half the trees in this study provided an opportunity to observe the fate of tubing over time. Thus, installed tubing was visually rated for position and condition on trees alive in the third- and fifth-year examinations.

At the third examination, 73 percent of tubes enclosing Douglas-firs were still upright; by the fifth examination, 63 percent were upright (table 12). By the third examination, 15 percent of Douglas-fir seedlings were growing through the mesh of the tube, and that increased to 20 percent by the fifth examination. Leaning tubes increased substantially from the third to the fifth examination, but numbers in the knockdown and off-the-tree categories hardly changed. By the fifth examina-tion, Upperten had 274 less upright tubes than Pitchfork, the next lowest (1,031 vs. 1,305). Over two-thirds of all tubes knocked off of Douglas-firs by the fifth exami-nation occurred at Upperten.

Only 31 percent of the larger tubes used with western hemlock were still upright at the third examination; by the fifth examination, 13 percent. Tubes found

Table 12—Third- and fifth-year position and condition of plastic mesh tubes on live trees

Tube	Species					
	Douglas-fir		Western hemlock		Total	
	Number observed by year					
Position:	3rd	5th	3rd	5th	3rd	5th
Upright	9,934	8,216	1,552	611	11,486	8,827
Leaning < 30%	579	1,036	136	90	715	1,126
Leaning > 30%	269	440	88	58	357	498
Knocked down	203	201	142	151	345	352
Off of tree	620	615	518	718	1,138	1,333
Tree through mesh	2,036	2,623	2,493	3,012	4,529	5,635
Total	13,641	13,131	4,929	4,640	18,570	17,771
Condition:						
Intact	13,039	10,373	4,201	2,383	17,240	12,756
Crumbling	58	2,200	176	1,606	234	3,806
Disintegrated	3	9	119	64	122	73
Off or gone	539	548	433	587	972	1,135
Total	13,639	13,130	4,929	4,640	18,568	17,770

off the tree numbered 518 at the third examination, 718 by the fifth examination. Despite use of a much larger tube, a greater percentage of western hemlocks were growing through the tube mesh than of Douglas-fir, 65 vs. 20 percent by the fifth examination.

To liberate protected trees, it is considered desirable that tubing disintegrate. The mesh tubing used was purported to do so. But 79 percent of tubes on Douglas-fir and 51 percent of those on hemlock were still intact at the fifth examination (table 12). Very few tubes on Douglas-fir showed crumbling or disintegration at the third examination, but 6 percent did on western hemlock. By the fifth examination, 17 percent of tubes around Douglas-firs and 36 percent of those around hemlocks were crumbling or disintegrating. Nearly twice as many tubes in stages of disintegration were found at Beaver and Upperten than on Pitchfork, respectively 1,349, 1,166, and 593. A surprisingly low number, 89, were in such stages on the northerly slope at Randall.

Height Growth

Total height was measured in centimeters for all 26,657 trees alive in the 10th year. The height for all trees averaged 512.1 cm (16.8 ft). Trees averaged tallest at Poposchultz, 643.5 cm, and shortest at Upperten, only 55.9 percent as tall, 359.4 cm (table 13).

Tubed trees averaged significantly taller than untubed trees (P < 0.001), but actually averaged only 8.5 inches taller at 10 years, 520.4 vs. 498.8 cm. Both tubed and untubed trees were tallest at Poposchultz and shortest at Upperten. Height growth had about the same trajectory on all sites (fig. 12). Total height nearly doubled between the seventh and 10th year for both tubed and untubed trees with the shortest ones on Upperten gaining relative more than those on other sites.

Site preparation tended to aid height growth (P = 0.195). On average, the burn and the spray-and-burn treatments tended to foster height growth more than spray alone, but the latter still averaged greater than for the control (table 14). But there were several exceptions to the general trend. At Pitchfork, the average height in the sprayed areas averaged less than in the controls, 431.2 vs. 501.1 cm. At Upperten, neither the burn nor the spray treatment differed much from the control. And at Bay's Wolfe, trees in both the burn and the spray-and-burn treatments averaged less height than in the control treatment.

Initial stock size influenced average height of Douglas-firs at 10 years (table 15). Container-grown Douglas-firs averaged significantly shorter than the combined average of the four bare-root stocks (P < 0.001); they averaged 72.5 cm (2.4 ft) shorter than large 2+0, the tallest bare-root stock, 509.0 vs. 581.5 cm.

At 10 years, average tree height differed significantly among all four sizes of bare-root Douglas-fir stock—large 2+0 taller than 2+1 (P = 0.105); medium 2 + 0 taller than small 2+0 (P = 0.005), and large 2+0 taller than small plus medium 2+0 (P < 0.001) (fig. 13). But there were several inconsistencies on a site-by-site basis; for example, trees from large 2+0 stock slightly exceeded height of those from 2+1 stock except at Beaver. Average height of tubed trees exceeded average height of untubed trees in 38 of the 42 stock type pairs. Heights of untubed trees averaged slightly taller than tubed trees for 2+1 transplants, and small and medium 2+0 Douglas-firs at Bay's Wolfe, and for container hemlock at Beaver (table 15).

Average height of all western hemlocks was significantly less (P < 0.001) at 10 years than for all Douglas-firs, 416.6 cm vs. 543.7 cm, an average difference of 127.1 cm (4.17 ft). Average heights of bare-root and container types of western hemlock did not differ significantly, 409.8 cm vs. 423.7 cm. On three sites, average height of hemlock from bare-root sources was greater than for container stock and the reverse was true on the other three sites.

Trees averaged significantly taller (P < 0.001) on areas given an aerial spraying for release, 529.2 vs. 494.6 cm (table 16). The release effect was very minor on Poposchultz however, 644.5 vs. 642.5 cm.

Table 13—Average height of untubed and tubed 10-year-old trees by site

Site	Untubed			Tubed			Total and average		
	Number	Centimeters	Standard error	Number	Centimeters	Standard error	Number	Centimeters	Standard error
Pitchfork	1,856	484.9	4.5	2,932	510.3	3.5	4,788	500.5	2.8
Beaver	1,758	420.5	4.1	2,707	449.2	3.2	4,465	437.9	2.5
Upperten	1,120	319.7	4.5	2,312	378.6	3.4	3,432	359.4	2.8
Randall	1,552	551.3	5.5	3,080	589.5	3.5	4,632	576.7	3.0
Poposchultz	2,527	618.1	3.7	3,018	664.8	3.4	5,545	643.5	2.5
Bay's Wolfe	1,419	485.2	5.5	2,376	478.9	4.4	3,795	481.2	3.4
Total and average	10,232	498.8	2.1	16,425	520.4	1.6	26,657	512.1	1.3

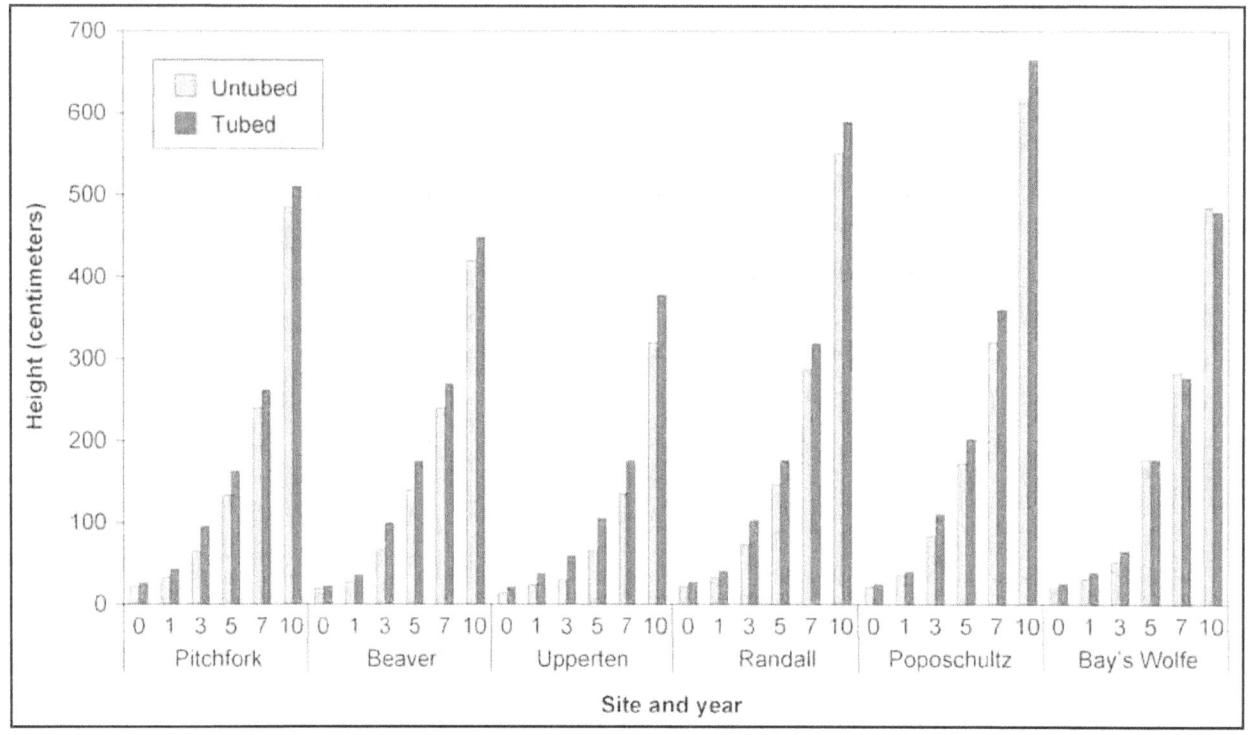

Figure 12—Average height of trees by site, year, and protection.

Table 14—Average height of 10-year-old trees by site and site preparation

Site	Site preparation														
	Control			Burn			Spray			Spray and burn			Total and average		
	Number	Centimeters	Standard error	Number	Centimeters	Standard error	Number	Centimeters	Standard error	Number	Centimeters	Standard error	Number	Centimeters	Standard error
Pitchfork	1,116	501.1	5.5	1,318	513.6	4.6	1,063	431.2	6.6	1,291	543.6	5.1	4,788	500.5	2.8
Beaver	934	355.8	5.1	1,059	392.1	4.2	1,271	476.4	4.7	1,201	501.4	5.0	4,465	437.9	2.5
Upperten	617	351.7	7.1	1,015	349.1	4.6	880	359.7	5.8	920	375.5	5.2	3,432	359.4	2.8
Randall	1,137	526.8	5.7	1,149	605.4	6.1	1,144	573.7	6.0	1,202	599.4	5.8	4,632	576.7	3.0
Poposchultz	1,396	530.7	4.3	1,483	729.3	4.3	1,244	567.1	4.9	1,422	731.7	4.0	5,545	643.5	2.5
Bay's Wolfe	693	475.3	8.8	666	436.6	8.3	1,110	554.7	6.3	1,326	445.2	4.9	3,795	481.2	3.4
Total and average	5,893	471.4	2.6	6,690	525.3	2.7	6,712	500.3	2.5	7,362	543.4	2.4	26,657	512.1	1.3

Table 15—Average height of 10-year-old trees by site, species, protection, and stock type

Species and stock type		Site						
		Pitchfork	Beaver	Upperten	Randall	Poposchultz	Bay's Wolfe	All
Douglas-fir:								
Transplant 2+1	Number	777	780	542	753	854	584	4,290
	Average (cm)	608.4	495.1	410.7	622.9	660.2	485.2	558.9
	Standard error	5.5	5.4	6.1	6.5	5.5	7.4	2.8
	Untubed	595.6	481.3	365.5	611.4	649.9	499.0	553.5
	Tubed	617.7	505.2	433.5	630.2	669.8	476.4	562.7
Large 2+0	Number	753	734	598	680	835	633	4,233
	Average (cm)	611.5	476.8	417.2	634.6	724.6	576.9	581.5
	Standard error	5.3	5.6	5.8	6.7	5.7	7.1	2.9
	Untubed	585.0	453.0	382.4	611.8	703.3	567.5	564.0
	Tubed	629.1	492.7	437.4	646.0	743.5	583.3	593.2
Medium 2+0	Number	736	680	572	678	823	566	4,055
	Average (cm)	554.8	444.0	401.4	569.3	701.0	532.0	543.5
	Standard error	5.7	5.7	6.2	7.1	5.7	7.9	3.0
	Untubed	544.4	421.1	339.3	535.1	682.4	533.1	528.0
	Tubed	561.6	458.5	435.0	587.3	716.9	531.4	553.4
Small 2+0	Number	736	612	484	633	779	542	3,786
	Average (cm)	515.2	406.6	379.8	578.5	657.3	501.4	518.2
	Standard error	6.1	6.1	6.5	7.2	5.9	8.0	3.1
	Untubed	495.6	376.3	313.0	526.8	631.1	520.2	497.6
	Tubed	530.1	423.2	417.0	600.8	680.5	490.6	531.1
Container	Number	637	561	466	638	803	553	3,658
	Average (cm)	433.2	396.6	343.2	605.5	649.9	533.8	509.0
	Standard error	6.0	6.8	6.3	7.2	6.0	7.6	3.3
	Untubed	398.3	359.5	303.5	545.7	623.7	524.1	484.7
	Tubed	454.3	421.8	358.2	631.6	673.0	539.8	523.6
Total	Number	3,639	3,367	2,662	3,382	4,094	2,878	20,022
	Average (cm)	548.7	448.3	392.7	602.9	679.0	527.0	543.7
	Standard error	2.8	2.7	2.8	3.1	2.6	3.5	1.4
	Untubed	529.8	425.2	345.0	570.3	658.5	530.0	528.2
	Tubed	561.6	463.4	417.3	619.4	697.1	525.1	553.8

Table 15—Average height of 10-year-old trees by site, species, protection, and stock type (continued)

Species and stock type		Site						
		Pitchfork	Beaver	Upperten	Randall	Poposchultz	Bay's Wolfe	All
Western hemlock:								
Bare root	Number	568	530	436	606	732	527	3,399
	Average (cm)	351.6	395.0	259.4	481.5	535.5	354.9	409.8
	Standard error	7.7	9.0	8.1	9.6	7.4	9.6	3.8
	Untubed	324.5	376.4	222.6	476.6	485.4	342.7	389.7
	Tubed	364.4	405.5	278.1	484.0	573.3	361.7	421.2
Container	Number	581	568	334	644	719	390	3,236
	Average (cm)	344.0	416.4	223.9	528.9	551.7	314.4	423.7
	Standard error	7.5	8.3	8.4	9.3	7.8	11.4	4.1
	Untubed	296.3	429.7	195.1	521.1	493.2	304.1	411.3
	Tubed	368.4	406.9	231.4	532.6	590.6	319.3	430.3
Total	Number	1,149	1,098	770	1,250	1,451	917	6,635
	Average (cm)	347.7	406.0	244.0	505.9	543.5	337.7	416.6
	Standard error	5.4	6.1	5.9	6.7	5.4	7.4	2.8
	Untubed	309.9	405.8	213.8	499.2	489.1	327.3	400.0
	Tubed	366.4	406.2	255.8	509.2	582.1	343.1	425.7

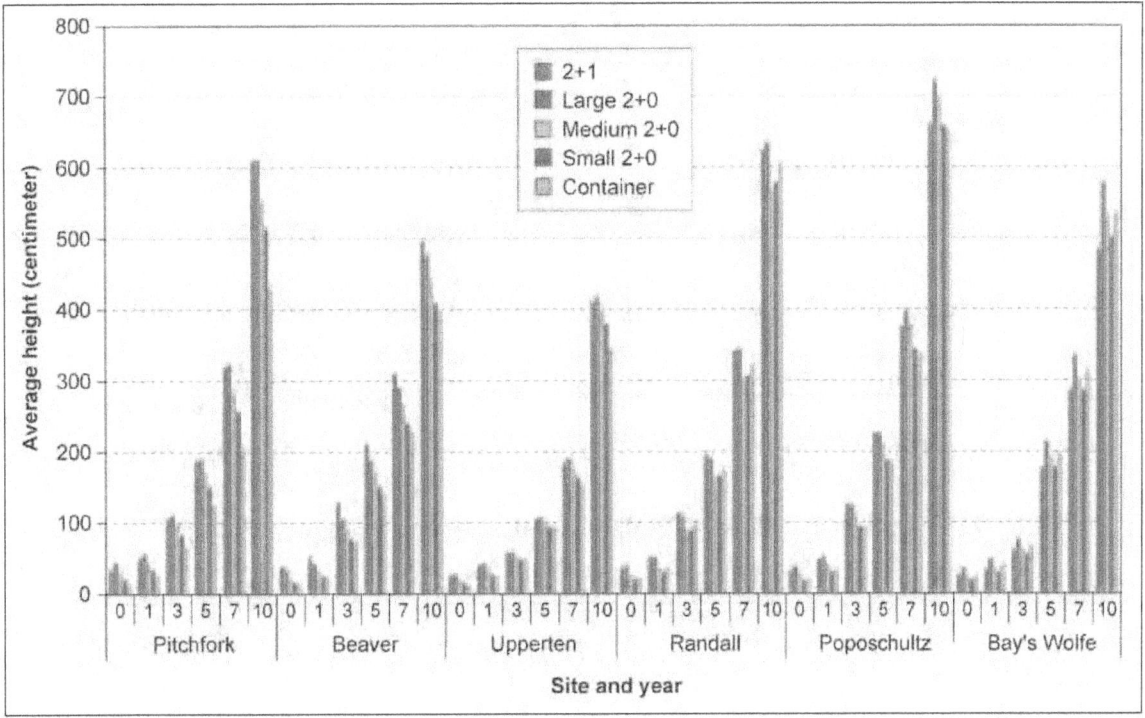

Figure 13—Average height of Douglas-fir by site, year, and stock type.

Table 16—Average height of 10-year-old trees by site and release treatment

Site	No release			Release			Total and average		
	Number	Centimeters	Standard error	Number	Centimeters	Standard error	Number	Centimeters	Standard error
Pitchfork	2,386	481.4	4.0	2,402	519.4	3.7	4,788	500.5	2.8
Beaver	2,317	418.3	3.4	2,148	459.0	3.7	4,465	437.9	2.5
Upperten	1,670	353.9	4.1	1,762	364.6	3.7	3,432	359.4	2.8
Randall	2,266	532.7	4.1	2,366	619.0	4.1	4,632	576.7	3.0
Poposchultz	2,782	642.5	3.5	2,763	644.5	3.6	5,545	643.5	2.5
Bay's Wolfe	1,766	464.0	5.2	2,029	496.3	4.5	3,795	481.2	3.4
Total and average	13,187	494.6	1.8	13,470	529.2	1.8	26,657	512.1	1.3

Spraying to release developing young trees had a positive effect in all four site preparation treatments ($P < 0.001$). The average height gain was least in the burn treatments, only 5.7 cm, and most in the spray only site preparation treatments, 66.8 cm:

	Average tree heights		
Site preparation	No release	Release	Difference
	Centimeters		
Control	457.8	484.4	26.6
Burn	522.5	528.2	5.7
Spray	466.0	532.8	66.8
Spray and burn	523.6	563.0	39.4
Average	494.6	529.2	34.6

All types of stock averaged some gain from release spraying (fig. 14). In only 4 of 28 pairs was average height of a stock type less in released areas than in unreleased areas—for 2+1 Douglas-fir in control areas, for medium and small Douglas-firs and bare-root hemlocks in burn areas (app. table 37).

There were no significant interactions in average height among protection, site preparation, and stock type treatments, but significant interactions with the release treatment. Notable interactions included site preparation and release ($P < 0.001$); protection and release ($P = 0.099$); and site preparation, protection and release ($P = 0.128$).

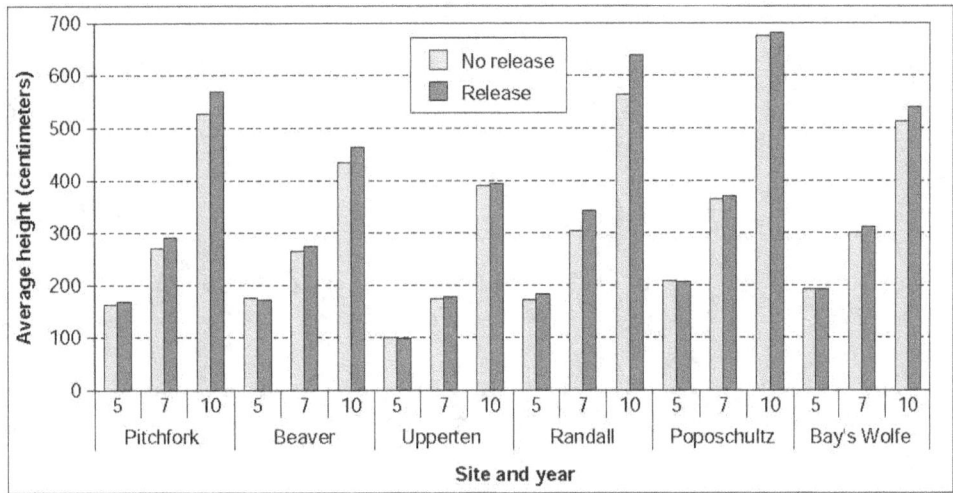

Figure 14—Average height of Douglas-fir by site, year, and release treatment.

Damage Effects

Damage observed on live trees at each examination was recorded by cause. A summary of tree damage by cause and the resulting average height of these trees is informative, despite the inherent subjective variations in assessing damage by observers of different skills and levels of observation. Degree of damage was not recorded; it had to appear more than trivial.

Considering damage evident from all causes on live 10-year-old trees, many more western hemlocks were damaged than Douglas-firs (table 17). Only 6.6 percent of all surviving Douglas-firs were visibly damaged compared to 24.8 percent of all western hemlocks. In terms of growth effects, heights of damaged Douglas-fir trees lowered total average height of the stand based on undamaged trees by only 543.7 vs. 556.7 cm. The difference was much greater for western hemlocks, 416.6 vs. 478.4 cm. Note that undamaged western hemlocks still averaged much less height growth than undamaged Douglas-firs.

Five factors caused most damage to Douglas-fir trees: serious distortion of growth through the mesh due to tube displacement, 589 trees (fig. 15); browsing by deer and elk, 256 trees; whipping of leaders from overtopping by alders or tall brush, 187 trees; bark chewing of various sorts, 101 trees; and clipping of terminals or side branches by mountain beaver, 99 trees. Damaged Douglas-firs averaged less height growth than undamaged trees except for those damaged by porcupines, where damaged trees averaged taller than undamaged trees, 601.8 cm vs. 556.7 cm. The apparent explanation is that porcupines climbed into taller-than-average Douglas-firs.

Table 17—Count and average height of undamaged and damaged 10-year-old trees by site and species

Species and damage agent	Site													
	Pitchfork		Beaver		Upperten		Randall		Poposchultz		Bay's Wolfe		All sites	
	Number	Centimeters	Number	Centimeters	Number	Centimeters	Number	Centimeters	Number	Centimeters	Number	Centimeters	Number	Centimeters
Douglas-fir:														
None	3,215	563.8	3,191	458.0	2,342	416.1	3,242	612.0	4,036	680.4	2,668	535.4	18,694	556.7
Clipped, unknown	1	51.0	4	49.5	0	0	0	0	2	315.0	4	128.8	11	126.7
Clipped, mountain beaver	31	342.7	15	67.9	11	97.6	34	334.8	0	0	8	126.6	99	253.7
Browsed	17	165.2	7	86.9	194	158.5	22	113.8	4	145.3	12	122.9	256	151.3
Trampled	4	20.5	0	0	0	0	1	433.0	0	0	0	0	5	103.0
Bark chewed	45	357.1	9	243.6	44	350.5	0	0	3	47.0	0	0	101	334.9
Foliage disease	1	177.0	0	0	0	0	1	600.0	1	421.0	2	472.0	5	428.4
Insects, terminal bud	1	395.0	1	649.0	0	0	0	0	0	0	1	598.0	3	547.3
Insects, foliage	0	0	2	247.5	1	300.0	0	0	2	753.0	1	559.0	6	476.7
Unknown	24	335.9	6	327.0	5	115.6	1	534.0	1	610.0	0	0	37	317.4
Tube injury	300	486.0	51	334.1	65	350.6	57	484.1	44	660.4	72	426.4	589	463.5
Whipped	0	0	81	293.1	0	0	15	501.9	1	805.0	90	438.9	187	382.8
Porcupine	0	0	0	0	0	0	9	500.3	0	0	20	647.5	29	601.8
Total	3,639	548.7	3,367	448.3	2,662	392.7	3,382	602.9	4,094	679.0	2,878	527.0	20,022	543.7
Western hemlock:														
None	601	393.2	962	432.8	328	371.8	1,074	545.8	1,357	556.6	665	405.2	4,987	478.4
Clipped, unknown	1	150.0	15	39.8	0	0	0	0	3	70.0	9	42.6	26	46.2
Clipped, mountain beaver	94	187.0	21	42.7	35	97.9	85	176.4	3	215.0	55	144.5	293	155.3
Browsed	19	88.9	5	80.8	322	150.7	5	153.4	3	75.0	60	101.2	414	139.3
Trampled	4	107.3	0	0	0	0	0	0	0	0	0	0	4	107.3
Bark chewed	359	337.7	4	180.8	49	200.4	19	262.2	45	270.7	23	189.1	499	307.2
Gopher	0	0	0	0	0	0	2	205.0	0	0	0	0	2	205.0
Foliage disease	1	272.0	0	0	0	0	0	0	0	0	0	0	1	272.0
Insects, foliage	0	0	1	422.0	0	0	1	740.0	1	473.0	0	0	3	545.0
Unknown	13	291.2	0	0	1	90.0	0	0	0	0	0	0	14	276.9
Tube injury	57	317.8	51	290.8	35	116.3	60	384.5	39	497.6	91	168.4	333	284.7
Whipped	0	0	39	297.7	0	0	3	342.0	2	200.0	5	459.6	49	312.9
Porcupine	0	0	0	0	0	0	1	172.0	0	0	9	425.1	10	399.8
Total	1,149	347.7	1,098	406.0	770	244.0	1,250	505.9	1,451	543.5	917	337.7	6,635	416.6
Grand total	4,788	500.5	4,465	437.9	3,432	359.4	4,632	576.7	5,545	643.5	3,795	481.2	26,657	512.1

Figure 15—Restrictions inflicted by tubing can distort growth and even cause stem breaks.

The same five factors caused the most damage to western hemlock, although the rankings were slightly different. For hemlock, bark chewing topped the list, 499 trees, followed by browsing, 414 trees, tube injury, 333 trees, clipping by mountain beavers, 293 trees, and whipping, 49 trees. These injuries all reduced average height of western hemlocks.

Mountain beavers and other agents clipped side branches and terminals of 110 Douglas-firs and 319 western hemlocks, sometimes leaving only living stubs 1 ft tall. The greater number of western hemlock clipped than Douglas-fir seems to demonstrate that western hemlocks are preferred by mountain beavers, but their smaller size and growth form might also be pertinent factors.

In limited instances, bull elk caused severe damage to several adjacent trees, particularly to western hemlocks (fig. 16). Apparently using his antlers, a bull damaged several trees in a row of hemlocks. Side branches were broken off or badly mauled and several hemlocks 10 ft tall or more appeared to have been ridden part way to the ground. Little or no damage was seen on Douglas-firs in adjacent rows. The apparent difference is that Douglas-firs were larger and had wider crowns, and had limbs in lower whorls that were more numerous, stiffer, and larger in diameter. They apparently offered more resistant to antlers than did the narrow-crowned western hemlocks.

Figure 16—Damage to western hemlock from antler rubbing by elk
at Pitchfork.

A look at tree height by slope position did not reveal any clear trends (table 18).
Plot location was used to allocate trees to slope position. On Pitchfork and Bay's
Wolfe, trees averaged taller on the upper slope, but the reverse was true for Beaver and Randall. On the other two sites, trees averaged somewhat taller on the
midslopes.

Initial heights of seedlings averaged lowest at Beaver and Upperten and so
did 10-year heights (table 18). But trees at Pitchfork and Randall, averaging tallest
initially, did not average tallest at 10 years. Instead, at Poposchultz seedlings of
intermediate initial height averaged much taller than all others at 10 years.

Different kinds of stem deformities seemed numerous in the developing 10-year
old stands. Thus, as part of the 10th-year examination, deformities were tallied by
kind. Slightly more than one-fifth of all live trees had some kind of physical factor

Table 18—Average tree height at year 0 and 10 by site and slope location

Site and year	Slope location							
	Lower		Middle		Upper		All slopes	
	Centimeters							
Year	0	10	0	10	0	10	0	10
Pitchfork	25.1	487.4	24.2	489.2	24.7	524.3	24.7	500.5
Beaver	21.9	487.2	21.3	444.6	21.9	390.2	21.7	437.9
Upperten	19.5	358.3	17.3	368.1	17.6	352.2	18.2	359.4
Randall	25.0	630.1	25.4	591.2	24.8	509.4	25.1	576.7
Poposchultz	24.2	648.3	22.8	656.3	24.8	625.9	23.9	643.5
Bay's Wolfe	22.8	358.4	23.9	498.1	25.2	531.5	24.0	481.2

that was rated a departure from an undamaged, vertical, single-stemmed tree. Deformity incidents differed little between Douglas-firs and western hemlocks, 21.1 vs. 23.9 percent (table 19). Adding the categories together, leader damage was by far the most common deformity—2,269 instances for Douglas-fir, 499 for western hemlock, representing 53.6 percent of all damage to Douglas-firs and 31.5 percent for western hemlocks. Forked stems, most likely the result of past leader damage, was the next most abundant deformity—22.1 percent for Douglas-firs and 50.8 percent for western hemlocks.

Most damage to Douglas-fir leaders was observed at Poposchultz, 557 instances and the least at Bay's Wolfe, 145 instances. On the other four units, leader damage ranged from 330 to 449 instances. Number of forked stems ranged from 61 on Beaver to 344 on Upperten. Many more leaning stems were found at Pitchfork and Beaver (112,127) than on the other sites.

Leader damage to western hemlock was more numerous on Beaver (119) and Upperten (184) than on the other four sites (40 to 62). Surprisingly, Poposchultz had many more forked stems (238) than found on other sites.

Tree Diameter

By the 10th year, 94 percent of study trees had a measurable diameter at breast height (DBH), 25,025 of 26,657. The average diameter ranged from 9.3 cm at Poposchultz to 4.9 cm at Upperten (3.7 to 1.9 in) (table 20).

Trees initially protected by tubing averaged significantly larger in diameter than those unprotected, 7.7 vs. 7.2 cm (P < 0.001). Among sites, average diameters for untubed trees ranged from 4.2 cm at Upperten to 8.8 cm at Poposchultz, a greater than two-to-one difference. Tubed trees averaged 5.2 cm to 9.7 cm at the same two sites, not quite a two-to-one difference.

Table 19—Growth deformities observed on live 10-year-old trees

Observed deformity	Species		
	Douglas-fir	Western hemlock	Total
	Number		
Dead terminal bud	69	10	79
No leader	116	95	211
Dead leader	112	36	148
Double leader	552	132	684
Lateral as leader	918	121	1,039
Multiple leaders	502	105	607
Late flush	15	0	15
Double flush	105	1	106
Forked stem	934	804	1,738
Dieback	218	126	344
Stem leans	309	56	365
Stem tipped	76	46	122
Stem split	20	18	38
Crown chlorotic	286	34	320
Undamaged	15,790	5,051	20,841
Total	20,022	6,635	26,657
Total damaged	4,232	1,584	5,816
Percent damaged	21.1	23.9	21.8

Table 20—Average diameter at breast height of 10-year-old trees by protection and site

Site	Untubed		Tubed		Total and average	
	Number	*Centimeters*	*Number*	*Centimeters*	*Number*	*Centimeters*
Pitchfork	1,731	7.5	2,774	7.9	4,505	7.7
Beaver	1,642	6.6	2,565	7.3	4,207	7.0
Upperten	912	4.2	2,009	5.2	2,921	4.9
Randall	1,477	7.7	2,982	8.7	4,459	8.3
Poposchultz	2,477	8.8	2,980	9.7	5,457	9.3
Bay's Wolfe	1,338	5.9	2,138	6.3	3,476	6.1
Total and average	9,577	7.2	15,448	7.7	25,025	7.5

For the whole study, tree diameters averaged less for areas without site preparation than for those that received site preparation, 6.8 vs. 7.6, 7.5 and 8.0 cm (table 21). If the null hypothesis of no difference is true, then the observed magnitude of difference is P = 0.293. Departures from the trend occurred on Pitchfork and mostly notably at Bay's Wolfe, where average tree diameter was much less in the spray-and-burn treatment than in the control, 4.7 vs. 6.8 cm. In contrast, at Poposchultz, the average diameter in the two burn treatments was much higher than in the other two treatments.

Diameter of western hemlock trees averaged significantly less than for Douglas-fir trees, 5.2 vs. 8.2 cm (P < 0.001) (table 22). Among sites, average diameters for Douglas-fir ranged from 5.3 cm at Upperten to 10.2 at Poposchultz, for western hemlock from 2.9 to 6.4 (fig. 17).

Diameters of bare-root Douglas-fir stock averaged significantly larger than for container stock 8.3 vs. 7.4 cm (P < 0.001), but not significantly larger between the two types of western hemlock stock, 5.0 vs. 5.3 cm (table 22). The 2+1 Douglas-fir stock exceeded the average diameter of the three 2+0 stock types, 8.7 vs. 8.2 (P < 0.003). Diameter of large 2+0 Douglas-fir stock averaged significantly larger (P < 0.001) than the average diameter of medium and small 2+0 stock, 8.8 vs. 7.9 cm and the latter two also differed from each other (P = < 0.002). Average diameter of container Douglas-fir stock was close to or even exceeded several averages for bare-root stock (fig. 18).

Tubed trees averaged larger in diameter than untubed trees in 40 of the 42 individual site-stock type pairs (table 22). At Bay's Wolfe, untubed small 2+0 Douglas-firs were larger than tubed trees and medium 2+0 averages were equal. At Beaver, untubed container hemlocks were larger and at Randall the tubed and untubed container hemlocks averaged the same diameter.

Diameters of released trees (species combined) averaged significantly larger than for those not released, 7.8 vs. 7.2 cm (P < 0.001). The trend was consistent for all sites except Poposchultz where the two averages were the same, 9.3 cm (table 23). On every site, Douglas-fir benefited from release, although the gain was very small on Upperten (fig. 19). Western hemlock also benefited from release, but results were more variable among sites.

A look at the tallest and largest diameter tree on each site provides insight not provided by averages. The salient finding is that the largest trees developed in varying combinations of species, stock type, and treatment. Four of the six tallest trees

Table 21—Average diameter at breast height of 10-year-old trees by site and site preparation

Site	Control		Burn		Spray		Spray and burn		Total and average	
	Number	Centimeters	Number	Centimeters	Number	Centimeters	Number	Centimeters	Number	Centimeters
Pitchfork	1,053	7.7	1,272	7.7	939	7.0	1,241	8.4	4,505	7.7
Beaver	849	5.6	1,005	6.0	1,206	7.7	1,147	8.3	4,207	7.0
Upperten	501	4.7	877	4.7	733	4.9	810	5.3	2,921	4.9
Randall	1,078	7.7	1,106	8.3	1,115	8.5	1,160	8.8	4,459	8.3
Poposchultz	1,367	7.1	1,475	10.5	1,203	8.2	1,412	11.0	5,457	9.3
Bay's Wolfe	597	6.8	566	6.0	1,046	7.6	1,267	4.7	3,476	6.1
Total and average	5,445	6.8	6,301	7.6	6,242	7.5	7,037	8.0	25,025	7.5

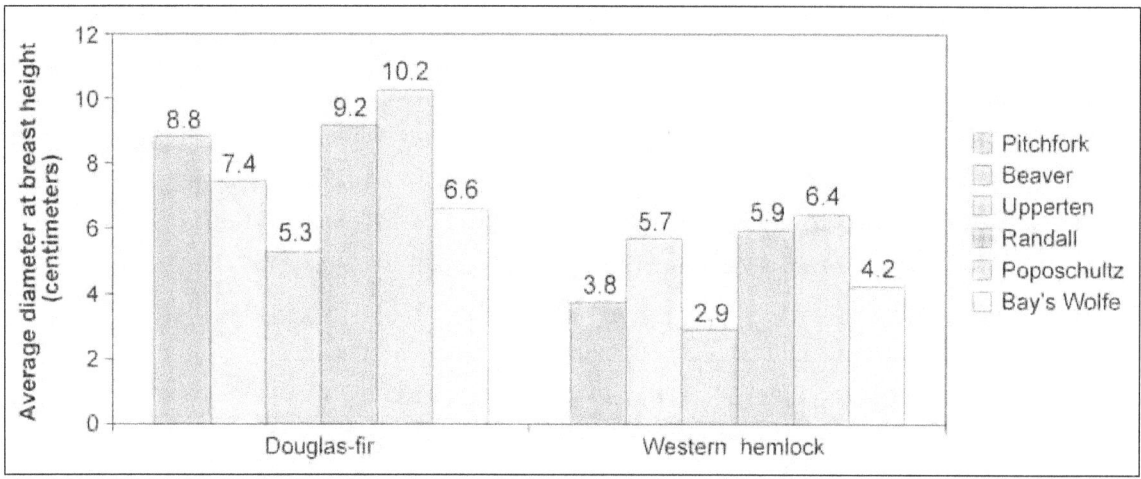

Figure 17—Average diameter at breast height of 10-year-old trees by species and site.

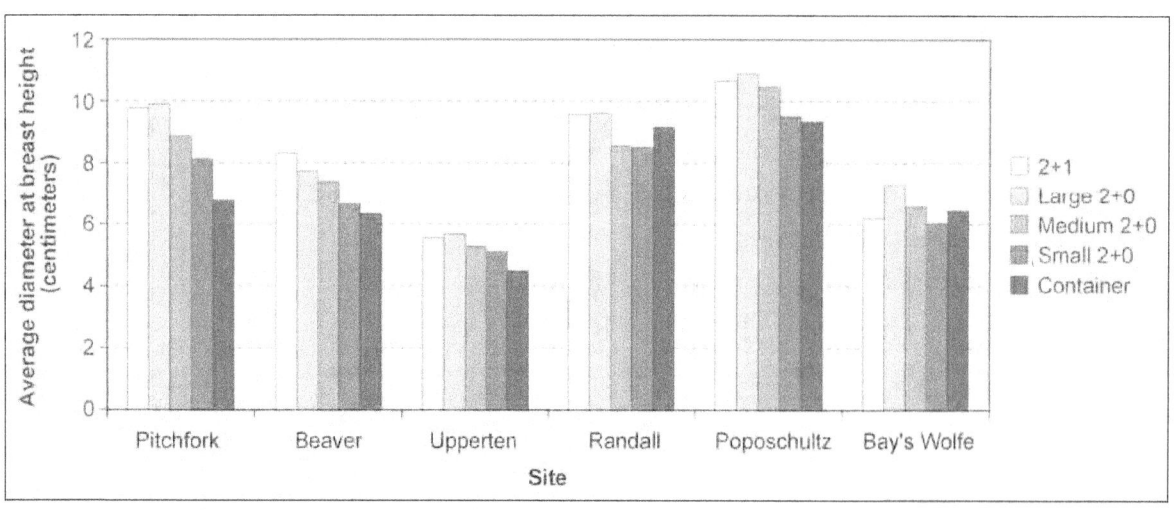

Figure 18—Average diameter at breast height of 10-year-old Douglas-firs by site and stock type.

Table 22—Average diameter at breast height (DBH) of 10-year-old trees by site, species, protection, and stock type

Species and stock type		Site						
		Pitchfork	Beaver	Upperten	Randall	Poposchultz	Bay's Wolfe	All
Douglas-fir:								
Transplant 2+1:								
Number		764	772	510	745	848	566	4,205
DBH in centimeters	All	9.8	8.4	5.6	9.7	10.7	6.2	8.7
	Untubed	9.5	8.1	4.8	9.2	10.4	6.1	8.5
	Tubed	10.1	8.6	6.0	10.0	11.0	6.4	8.9
Large 2+0:								
Number		750	723	562	679	834	628	4,176
DBH in centimeters	All	9.9	7.7	5.7	9.7	10.9	7.4	8.8
	Untubed	9.3	7.1	4.9	9.0	10.5	7.2	8.3
	Tubed	10.4	8.2	6.1	10.0	11.3	7.5	9.1
Medium 2+0:								
Number		719	658	529	658	820	550	3,934
DBH in centimeters	All	8.9	7.5	5.3	8.6	10.5	6.6	8.1
	Untubed	8.7	7.0	4.3	7.6	10.0	6.6	7.8
	Tubed	9.1	7.8	5.9	9.1	11.0	6.6	8.4
Small 2+0:								
Number		710	588	435	620	772	523	3,648
DBH in centimeters	All	8.2	6.7	5.1	8.6	9.6	6.1	7.6
	Untubed	7.8	5.8	4.0	7.2	9.0	6.2	7.1
	Tubed	8.4	7.2	5.7	9.2	10.0	6.0	7.9
Container:								
Number		607	524	418	620	795	545	3,509
DBH in centimeters	All	6.8	6.3	4.5	9.2	9.4	6.5	7.4
	Untubed	6.0	5.5	3.8	8.0	8.9	6.3	6.9
	Tubed	7.3	6.9	4.8	9.7	9.9	6.6	7.8
Total:								
Number		3,550	3,265	2,454	3,322	4,069	2,812	19,472
DBH in centimeters	All	8.8	7.4	5.3	9.2	10.2	6.6	8.2
	Untubed	8.4	6.9	4.4	8.3	9.8	6.5	7.8
	Tubed	9.1	7.8	5.7	9.6	10.7	6.7	8.4
Western hemlock:								
Bare root:								
Number		480	445	279	537	703	401	2,845
DBH in centimeters	All	3.8	5.6	3.1	5.7	6.2	4.3	5.0
	Untubed	3.1	5.2	2.7	5.5	5.2	3.6	4.5
	Tubed	4.1	5.8	3.3	5.8	6.9	4.8	5.3
Container:								
Number		475	497	188	600	685	263	2,708
DBH in centimeters	All	3.8	5.8	2.6	6.1	6.7	4.1	5.3
	Untubed	3.3	5.9	1.9	6.1	5.5	3.3	5.0
	Tubed	4.0	5.7	2.8	6.1	7.4	4.6	5.5
Total:								
Number		955	942	467	1,137	1,388	664	5,553
DBH in centimeters	All	3.8	5.7	2.9	5.9	6.4	4.2	5.2
	Untubed	3.2	5.6	2.5	5.8	5.3	3.5	4.8
	Tubed	4.0	5.7	3.0	6.0	7.1	4.7	5.4

Table 23—Average diameter at breast height of 10-year-old trees by site and release treatment

Site	No release		Release		Total and average	
	Number	*Centimeters*	*Number*	*Centimeters*	*Number*	*Centimeters*
Pitchfork	2,209	7.5	2,296	8.0	4,505	7.7
Beaver	2,160	6.6	2,047	7.5	4,207	7.0
Upperten	1,398	4.8	1,523	5.0	2,921	4.9
Randall	2,165	7.4	2,294	9.2	4,459	8.3
Poposchultz	2,733	9.3	2,724	9.3	5,457	9.3
Bay's Wolfe	1,584	5.8	1,892	6.4	3,476	6.1
Total and average	12,249	7.2	12,776	7.8	25,025	7.5

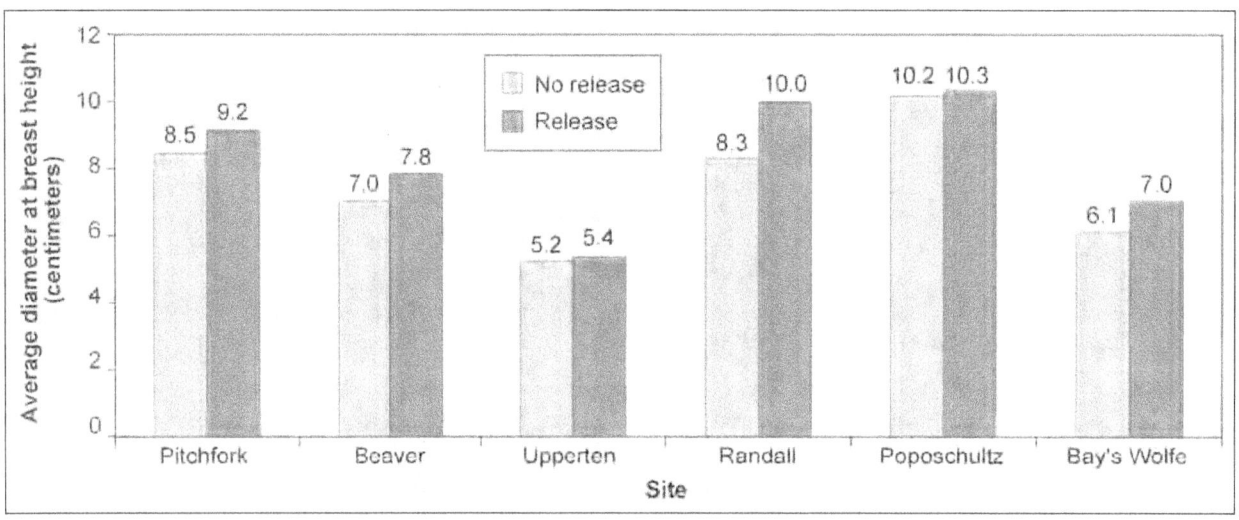

Figure 19—Average diameter at breast height of 10-year-old Douglas-firs by site and release treatment.

started in containers and two of these were western hemlocks. Tallest tree per site at 10 years, its diameter and treatment history:

Site	Height	Diameter	Stock type and treatment
	Centimeters		
Pitchfork	999	13.2	Large 2+0 Douglas-fir, tubed, control, no release
Beaver	1110	16.3	Container western hemlock, tubed, spray and burn, release
Upperten	890	12.3	Container Douglas-fir, tubed, spray, no release
Randall	1063	14.5	Container Douglas-fir, tubed, burn, release
Poposchultz	1188	18.0	Large 2+0 Douglas-fir, untubed, burn, release
Bay's Wolfe	1035	13.6	Container western hemlock, tubed, spray, no release

Largest diameter tree per site, its height and treatment history:

Site	Height	Diameter	Stock type and treatment
Pitchfork	714	20.1	2+0 medium Douglas-fir, untubed, spray and burn, no release
Beaver	843	19.2	Bare-root western hemlock, untubed, spray, release
Upperten	844	14.9	Large 2+0 Douglas-fir, tubed, control, no release
Randall	990	20.5	Large 2+0 Douglas-fir, untubed, spray, release
Poposchultz	905	20.9	Large 2+0 Douglas-fir, tubed, burn, no release
Bay's Wolfe	777	16.7	2+1 Douglas-fir, tubed, spray, release

Among the six sites, the tallest tree occurred in all four site preparation treatments as well as in both protection and release treatments. Regarding largest diameter trees, a different but similar mix of stock types and treatments are represented.

Stand Analysis

In foregoing sections, stand statistics for average survival, height, and diameter have been reported by protection, site preparation, stock type, and release treatments. Although each average describes one feature of the 10-year-old stands, an integration is needed to gain a full understanding of treatment effects. Such integration was made by using average height and DBH to estimate average volume per tree for each treatment based on the formula for volume of a cone.[2]

---

[2] Use of diameter at breast height (DBH) as the base of the cone was necessary because no diameter was available at the ground line from which height was measured. The resulting volume data are lower than actual volumes, but are on a comparable basis for treatment comparisons.

An assumed full stand of 400 trees per acre was reduced by the average percent survival per treatment. The resulting number of live trees per acre was then multiplied by the average volume per tree to arrive at average cubic volume per acre at 10 years. Assuming full stocking of 400 trees per acre seemed reasonable and convenient. An integration could be made just as readily using a different full stocking basis.

Tubed trees averaged taller in height and larger in diameter, and many more survived, resulting in almost twice as much volume as untubed trees at 10 years (table 24, fig. 1). The spray-and-burn site preparation treatment shows a similar gain over the control, 1.00 to 1.99. The burn and the spray treatments produced about half again as much volume as the control. Release spraying yielded about one-fourth more volume than trees not released. Thus, every treatment yielded a substantial volume gain relative to no treatment.

At 10 years, stand closure is well underway and many of the smaller trees will soon be crowded out. Thus, primary interest focuses on the larger trees, those likely to be the stand components in the future. How large are they at 10 years and how did they respond to the treatments tested in this study? A comparison has been made based on the tallest 90, 75, and 50 percent of the trees in each treatment.

Table 24—Volume per acre at age 10 for stands resulting from different treatments

Treatment	Average height	Average DBH	Average volume per tree	Survival	Trees per acre	Volume per acre	Relative volume
	Centimeters	Centimeters	Cubic centimeters	Percent	Number	Cubic meters	
Protection:							
Untubed	498.8	7.2	6 769.6	50.5	202	1.367	1.00
Tubed	520.4	7.7	8 097.9	82.2	329	2.658	1.94
Site preparation:							
Control	471.4	6.8	5 706.6	58.5	234	1.335	1.00
Burn	525.3	7.6	7 943.4	66.5	266	2.113	1.58
Spray	500.3	7.5	7 367.5	66.7	267	1.967	1.47
Spray and burn	543.4	8.0	9 104.8	73.1	292	2.659	1.99
Release:							
No release	494.6	7.2	6 712.6	65.5	262	1.759	1.00
Release	529.2	7.8	8 429.1	66.9	268	2.259	1.28

DBH = Diameter at breast height.

In both the released stands and those not released, the tallest half of the trees averaged just over 1.6 m taller and 3.0 cm larger in diameter than averages for the full stand (table 25). For both height and diameter, trees given a release treatment averaged larger than those not released; height growth averaged about one-third m greater and DBH 0.7 cm larger. Concerning rankings, the spray-and-burn site preparation treatment maintained highest position in all comparisons and the control the lowest except for one—in average tree height for the tallest 50 percent not released, the spray treatment was lowest with trees in the control treatment not much taller.

Stocking

Tree distribution and density were determined on five sites when study stands were 13 years old. Each of the eight site preparation-release combinations per unit was sampled. Most subunits were sampled by 22 or more 1/250 acre circular plots (7.45-ft. radius). Using this size plot, actual stocking is compared to a fully stocked stand of 250 well-spaced trees per acre. After planted trees were tallied, each plot was searched for established, readily visible natural reproduction, but not for very small seedlings that might be present.

Stocking of planted trees averaged 81.5 percent for all site preparation-release areas combined, and nearly 5 percent less, 76.8 percent, for areas not released (table 26). Additional plots stocked by naturally established conifers, 4.0 percent, and by hardwoods, 3.4 percent, increased total stocking to 84.2 percent in areas without release. In released areas, naturally established conifers increased stocking by 3.2 percent, hardwoods by only 0.6 percent for a total of 85.3 percent.

In both no release and release areas, stocking of planted trees averaged lower in the control than in site-prepared areas (table 26). Stocking of naturally established conifers also averaged lower in the control treatment than elsewhere, but the reverse was true for hardwoods. In all treatments, the combined stocking of naturally regenerated conifers and hardwoods was much lower than for planted trees. And of course, the naturals varied greatly in height and diameter from conifers as short as 1 ft to others that matched planted tree height and diameter. Many hardwoods were taller than plantation trees; the tallest alder and cherry were estimated to be 50 ft.

Among the five sites, stocking of planted trees ranged from the lowest, 47.4 percent for the control-no release area at Upperten to a high of 96.0 percent for all three site preparation-release treatments at Poposchultz. Stocking of planted trees in all but 9 of the 40 treatment-release combinations was higher than 70 percent. Six of those with less than 70 percent stocking were in control areas; one each was in burn-release and spray-release areas at Beaver and Upperten and the third in the

Table 25—Average height and diameter of the largest 90, 75, and 50 percent of 10-year-old trees in site preparation and release treatments

Site preparation	Stand fraction							
	All		Tallest 90 percent		Tallest 75 percent		Tallest 50 percent	
	Mean Centimeters	*Rank*	*Mean Centimeters*	*Rank*	*Mean Centimeters*	*Rank*	*Mean Centimeters*	*Rank*
Total height:								
No release:								
Control	457.8	4	499.4	4	552.6	4	633.7	3
Burn	522.5	2	564.6	2	614.3	2	693.6	2
Spray	466.0	3	506.9	3	554.9	3	625.3	4
Spray and burn	523.6	1	565.9	1	617.2	1	700.2	1
Average	494.6		534.2		584.7		663.2	
Release:								
Control	484.4	4	522.4	4	565.7	4	628.7	4
Burn	528.2	3	573.1	3	627.3	2	717.8	2
Spray	532.8	2	576.9	2	627.0	3	699.3	3
Spray & Burn	563.0	1	605.4	1	653.6	1	729.0	1
Average	529.2		569.5		618.4		693.7	
Diameter at breast height:								
No release:								
Control	6.5	4	7.1	4	8.0	4	9.4	4
Burn	7.5	2	8.2	2	9.1	2	10.5	2
Spray	6.8	3	7.5	3	8.3	3	9.6	3
Spray and burn	7.7	1	8.4	1	9.4	1	11.1	1
Average	7.2		7.8		8.7		10.2	
Release:								
Control	7.1	4	7.8	4	8.6	4	10.0	4
Burn	7.7	3	8.5	3	9.4	3	11.0	3
Spray	8.1	2	8.8	2	9.7	2	11.2	2
Spray and burn	8.3	1	9.0	1	9.9	1	11.5	1
Average	7.8		8.5		9.4		10.9	

Table 26—Average stocking of planted and naturally established trees by site preparation and release treatments

Site preparation	Release	Planted trees	Natural		Total stocking	Only naturals
			Conifers	Hardwoods		
		- - - - - - - - - - - *Percentage of stocking* - - - - - - - - - - -				
Control	0	63.5	10.9	28.5	75.2	36.5
	1	74.0	15.7	11.0	78.0	25.2
Burn	0	81.7	24.6	17.5	88.1	38.8
	1	83.3	27.0	4.0	89.7	31.0
Spray	0	73.7	22.0	12.7	83.1	31.4
	1	85.8	16.5	5.5	90.6	20.5
Spray and burn	0	90.0	20.0	10.0	91.7	29.2
	1	82.8	18.9	4.9	82.8	21.3
Average	0	76.8	19.2	17.6	84.2	34.1
	1	81.5	19.5	6.4	85.3	24.5

spray-no release area at Beaver. Naturally established conifers raised conifer stocking in five of these nine treatment combinations above 70 percent, leaving only four treatment combinations—both control treatments in Upperten, and the control-no release and burn-release treatments in Beaver under 70 percent stocking. Counting hardwood stocking on plots devoid of conifers brought only one of these four, the burn-release treatment at Beaver, above 70 percent stocking.

Distribution of trees within individual treatment combinations ranged from good to excellent. A tally of voids, defined as three or more consecutive unstocked plots, revealed only 15 voids among the 1,003 plots sampled. There were only two voids of five consecutive unstocked plots, one each in no-release and release areas of the control in Upperten. There were four voids of four plots each, two in control-no release areas of Upperten and Randall, the other two in spray-no release areas of Beaver and Poposchultz. There were nine voids with three unstocked plots in a row—six in control areas, one in a spray-release area and two in spray and burn–no release areas. Number of voids totaled 7 for Upperten, 3 for Beaver, 3 for Pitchfork, and 1 each for Randall and Poposchultz.

At 13 years, planted trees on study sites averaged more than 300 per acre, based on numbers tallied in survey plots and expressed on a per acre basis. With naturally established conifers and hardwoods included, averages per acre were essentially the same for no-release and release areas, 348 and 349:

| Site preparation | Release | Planted | Natural regeneration | | Total |
			Conifer	Hardwood	
			Trees per acre		
Control	0	245	9	29	283
	1	289	12	6	307
Burn	0	319	18	34	371
	1	347	24	6	377
Spray	0	284	30	6	320
	1	337	16	6	359
Spray and burn	0	417	4	0	421
	1	348	2	0	350
Average	0	316	15	17	348
	1	330	14	5	349

The number of planted trees was lowest in the control-no release treatment and highest in the spray-and-burn no-release treatment. Nearly all naturally regenerated conifers were Douglas-firs. The natural conifers tallied for all treatments totaled: Douglas-fir 54, Sitka spruce 2, western hemlock 1. The tally for hardwoods: red alder 35, cascara buckthorn 9, cherry 1. Fewer naturally established conifers were found in the spray-and-burn than in the other treatments. Hardwoods occurred in the same three treatments, but were notably less in release areas than in no-release areas.

Vegetation Dynamics

Cover

Development of vegetative cover was measured along transect lines eight times during the study. The vegetation present shortly before site preparation was measured on all six sites, designated as the "0" year. A repeat examination later the same year soon after broadcast burning was possible only on Randall, Poposchultz and Bay's Wolfe. Thus, examination one data represents only these three sites. All sites are represented by pre- and post-release and subsequent examinations.

In aggregate, the full complement of transects totaled 12,000 ft of slope distance per examination, or 2,000 ft per site, 3,000 ft per site preparation treatment and 1,500 per release treatment (fig. 20). Examination one data has half that basis.

Slash increments not covered by vegetation were measured at every examination, and in most examinations, so were increments of bare ground. Because these

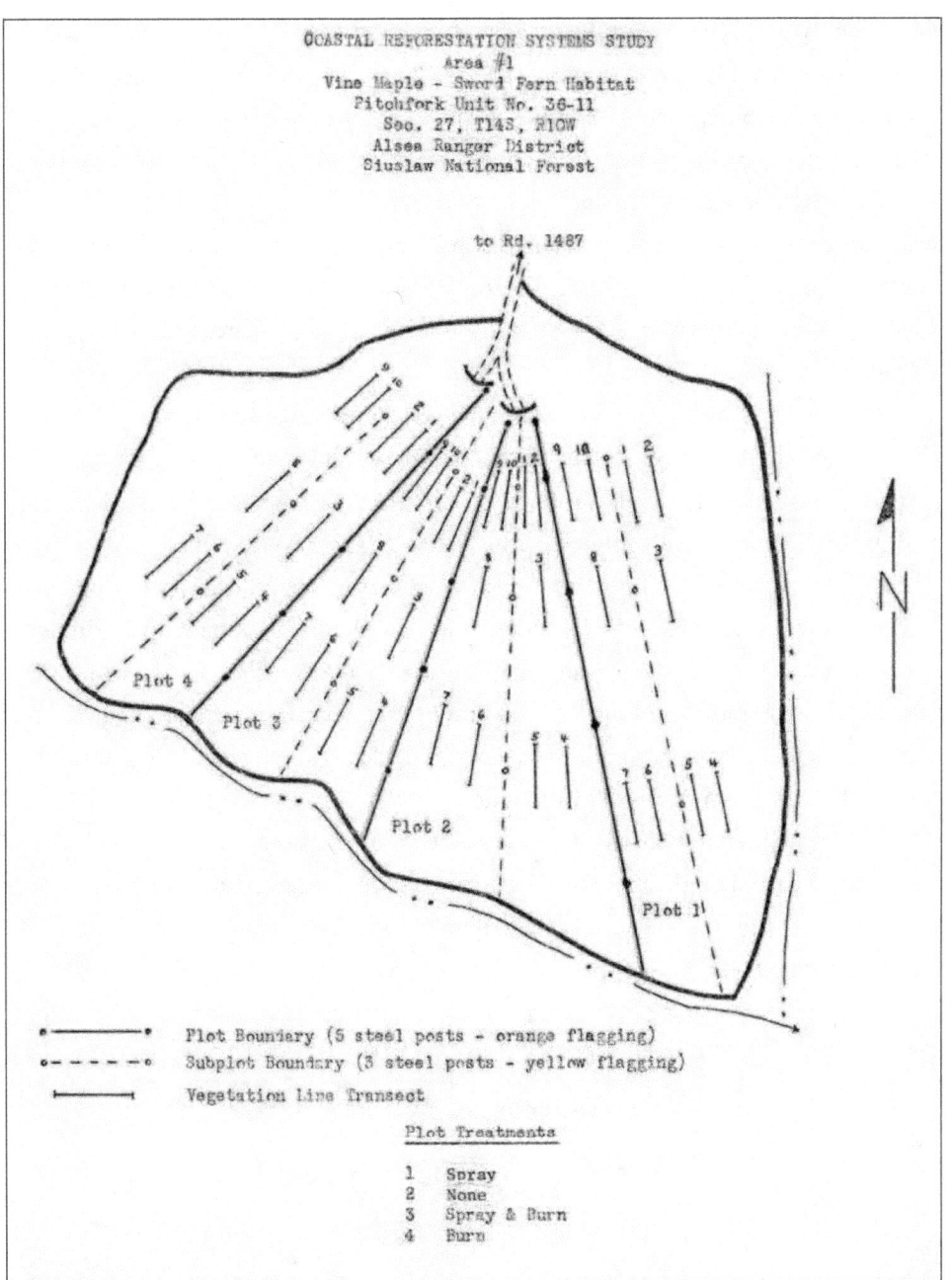

Figure 20—Schematic of vegetation transect locations at Pitchfork; typical arrangement within site preparation and release segments.

increments have no layering effect they were used to determine total initial cover of vegetation (total length of transect lines, 100 percent, less percent slash and bare ground equals percent total vegetative cover). Cover for individual species was calculated as a percent of the total length of all cover.

Vegetation data for all examinations were summed for release and no-release transects even though release treatment applies only to the fourth examination onward. This choice was more than a summation convenience; it also made it possible to compare vegetation summaries from the same sample areas before and after release spraying.

Before site preparation, study sites averaged 52 percent live vegetative cover (fig. 21). Assorted slash covered an additional 38 percent of the surface and about 10 percent of the surface area was bare ground. Broadcast burning half of each site and spraying another quarter reduced the live vegetation average about 22 percent and the slash surface by 13 percent (table 27). Bare surface increased to 45 percent. Later release spraying half of each study area caused only a minor decrease in live vegetation cover, and equally minor increases in uncovered slash and bare ground (release between third and fourth examination). Rapid development of annual species and residual and new woody species increased average vegetative cover to 78 percent or more from the third examination onward.

Before site preparation, live vegetative cover ranged from 38 percent at Beaver to 64 percent at Bay's Wolfe (table 27). By the second examination, vegetative cover had increased, ranging from 3.2 percent gain at Pitchfork to 21 percent gain at Beaver and Randall.

Initial live vegetative cover averaged higher on areas designated as controls or for spraying only than for those to be broadcast burned:

Site preparation	Total live cover at examination			
	0	1	2	3
	Percent			
Control	60.4	57.3	55.8	82.4
Burn	43.6	20.4	65.4	77.7
Spray	55.6	56.6	48.8	81.3
Spray and burn	42.0	5.9	55.9	75.4

The largest difference in total initial cover, 18 percent, was between the control and spray-and-burn treatment. Data for examinations 0 to 3 indicate spraying reduced total live cover very little. At 10 years, total live cover averaged 95 percent or more in all treatments (fig. 22, table 27).

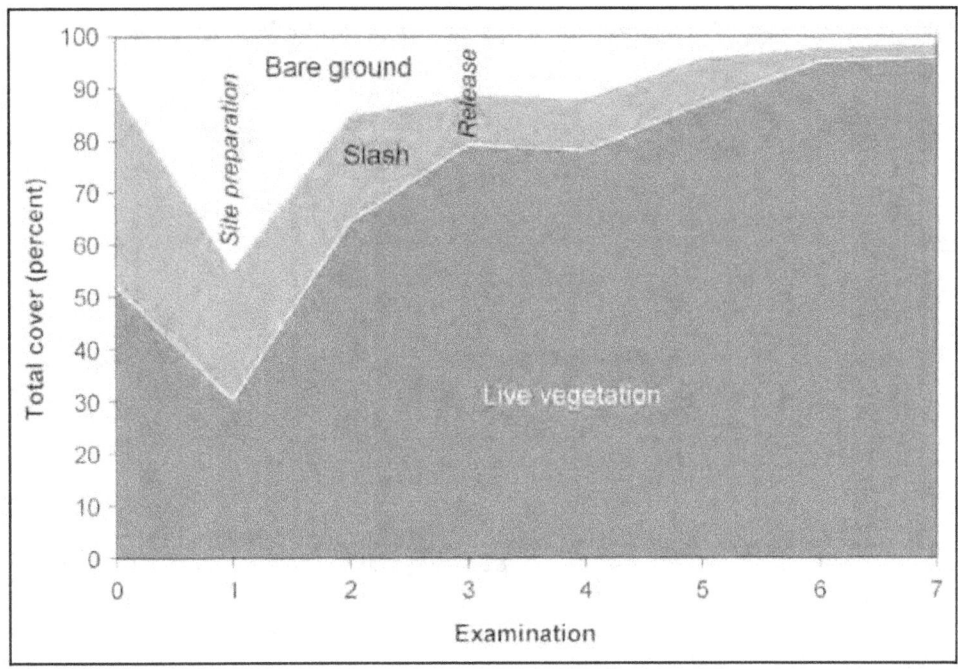

Figure 21—Surface cover trends over 10 years; averages for all sites combined.

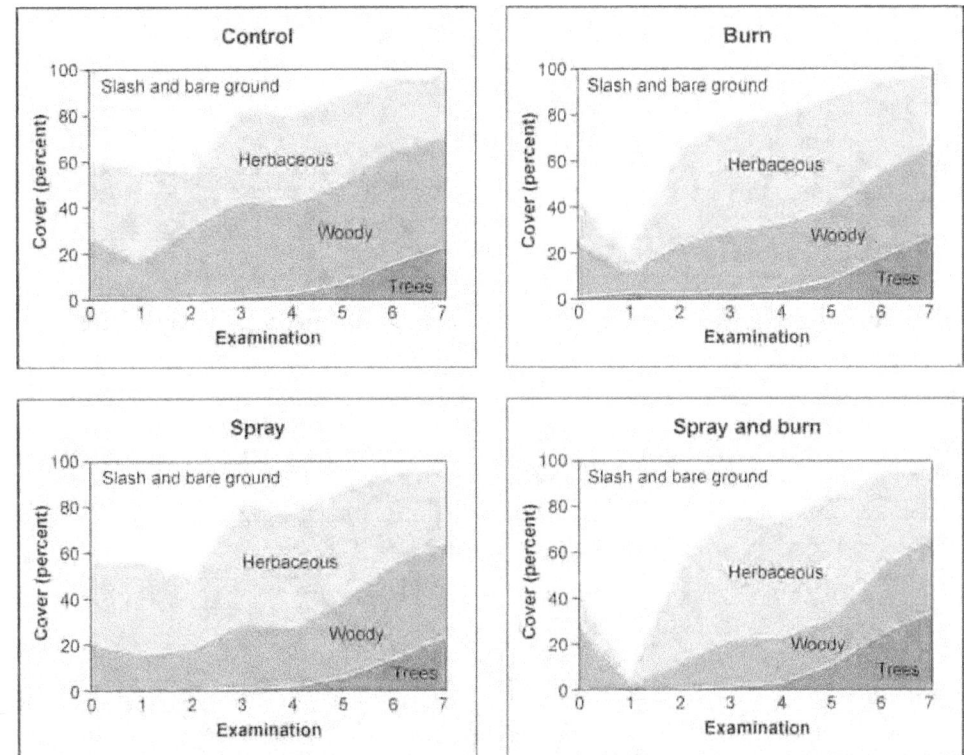

Figure 22—Cover development in each site preparation treatment over 10 years: trees, woody, herbaceous, and total live cover.

Table 27—Average surface cover over 10 years by site and examination

Site	Surface	Examination							
		0	1	2	3	4	5	6	7
		Percent							
Pitchfork	Live vegetation	41.1	—	44.3	80.2	68.5	89.9	88.5	94.8
	Slash	45.9	—	26.3	7.9	10.4	5.3	4.5	2.1
	Bare ground	13.0	—	29.4	11.9	21.1	4.8	7.0	3.1
Beaver	Live vegetation	38.4	—	59.1	72.7	77.0	88.8	95.3	96.9
	Slash	50.0	—	37.7	11.8	8.8	6.1	2.5	1.3
	Bare ground	11.6	—	3.2	15.5	14.2	5.1	2.2	1.8
Upperten	Live vegetation	52.2	—	57.6	69.9	61.0	82.2	94.0	94.1
	Slash	40.4	—	27.0	9.8	16.9	11.0	4.5	3.2
	Bare ground	7.4	—	15.4	20.3	22.1	6.8	1.5	2.7
Randall	Live vegetation	61.5	31.7	82.1	87.7	86.7	86.5	97.3	98.2
	Slash	23.8	23.8	5.2	5.2	5.2	7.8	1.6	0.6
	Bare ground	14.7	44.5	12.7	7.1	8.1	5.7	1.1	1.2
Poposchultz	Live vegetation	54.7	23.1	71.3	85.9	88.9	88.1	97.1	99.4
	Slash	45.3	21.8	9.9	9.9	8.5	10.3	2.4	0.2
	Bare ground	0	55.1	18.8	4.2	2.6	1.6	0.5	0.4
Bay's Wolfe	Live vegetation	63.9	36.6	72.5	78.9	85.8	91.7	98.4	92.0
	Slash	24.1	29.6	17.3	12.9	11.0	8.0	1.2	8.0
	Bare ground	12.0	33.8	10.2	8.2	3.2	0.3	0.4	0.0
Average[a]	Live vegetation	52.0	30.5	64.5	79.2	78.0	87.9	95.1	95.9
	Slash	38.3	25.1	20.6	9.6	10.1	8.1	2.8	2.6
	Bare ground	9.8	44.5	15.0	11.2	11.9	4.1	2.1	1.5

[a] Some groups of three surface conditions do not round to 100 percent.

Initial cover of woody shrubs was reduced in all site preparation treatments:

Woody cover at examination

Site preparation	0	1	2	3	Ranking
	Percent				
Control	26.9	17.3	31.1	42.0	4
Burn	23.7	9.8	21.6	27.1	2
Spray	20.3	15.9	17.7	28.1	3
Spray and burn	28.0	2.5	11.8	20.4	1

A 9.6-percent reduction in woody cover in control areas from the first to the second examination was not anticipated and exceeds the reduction observed in sprayed areas, 4.4 percent. Woody cover was reduced from 23.7 percent to 9.8 percent in burned areas and from 28.0 to 2.5 percent in spray-and-burn areas. By the third examination, woody cover had increased in all treatments, with the control areas averaging 42.0 percent and the spray-and-burn areas half as much, 20.4 percent.

At 10 years, these differing amounts of tree cover appear attributable to the woody cover differences measured in the third examination:

			Live cover at 10 years		
Site preparation	Total	Woody	Trees	Conifers	Ranking
			Percent		
Control	97.2	47.9	23.0	12.0	4
Burn	98.5	39.7	27.7	18.8	2
Spray	96.4	40.8	23.7	18.2	3
Spray and burn	96.7	32.1	34.0	23.5	1

Although total vegetative cover differed little between site treatments at 10 years, there were still notable differences in woody shrub cover and the cover gained by trees. The rankings for shrub cover remained the same, but tree cover ranked just the opposite. The cover by all trees and by conifers was highest where woody cover was lowest.

Herbaceous species were an important cover component in all site preparation treatments. They increased in all site treatments, peaking at 40 percent in the control by the first examination, and reaching around 50 percent by the third to fifth examinations in the other three site preparation treatments (fig. 22). By the seventh exam, herbaceous cover had declined to around 30 percent as successional trends set in.

Spraying glyphosate for release produced a minor and variable effect on total vegetative cover (fig. 23). Total cover for the examination just before and after release in each site preparation averaged:

	Release effect on total cover	
Site preparation	Exam 3	Exam 4
	Percent	
Control	80.7	71.8
Burn	77.5	79.0
Spray	79.8	73.7
Spray and burn	75.0	71.8

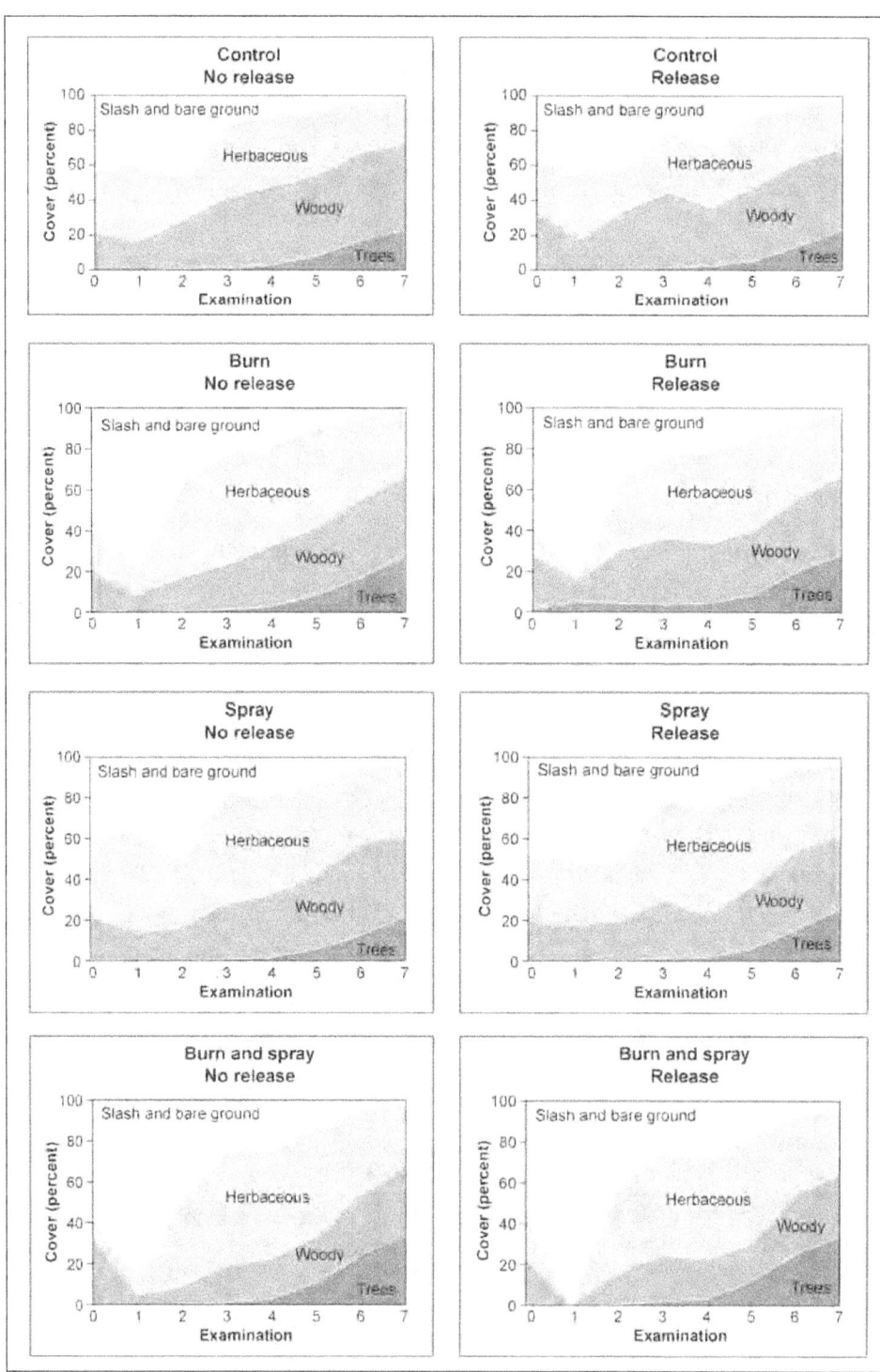

Figure 23—Influence of release on amount and composition of cover in each site preparation treatment.

Release spraying reduced the total cover in three treatments, but not in the burn treatment.

Spraying reduced the woody component of the vegetation cover in all treatments. Some release effects still appear evident at 10 years when compared to woody cover percentage for adjacent areas not released:

	Release effect on woody cover			
	Release			**No release**
Site preparation	**Exam 3**	**Exam 4**	**Exam 7**	**Exam 7**
	Percent			
Control	43.5	33.3	47.2	48.6
Burn	32.3	29.1	39.0	40.5
Spray	28.8	21.0	35.8	45.8
Spray and burn	22.7	19.9	30.7	33.6

Woody vegetation cover was much lower in spray-and-burn areas than elsewhere.

By the 10th year, total tree cover differed little between areas not released and released but substantially among site preparation treatments:

	Total tree cover		**Conifer cover**	
Site preparation	**No release**	**Release**	**No release**	**Release**
	Percent			
Control	22.8	23.1	11.0	13.1
Burn	27.4	28.0	18.7	18.9
Spray	21.5	25.8	14.9	21.4
Spray and burn	34.5	33.6	23.4	23.6

Total tree cover as well as conifer cover were higher on areas prepared by broadcast burning than for the control. Only in areas site prepared by spraying did conifer and total tree cover benefit appreciably from a release spray.

Species Found

Forty-six individual species or species groups were found along line transects (table 28). Woody shrub and tree species were individually identified and tallied except for blue and red elderberry (*Sambucus* spp), Oregon grape (*Berberis* spp.), and cherry (*Prunus* spp.). Several herbaceous species were tallied by genus groups including thistles (*Cirsium* spp.), fireweeds (*Epilobium* spp.), grass (*Gramineae* spp.) lotus (*Lotus* spp.) lupines (*Lupinus* spp.), candy flower (*Montia* spp.), and senecio (*Senecio* spp.). Annual plants of infrequent occurrence were tallied under

Table 28—Species and groups tallied along line transects

Scientific name[a]	Abbreviation	Common name
Abies grandis (Dougl. ex D. Don) Lindl.	ABGR	Grand fir
Acer circinatum Pursh	ACCI	Vine maple
Acer macrophyllum Pursh	ACMA	Bigleaf maple
Adiantum pedatum L.	ADPE	Maidenhair fern
Alnus rubra Bong.	ALRU	Red alder
Athyrium filix-femina (L.) Roth	ATFI	Lady-fern
Baccharis pilularis DC.	BAPI	Chaparral broom
Berberis spp.	BESP	Oregongrape
Blechnum spicant (L.) Roth	BLSP	Deer-fern
Cirsium spp.	CISP	Thistle
Corylus comuta var. *californica* (A. DC.) Sharp	COCO	California hazel
Dicentra formosa (Andr.) Walp.	DIFO	Bleedingheart
Digitalis purpurea L.	DIPU	Foxglove
Epilobium spp.	EPSP	Fireweed
Gaultheria shallon Pursh	GASH	Salal
Gramineae spp.	GRSP	Grass
Herbaceous	HEMI	Miscellaneous herbaceous
Holodiscus discolor (Pursh) Maxim.	HODI	Ocean-spray
Libocedrus decurrens Torr.	LIDE	Incense cedar
Lotus spp.	LOSP	Deervetch
Lupinus spp.	LUSP	Lupine
Menziesia ferruginea Smith	MEFE	False azalea
Montia spp.	MOSP	Candy flower
Physocarpus malvaceus (Greene) Kuntze	PHMA	Ninebark
Picea sitchensis (Bong.) Carr.	PISI	Sitka spruce
Polystichum munitum (Kaulf.) Presl	POMU	Sword-fern
Prunus spp.	PRSP	Cherry and plum
Pseudotsuga menziesii (Mirb.) Franco	PSME	Douglas-fir
Pteridium aquilinum (L.) Kuhn.	PTAQ	Bracken-fern
Rhamnus purshiana DC.	RHPU	Cascara buckthorn
Rhododendron macrophyllum	RHMA	Pacific rhododendron
Ribes bracteosum Dougl.	RIBR	Stink currant
Ribes sanguineum Pursh	RISA	Red flowering currant
Rosa gymnocarpa Nutt.	ROGY	Little wood rose
Rubus laciniatus Willd.	RULA	Evergreen blackberry
Rubus leucodermis Dougl.	RULE	Black raspberry or blackcap
Rubus parviflorus Nutt.	RUPA	Thimbleberry
Rubus procerus Muell.	RUPR	Himalayan blackberry
Rubus spectabilis Pursh	RUSP	Salmonberry

Table 28—Species and groups tallied along line transects (continued)

Scientific name[a]	Abbreviation	Common name
Rubus ursinus Cham. & Schlecht.	RUVI	Trailing blackberry
Sambucus spp.	SA	Elder
Senecio spp.	SESP	Groundsel
Symphoricarpos albus (L.) S.F. Blake	SYAL	Common snowberry
Tsuga heterophylla (Raf.) Sarg.	TSHE	Western hemlock
Vaccinium ovatum Pursh	VAOV	Evergreen huckleberry
Vaccinium parvifofium Smith	VAPA	Red huckleberry

[a] Scientific nomenclature used throughout study records. Several species have since been renamed.

a miscellaneous herbaceous designation. In summarizing woody and herbaceous cover, all perennial vines were classed as woody, all ferns as herbaceous.

Though in its niche every species exerts competitive influence on vegetation development, our primary focus was on those species whose occurrence is common enough to be major competition during tree establishment. To identify those species, the percentage cover for each species and species group found along 40 transect lines on each of six sites and in seven or eight examinations was summed. The aggregated percentage totaled more than 1,000 percent for two tree species, five woody shrubs, and five herbaceous groups. Only four more species totaled in the 500 to 1,000 percent range. The cover development of these 16 species following site preparation and release treatments is given primary attention.

Nine tree species were found along the transect lines; only Douglas-fir and western hemlock had been planted. The other seven established naturally, but among these only red alder became a widespread dominant. Sitka spruce, cherry species, and cascara buckthorn were found on several sites, but bigleaf maple, grand fir, and incense cedar were found only in a single treatment, sometimes in only one examination (app. table 38).

Conifer cover essentially developed from planting onward, whereas red alder was a minor cover component from the start in 6 of 24 treatment quarters (app. table 38). By 10 years, red alder cover averaged highest where not released in the spray-and-burn treatments, 21.6 percent, and only slightly less in several other treatments (table 29). Spraying for release seems to have slowed red alder development as its cover averaged lower in released areas than in areas not released.

At 10 years, Douglas-fir cover averaged about 20 percent in control treatments and nearly twice that much in the spray-and-burn treatments (table 29). Next highest cover of Douglas-fir was in the burn treatments and was nearly equaled in release areas of the spray treatments. Cover of western hemlock averaged much higher with release than without except in the spray-and-burn treatment.

Table 29—Species comprising major fractions of vegetative cover during the decade by site preparation and release treatments

Ranking[a]	Species	Release	Control								Burn							
			0	1	2	3	4	5	6	7	0	1	2	3	4	5	6	7
			Percent															
Trees:																		
6	PSME	0	0	0	0.1	0.2	0.7	3.4	9.1	20.7	0	0	0.1	0.5	1.2	5.4	19.3	36.3
		1	0	0	0.1	0.4	1.1	2.9	11.8	19.0	0	0	0.1	0.2	0.2	3.3	18.7	32.2
10	ALRU	0	0	0	0	0.8	2.2	7.2	16.1	19.1	0.5	0	0.2	1.1	2.0	6.4	11.5	17.2
		1	0	0	0	0.5	1.2	3.7	9.2	16.4	0.6	1.6	3.6	4.9	4.7	7.8	14.8	16.5
16	TSHE	0	0	0	0.1	0.1	0.1	0.2	0.6	1.9	0	0	0	0.2	0.3	0.4	1.0	1.0
		1	0	0	0.1	0.1	0.4	1.2	2.5	5.7	0	0.1	0	0.1	0.2	0.6	2.6	4.8
Woody shrubs:																		
1	RUSP	0	11.3	4.1	16.7	23.0	25.3	31.0	34.0	31.4	12.9	1.2	9.9	14.6	18.4	21.5	28.6	30.9
		1	15.7	2.1	20.5	28.6	13.3	22.9	26.4	30.3	20.9	2.9	17.5	27.8	20.0	23.0	29.7	36.0
7	GASH	0	2.1	1.4	3.0	11.8	13.8	17.0	20.5	21.5	3.3	0	1.5	5.5	9.4	11.0	14.5	18.1
		1	1.5	0.9	1.0	4.5	8.4	9.9	15.3	13.7	2.5	0	2.0	4.5	7.7	7.8	11.1	12.9
9	RUVI	0	2.2	0.5	7.7	8.1	9.0	8.5	12.2	13.2	0.3	0	0.3	1.2	1.8	3.6	6.9	8.0
		1	3.5	2.2	5.8	7.9	6.4	10.3	14.7	16.0	0	0.1	0.9	2.0	2.9	4.9	6.5	6.1
11	RUPA	0	0	0	0.6	3.3	4.1	4.7	8.1	7.6	0	0	0.8	3.2	5.0	7.3	12.0	12.6
		1	0	0	0.7	2.8	1.6	4.4	7.4	9.2	0.3	0	1.3	4.2	2.6	6.3	10.2	12.8
12	ACCI	0	4.0	0.4	4.7	4.7	6.3	7.5	9.3	13.8	2.3	0.7	0.4	0.8	0.6	1.5	1.7	1.3
		1	6.6	2.0	7.9	8.8	7.6	6.8	8.1	7.8	3.9	0.1	0.4	0.5	0.3	0.3	1.1	1.6
Herbaceous species:																		
2	GRSP	0	4.3	4.9	11.7	12.9	12.6	10.0	8.5	9.7	2.6	2.6	7.3	36.4	37.1	29.4	26.2	18.4
		1	3.9	3.0	10.1	12.8	11.4	13.3	12.8	7.8	4.2	5.2	12.0	29.4	36.6	30.5	33.8	21.1
3	POMU	0	11.3	3.4	9.6	14.2	15.0	16.6	19.8	23.6	8.2	3.1	5.6	10.6	11.8	14.1	18.4	19.9
		1	7.4	1.1	6.6	8.9	11.2	13.1	15.6	16.3	4.2	2.1	2.7	4.4	5.3	6.3	9.9	12.8
4	HEMI	0	7.6	1.7	9.7	4.9	4.6	7.6	9.0	7.2	7.4	0.3	8.7	10.6	8.4	16.0	23.5	11.0
		1	3.5	1.0	8.3	6.5	9.9	10.0	16.7	12.5	3.1	1.0	6.0	5.3	8.9	14.1	16.9	14.5
5	PTAQ	0	7.4	4.4	12.0	21.0	21.8	18.4	14.5	8.4	1.0	0	2.6	5.1	4.1	5.2	5.7	5.9
		1	8.0	5.2	9.3	12.7	9.7	9.0	9.3	8.2	0.2	0	3.6	4.7	3.3	3.3	5.8	4.5
8	SESP	0	5.5	0.5	7.6	3.2	5.3	7.8	1.3	0.4	7.8	0	20.2	5.8	6.0	7.1	5.1	1.4
		1	4.6	1.6	5.4	5.4	10.3	12.0	1.5	0.2	10.2	1.4	9.5	7.4	8.7	11.5	3.5	2.0
13	EPSP	0	2.4	2.0	5.9	4.2	1.4	0.8	0.2	0	0	0.5	7.2	8.1	5.8	1.1	0.2	0.2
		1	3.1	3.4	6.3	3.9	0.7	1.3	0.2	0	0.1	0.8	7.1	5.9	1.4	1.2	0	0
14	DIPU	0	0	0	0.4	2.0	2.4	3.6	1.4	3.6	0	0	0.1	1.5	2.1	4.3	1.1	1.7
		1	0	0	0.6	1.7	0.2	4.5	2.4	3.7	0	0	1.9	2.0	0.2	4.6	2.8	4.2
15	MOSP	0	5.6	1.3	3.1	0	0.1	0	0	0.3	10.2	0	3.4	0	0	0	1.1	0.1
		1	2.8	0.3	1.2	0	0.1	0	0.2	0.1	9.3	1.2	1.5	0	0	0	0	0.1

Table 29—Species comprising major fractions of vegetative cover during the decade by site preparation and release treatments (continued)

Ranking[a]	Species	Release	Spray								Spray and burn							
			0	1	2	3	4	5	6	7	0	1	2	3	4	5	6	7
			Percent															
Trees:																		
6	PSME	0	0	0	0	0.4	1.2	3.9	11.5	22.4	0	0	0.1	0.7	1.6	5.4	24.0	37.7
		1	0	0	0.1	0.7	0.8	4.3	15.8	30.2	0	0	0.1	0.7	1.9	7.6	24.6	39.4
10	ALRU	0	0.3	0	0	0.1	0.2	2.5	7.3	12.8	0	0	0	0.3	1.4	7.6	17.4	21.6
		1	0	0	0	0.1	0.2	0.8	3.3	8.5	0.1	0	0.1	1.5	1.4	8.7	16.9	18.4
16	TSHE	0	0	0	0.1	0.3	0.6	1.5	3.1	7.4	0	0	0	0.3	0.4	1.9	5.2	8.0
		1	0	0	0	0.2	0.8	3.2	7.4	13.7	0	0	0	0.1	0.1	0.2	2.8	6.5
Woody shrubs:																		
1	RUSP	0	10.2	3.2	13.8	21.7	22.5	25.4	28.9	32.1	17.8	0	4.2	11.3	11.8	14.8	20.8	26.5
		1	11.3	5.9	15.8	27.6	14.8	22.9	31.8	29.5	13.8	0	5.8	12.6	7.8	8.1	11.4	16.7
7	GASH	0	1.0	1.0	0.8	2.9	6.2	11.1	17.7	20.8	0.6	0	0.5	1.3	1.7	3.5	5.9	6.2
		1	1.2	0.2	0.6	1.7	4.9	8.0	11.2	12.8	0.7	0	1.2	2.6	4.6	6.8	11.0	14.8
9	RUVI	0	2.5	0	0.2	3.0	4.5	8.3	17.7	16.6	0	0	0.3	0.7	1.1	2.1	5.6	5.6
		1	0.4	0	0.3	1.0	1.4	4.4	9.8	12.4	0.1	0	0.8	2.4	3.3	4.3	12.2	13.3
11	RUPA	0	0	0	0.1	1.1	1.1	2.2	7.2	10.0	0	0	0.2	3.8	7.1	8.5	20.3	19.1
		1	0	0.1	0.0	0.7	0.6	2.7	6.7	9.2	0	0	0.4	4.2	3.5	3.4	12.9	7.9
12	ACCI	0	4.2	1.2	2.8	2.4	3.0	2.4	4.1	5.2	14.1	0.9	0.5	0.4	0.4	0.6	1.1	1.0
		1	1.4	0.3	2.4	3.2	2.1	2.4	4.0	3.8	3.5	0	1.7	1.2	1.2	2.2	2.5	2.2
Herbaceous species:																		
2	GRSP	0	5.4	6.0	18.8	20.3	17.4	15.8	18.6	12.8	0.2	0	3.6	37.8	43.2	30.3	33.3	17.9
		1	2.8	2.6	8.2	14.5	14.1	11.4	17.5	13.0	2.4	0.1	1.0	28.4	32.6	31.3	29.5	22.7
3	POMU	0	6.3	3.8	8.6	9.9	10.1	11.7	17.6	19.2	9.0	0	3.6	5.5	7.7	8.7	11.1	14.8
		1	8.3	4.6	11.4	17.1	19.8	19.0	27.6	29.8	9.7	0.3	2.1	3.2	4.5	4.6	8.8	9.5
4	HEMI	0	4.1	2.3	6.5	3.7	5.4	9.0	13.6	12.1	1.0	0	2.0	4.6	7.3	17.6	24.0	17.9
		1	3.8	0.8	4.7	6.4	6.1	7.9	14.0	17.8	2.3	0.1	3.5	6.3	8.9	18.0	19.6	24.1
5	PTAQ	0	7.6	7.8	17.7	27.0	23.8	16.4	15.0	10.3	0.2	0	0.7	3.2	4.2	5.1	5.3	2.8
		1	4.8	2.8	9.5	19.7	11.5	11.4	8.9	6.1	2.1	0	2.3	6.7	4.1	3.2	5.8	2.7
8	SESP	0	3.6	0.2	5.6	4.5	10.1	9.7	1.5	0.3	0.9	0	11.6	9.9	6.4	12.5	5.0	1.1
		1	1.5	0	4.9	4.1	15.4	14.7	0.5	1.0	2.1	0.2	14.8	6.7	11.6	15.1	6.0	1.0
13	EPSP	0	0.1	1.2	2.2	5.0	3.7	1.7	0.2	0	0	0	9.4	8.4	3.9	1.4	2.6	0
		1	0	0.6	2.4	4.7	1.2	2.6	0.2	0	0.2	0	11.2	6.9	1.9	1.3	1.6	0.1
14	DIPU	0	0	0	1.0	2.3	1.1	5.9	2.5	5.2	0	0	0.1	2.2	2.4	4.8	2.7	3.3
		1	0	0	0.4	1.0	0.5	9.0	5.5	6.5	0	0	0.0	2.5	0.8	10.6	3.4	2.9
15	MOSP	0	3.5	0.1	2.1	0.1	0	0	0.1	0	9.1	0	9.7	0.2	0	0	0	0
		1	6.8	0.2	4.8	0.2	0.1	0	0	0.1	4.9	0	6.8	0.1	0	0	0	0

[a] Ranked on basis of aggregated cover from highest downward.

See table 28 for species codes.

Salmonberry was the most prominent cover component in all site preparation treatments at the start of the study, ranging from 10.8 to 16.9 percent cover (table 29). Though reduced to 5.9 percent or less by site preparation (first examination), by the 10th year its cover averaged more than 30 percent in all treatments except the spray-and-burn treatment (fig 24). In the latter treatment, salmonberry cover averaged about five percent lower than in other no-release areas, and just over half as much as in release areas of the other treatments. Although average cover of salmonberry was reduced substantially by release spraying—reductions between the third and fourth examinations—its recovery appears unhampered to become similar to 10th-year coverage in no-release areas except in the spray-and-burn treatments.

Another woody shrub, salal, was present at low levels initially, declined in cover in all treatments during site preparation and then increased to noteworthy levels by year 10. Though no dip in salal cover is shown after release treatment, release areas averaged less salal cover than no-release areas except in the spray-and-burn treatment, where averages were reversed. Salal coverage at 10 years ranged from 12.8 to 14.8 percent in release areas of the four site treatments and 18.1 to 21.5 for no-release areas in all but the spray-and-burn treatment where it averaged only 6.2 percent.

Figure 24—Salmonberry, the most prominent woody shrub, rapidly formed a tall, dense cover 3 years after broadcast burning on the Beaver site.

The other three woody species differed in response to treatment. Trailing blackberry cover was reduced by site preparation and attained highest coverage in the control and spray treatments, around 15 percent. A slight dip resulting from release seems evident only in the control treatment. Thimbleberry was hardly present initially, was reduced by release spraying, and gained highest coverage, 20.3 percent, in the no-release areas of the spray-and-burn treatment. Vine maple cover initially averaged highest in no-release areas of the spray-and-burn treatment, was markedly reduced by site preparation and also some by release treatment. It reached top coverage at 10 years in the no-release control areas, 13.8 percent, and only 1.0 percent in the no-release spray-and-burn treatment where initially its cover had been 14.1 percent.

Grass was the most common herbaceous species and its coverage was second only to salmonberry. Grass cover peaked around the third or fourth examination, and varied substantially among site treatments—lowest in control areas (12.9 percent) and highest in spray-and-burn no-release areas (43.2 percent). It retained substantial coverage even in the 10th year, slightly under 9 percent in the control to around 20 percent in the burn and spray-and-burn no-release treatments.

Sword-fern, the third most prominent species, was present in all treatments at the start of the study, averaging from 6.2 to 9.4 percent of total cover. Though reduced during the site preparation interval even in the control, its coverage shows a steady increase with 10th year averages ranging from 12.2 to 24.5 percent. Site preparation reduced sword-fern cover, but reduction by release spraying is not evident. Initial differences in average cover between no-release and release areas were maintained except in the spray-and-burn treatment with the most drastic reduction and least recovery.

As an aggregation of various species, the miscellaneous herbaceous category provided important coverage. Site preparation reduced cover of these species, but their cover increased to peak by the sixth examination, reaching around 24 percent in burn, and spray-and-burn no-release treatments. By the 10th year, miscellaneous cover tended to be somewhat higher in released areas.

In contrast to sword-fern, bracken-fern varied more, including some reduction following release treatment. Though somewhat inconsistent, bracken-fern coverage peaked about mid-decade. Its initial presence was lowest in the burn and spray-and-burn treatments. The average gain in cover was much lower in the spray-and-burn than in the other three site preparation treatments.

Groundsel and fireweed peaked during the decade and provided little cover by the 10th year. In particular, fireweed peaked from 6 to 11 percent cover soon after site preparation. Peak coverage of groundsel was more variable, occurring at the second to fifth examination with the highest cover, 20.2 percent, in no-release burn areas.

Purple foxglove was not present before site preparation. It gained coverage through most of the decade, peaking at the fifth examination with 10.6 percent the highest in released spray-and-burn areas. Candy flower cover trended just the opposite of purple foxglove. Generally, highest cover of candy flower was found before site preparation and the percentage tended downward from then on except in the spray-and-burn treatment where it reached 9.7 percent at the second examination.

Live Biomass

Each examination included collection of all live vegetation found within a set of circular plots, each encompassing a 2 ft^2 area. All vegetation occurring within the sample, including any over-hanging the plot, was collected. If study trees were within the plot, they were left intact and an equivalent tree sample was collected nearby. The same substitution was made when other vegetation was unreachable.

Center points around which successive samples were taken were located at a right angle to, and 5 ft from, the 10-, 25- and 40-ft mark along each transect line. A point straight uphill from the sample center point was designated as 12 o'clock and samples were collected clockwise at 2, 4, and 6 o'clock etc., in successive examinations.

Three samples were taken per transect line so in each examination (except 0 and 1) each release treatment was represented by 15 samples, each site preparation treatment by 30, and each site by 120, or 720 for all sites combined. Examination 1 included only three sites, so year 1 data are based on Randall, Poposchultz, and Bay's Wolfe. The initial examination had several occurrences where less than 15 samples were taken; data compilation was adjusted as necessary. At each sample point the collected live above-ground vegetation was bagged separately as herbaceous, woody shrub, or tree material. After oven-drying, woody and tree material larger than one-fourth inch in diameter was separated out and weighed as a subset within the category.

Before site preparation (examination 0), live biomass averaged much less on areas designated for control or spray treatment than for those to be burned or sprayed and burned (see tabulation on page 56), a direct contrast to live cover data. Biomass averages for no-release and release areas combined varied more than 3 to 1 before site preparation:

Site preparation	Biomass per acre by examination		
	0	1	2
	Kilograms		
Control	1 171	206	1 327
Burn	2 664	88	495
Spray	847	134	513
Spray and burn	2 661	17	283

By the second examination, the control areas averaged more than twice as much total live biomass as in burned areas and over four times as much as in areas sprayed and burned.

Site preparation greatly reduced woody biomass to become the smaller component of total live vegetation. Before site preparation, woody biomass greatly exceeded herbaceous biomass in control and spray-and-burn areas, was nearly an equal component in spray site preparation areas, and was a smaller component in burn areas (table 30). After site preparation (second examination), the control areas still averaged less herbaceous than woody biomass (472 vs. 846 kg), but woody biomass averaged substantially less than herbaceous biomass in the other three site preparation treatments, 321 vs. 97 in burn areas, 320 vs. 169 in spray areas and 257 vs. 25 in spray-and-burn areas.

Spraying glyphosate for release in the fall (between the third and fourth examination) reduced vegetative biomass in every site preparation treatment. The effect differed among treatments as shown by a before and after comparison of total biomass averages:

Total biomass per acre by site preparation and release treatment:

Release	Control		Burn		Spray		Spray and burn	
	0	1	0	1	0	1	0	1
	Kilograms							
Exam 3	1181	1023	749	804	976	1052	670	706
Exam 4	1151	867	835	642	930	714	516	418
Exam 5	1653	1140	1062	1070	1338	936	927	914
Exam 7	2622	1961	2022	2278	2160	1870	1721	2670

Total live biomass in the fourth examination averaged about 160 kg less than in the third examination in the release areas of the control and burn treatments, 288 kg less in the spray-and-burn treatments and 338 kg less where only spray had been used for site preparation. Areas in three of the four site preparation treatments not given release also showed some reduction in biomass in the fourth examination, the largest reduction being in spray-and-burn treatments, averaging 154 kg. By the fifth

Table 30—Average dry weight of live vegetation at each examination by site preparation and release treatments

Treatment and exam	Release	Herbaceous total	Woody shrubs Total	Woody shrubs >1/4"	Trees Total	Trees >1/4"	Total Total	Total >1/4"
				Kilograms per acre				
Control:								
0	0	372.3	487.2	3.1	15.2	0	874.7	3.1
0	1	296.0	1 171.2	1.9	.5	0	1 467.7	1.9
1	0	93.0	193.5	132.6	0	0	286.4	132.6
1	1	86.9	35.8	1.5	3.6	0	126.3	1.5
2	0	534.9	291.8	58.3	2.2	0	828.9	58.3
2	1	408.9	1 399.3	52.3	16.3	0	1 824.4	52.3
3	0	555.9	485.4	43.4	140.0	49.9	1 181.2	93.3
3	1	512.4	432.8	28.1	77.5	23.7	1 022.8	51.8
4	0	420.0	653.0	41.7	78.4	23.6	1 151.4	65.3
4	1	365.4	380.5	31.6	121.1	48.8	867.1	80.4
5	0	455.3	902.0	132.7	295.5	61.4	1 652.8	194.1
5	1	418.4	555.3	79.9	166.7	50.1	1 140.4	130.0
6	0	353.9	999.2	264.8	240.7	98.6	1 593.9	363.4
6	1	285.4	824.6	158.5	291.3	171.2	1 401.3	329.7
7	0	321.7	1 524.5	470.9	775.5	294.4	2 621.6	765.3
7	1	282.2	1 172.1	293.4	506.7	224.9	1 961.0	518.3
Spray:								
0	0	330.3	137.3	1.2	2.5	0	470.2	1.2
0	1	542.3	669.4	116.5	11.2	0	1 222.9	116.5
1	0	104.7	81.5	41.1	1.9	0	188.1	41.1
1	1	35.5	43.5	21.6	0	0	79.0	21.6
2	0	410.3	139.6	8.9	32.6	3.4	582.5	12.3
2	1	228.9	198.9	29.5	14.9	0	442.6	29.5
3	0	576.6	393.0	31.4	6.3	0	976.0	31.4
3	1	620.6	402.0	18.0	29.3	.5	1 051.8	18.5
4	0	434.0	466.7	64.7	28.9	1.0	929.6	65.7
4	1	343.0	352.2	50.6	18.3	1.7	713.6	52.3
5	0	420.0	820.5	221.6	97.7	58.2	1 338.2	279.8
5	1	510.8	399.1	62.7	25.7	6.1	935.6	68.8
6	0	379.9	1 013.1	469.2	90.5	17.2	1 483.5	486.4
6	1	306.3	678.9	152.6	42.9	.6	1 028.1	153.2
7	0	216.3	1 384.5	543.3	559.4	181.9	2 160.3	725.2
7	1	416.1	1 134.4	372.8	319.7	109.9	1 870.2	482.7

Treatment and exam	Release	Herbaceous total	Woody shrubs Total	Woody shrubs >1/4"	Trees Total	Trees >1/4"	Total Total	Total >1/4"
				Kilograms per acre				
Burn:								
0	0	1 634.8	986.0	415.6	.9	0	2 621.7	415.6
0	1	1 592.3	1 104.6	415.7	9.7	1.6	2 706.6	417.3
1	0	24.5	7.7	1.4	2.0	.9	34.3	2.3
1	1	31.5	19.9	5.5	91.0	81.5	142.3	87.0
2	0	335.5	79.2	0	1.4	0	416.1	0
2	1	305.5	114.3	7.5	153.8	47.0	573.5	54.5
3	0	555.8	190.1	16.2	2.9	0	748.8	16.2
3	1	427.0	358.7	24.2	18.6	0	804.3	24.2
4	0	332.4	485.1	41.4	17.4	2.2	834.9	43.6
4	1	247.3	348.1	63.9	46.6	12.4	642.0	76.3
5	0	412.2	526.5	22.2	123.6	27.1	1 062.3	49.3
5	1	326.6	559.9	108.8	183.6	21.9	1 070.1	130.7
6	0	353.1	588.5	114.0	358.0	169.3	1 299.6	283.3
6	1	250.7	925.0	104.1	875.4	509.8	2 051.1	613.9
7	0	258.9	1 060.0	200.9	702.6	350.3	2 021.6	551.2
7	1	112.8	1 055.4	279.1	1 110.2	635.6	2 278.3	914.7
Spray and burn:								
0	0	326.3	2 024.9	862.0	0	0	2 351.2	862.0
0	1	385.1	2 585.7	853.8	0	0	2 970.8	853.8
1	0	0	33.6	2.0	0	0	33.6	2.0
1	1	.3	.3	0	0	0	.3	0
2	0	275.4	17.9	0	0	0	293.4	0
2	1	238.0	32.4	0	1.5	0	272.0	0
3	0	552.3	117.5	6.5	.4	0	670.2	6.5
3	1	490.5	211.1	19.8	4.6	0	706.2	19.8
4	0	335.1	163.0	5.1	17.9	.5	516.1	5.6
4	1	203.3	176.7	12.8	38.1	3.5	418.1	16.3
5	0	431.5	382.4	54.9	113.0	24.3	926.9	79.2
5	1	436.0	376.4	44.3	101.7	20.5	914.0	64.8
6	0	316.3	529.9	46.2	156.8	31.3	1 003.0	77.5
6	1	248.1	449.5	55.3	434.7	195.3	1 132.2	250.6
7	0	175.8	735.0	122.3	810.3	304.0	1 721.1	426.3
7	1	194.5	543.6	47.7	1 932.0	1 244.6	2 670.1	1 292.3

examination, total biomass was about equal in no-release and release areas of burn or spray-and-burn treatments, but still less in release areas of the control and spray treatments, and the differences continued to the seventh examination. In the burn and spray-and-burn treatments, release spraying seems to have had an opposite long-term effect—for these, total live biomass in release areas was greater in the seventh examination than in areas not released.

Spraying for release reduced herbaceous biomass in the fourth examination more than it reduced woody biomass, averaging 223 vs. 37 kg less for the four site preparation treatments (table 30):

| | Biomass changes after release | | | | | | | |
| | Control | | Burn | | Spray | | Spray and burn | |
Site preparation	Herbaceous	Woody	Herbaceous	Woody	Herbaceous	Woody	Herbaceous	Woody
	Kilograms							
Exam 3	512	433	427	359	621	402	491	211
Exam 4	365	381	247	348	343	352	203	177
Reduction	147	52	180	11	278	50	288	34
Exam 5	418	555	327	560	511	399	436	376
Exam 7	282	1172	113	1055	416	1134	195	544

Herbaceous biomass increased between the fourth and fifth examination in released areas of all site preparation treatments, but then markedly declined by the seventh examination. In contrast, woody biomass was only slightly reduced by release spraying and gained substantially thereafter to over 1000 kilograms per acre in all site preparation treatments except spray and burn. Woody vegetation clearly was affected by the release spraying; swaths of browned foliage on dominant salmonberry were visual evidence that woody species experienced at least a temporary setback (fig. 6).

Tree biomass developed slowly, with both first appearance and seventh examination quantities differing by site preparation and release treatments (table 30). Widely spaced trees probably caused more sample variability than did other, more uniformly distributed vegetation. But, trends and 10th-year results still seem most informative. In the two burn site preparation treatments, tree biomass at 10 years in release areas exceeded that in no-release areas. For the spray-and-burn treatment, the biomass in the released areas averaged more than twice as much. In contrast, in the spray only treatment, tree biomass at the second examination was greater in no-release areas and was substantially greater at the 10th year, despite a big reduction in the third examination. Only in the release areas of the spray-and-burn treatment did tree biomass exceed more than half the total biomass, 72.4 percent.

Woody and tree biomass greater than one-fourth-inch in diameter after oven drying was considered a rough demarcation for biomass no longer palatable as browse. In all treatments except spray-and-burn, some woody biomass larger than one-fourth inch was present from the first sampling onward. For the spray-and-burn treatment there is a noticeable gap between the first and third examinations. Tree biomass larger than one-fourth inch generally showed a steady progression from the third and fourth examination onward. In the 10th year, biomass greater than one-fourth inch diameter averaged 26 percent of the total biomass in the release areas of the control and spray treatments, 40 percent in the burn treatment, and 48 percent in the spray-and-burn treatment.

Vegetation Density and Height

Stem counts of trees, woody shrubs, and ferns were made on milacre plots adjacent to each line transect. Milacres were located at a right angle to and 10 ft away from the 0, 25, and 50 foot-mark along each transect line. Number of milacres per site and treatment were the same as already enumerated for biomass samples.

Height of each species found on a milacre was based on the average height of crown rather than on a midpoint of the tallest and shortest stem. A single height value was recorded for each species on a milacre, whereas the stem count included multiple stems and perhaps more than one plant of the same species.

A difference in summary techniques should be kept in mind when evaluating data for individual species. The number of stems per species and calculation of its average height are based on the combined total of stems measured in release and no-release segments of all four site preparation treatments. Data for the main species, however, are presented separately for no-release and release areas in each site preparation treatment. Comments for individual species are based on how a species developed from its initial presence before site preparation to year 10.

Evaluating effects of release spraying involves some uncertainties. The number of stems and average height just before and after release are the primary basis, but what happened in the adjacent no-release area can reinforce or confuse the evaluation. At least three factors may have reduced height or hindered height growth: (1) a likely setback from release spraying, (2) height changes caused by browsing animals, particularly for such favored species as red huckleberry and elder, and (3) competition from other species developing nearby. Thus, the author's comments about release effects on average height of individual species are best estimates. The uniformity of response to release in several site preparation treatments strengthens the estimate.

Eight tree species were found and measured on milacre plots (table 31). The planted species, Douglas-fir and western hemlock, constituted 81 percent of the tree count total at the third examination, but only 66 percent at the seventh examination. Red alder, the main volunteer species, doubled in numbers and averaged one-third taller than Douglas-fir and twice as tall as western hemlock at 10 years. Cherry and cascara buckthorn, desired components for wildlife, were also present in quantity. Three species, bigleaf maple, Sitka spruce and incense cedar were only incidental occurrences.

Trees constituted a very minor portion of the total number of stems per acre (table 32). Tree numbers peaked about the fifth or sixth examination and declined by the seventh examination, except in the areas given spray site preparation and no release.

Only a few red alders were present before site preparation, but it established in all treatments afterward (table 33). Red alder averaged tallest, 26.4 ft. in control areas with no release. The second tallest alder average, 23.2 ft, was in burn areas with no release. Alders were most numerous in spray-and-burn areas, and the only instance where they averaged taller in release areas. At ten years, red alders averaged taller than the Douglas-firs in all treatments.

Cherry was found from the fourth examination onward. It was most numerous and tallest on burned areas.

Responses of Douglas-fir and western hemlock to site preparation and release should be viewed under conifer development where the data bases are much larger.

Twenty-one woody shrub species were found on milacre plots, but only nine were reasonably common components of the dominant shrub cover (tables 31 and 33). The number of shrub stems per acre changed greatly over the decade from a low of 6,080 initially in the spray-and-burn-release treatment to a high of 66,378 in the fourth examination of the control-no release treatment (table 32). In all instances but the spray-and-burn-release treatment, the shrub count peaked before the end of the decade.

Both site preparation and release effects are evident in stem counts of woody shrubs, and results vary among treatments (table 32). In the control-no-release treatment, the initial numbers were somewhat higher than in the release segment, peaked the highest of all in the fourth examination and then declined to 6,089 stems less than in the release segment by the seventh examination. In the burn treatment, the release segment had more than twice as many stems as the no-release segment initially, both segments were reduced 70 percent or more by burning, and the release segment was reduced again by release spraying, yet by the 10th year,

Table 31—Number of stems and average height for species found on milacre plots in pre- and post-release examinations

		Examination					
		3		4		7	
Common name	Abbr.	Stems	Average height	Stems	Average height	Stems	Average height
		Number	Feet	Number	Feet	Number	Feet
Trees:							
Douglas-fir	PSME	181	3.02	258	3.85	235	12.53
Red alder	ALRU	43	5.74	59	9.06	89	18.89
Western hemlock	TSHE	47	1.62	61	2.50	64	9.05
Cherry	PRSP			30	1.35	34	4.34
Cascara buckthorn	RHPU	10	3.57	18	3.59	26	4.99
Sitka spruce	PISI					4	4.13
Bigleaf maple	ACMA					1	1.10
Incense cedar	LIDE	2	1.95				
Woody shrubs:							
Salmonberry	RUSP	379	2.77	382	2.43	431	4.13
Thimbleberry	RUPA	255	1.17	261	1.37	315	3.02
Trailing blackberry	RUVI	161		216		358	
Salal	GASH	128	0.88	137	0.87	194	1.77
Vine maple	ACCI	95	2.50	94	3.21	92	4.50
Elder, red or blue	SA	102	2.93	126	2.95	72	4.63
Red huckleberry	VAPA	64	1.89	107	1.90	64	3.14
Oregongrape	BESP	18	0.80	29	1.00	35	1.40
Evergreen huckleberry	VAOV					36	3.55
Blackcap	RULE					2	2.40
Ocean-spray	HODI	3	1.20	8	3.47	21	3.80
California hazel	COCO	5	6.81	8	5.15	9	8.42
False azalea	MEFE	4	0.44	2	2.55	10	2.55
Himalayan blackberry	RUPR					5	
Chaparral brown	BAPI			2	2.70	3	3.30
Stink currant	RIBR	2	3.35	3	3.83		
Evergreen blackberry	RULA					8	
Little wood rose	ROGY			2	1.85	2	4.00
Red flowering currant	RISA					5	5.00
Pacific rhododendron	RH	1	2.30	1	2.40	1	3.80
Common snowberry	SYAL					2	1.35
Ferns:							
Sword-fern	POMU	423	2.20	450	2.15	524	2.49
Bracken-fern	PTAQ	203	2.79	196	2.63	161	3.82
Deer-fern	BLSP					10	1.30
Lady-fern	ATFI					11	2.01
Maidenhair fern	ADPE			1	0.60		

[a] Listed by highest number downward in each group.

Table 32—Stems per species group by examination, site preparation, and release treatments

Site preparation and examination	Species group							
	Ferns		Woody shrubs		Trees		Total	
	No release	Release	No release	Release	No release	Release	No release	Release
	Number of stems per acre							
Control:								
0	14,919	9,359	14,796	13,658	22	3,506	29,737	26,522
1	16,911	10,800	12,333	14,578	0	0	29,244	25,378
2	22,978	18,289	24,089	37,911	567	989	47,634	57,189
3	40,155	36,011	47,467	49,733	867	845	88,489	86,589
4	45,555	35,500	66,378	36,944	900	1,255	112,834	73,700
5	60,622	56,184	53,322	52,300	2,000	1,417	115,945	109,900
6	65,433	59,389	52,367	45,400	789	1,133	118,589	105,923
7	73,556	56,689	43,600	49,689	778	1,022	117,933	107,400
Burn:								
0	5,867	3,667	9,300	19,234	33	811	15,200	23,712
1	7,733	6,845	1,955	5,845	0	556	9,689	13,245
2	16,544	12,011	18,011	25,334	433	667	34,989	38,012
3	22,844	13,033	21,155	33,033	633	889	44,633	46,955
4	26,078	19,400	23,556	26,567	1,034	1,056	50,667	47,023
5	46,555	28,000	33,744	34,778	1,745	1,478	82,044	64,256
6	40,911	30,267	40,389	43,444	1,045	923	82,345	74,633
7	39,511	32,178	36,777	38,878	812	934	77,100	71,989
Spray:								
0	13,382	11,915	12,067	8,008	0	11	25,448	19,934
1	14,889	27,533	14,445	11,578	156	0	29,489	39,111
2	27,078	36,289	17,756	14,111	245	267	45,078	50,667
3	31,600	41,311	32,456	33,555	444	367	64,500	75,233
4	35,289	51,311	44,211	27,833	733	678	80,234	79,822
5	44,700	75,733	46,422	33,756	1,000	967	92,122	110,456
6	44,511	76,600	53,778	43,611	978	700	99,267	120,912
7	55,900	88,567	43,078	37,056	1,089	745	100,067	126,367
Spray and burn:								
0	9,361	12,859	6,530	6,080	33	84	15,924	19,023
1	0	1,311	67	200	0	0	67	1,511
2	10,711	10,034	9,700	14,034	323	333	20,734	24,400
3	18,233	19,734	19,300	32,278	734	1,122	38,267	53,134
4	17,325	19,378	19,872	22,856	1,553	1,122	38,750	43,356
5	32,089	28,733	29,722	26,111	2,056	1,756	63,867	56,600
6	30,300	29,322	33,522	39,711	2,367	2,011	66,189	71,044
7	31,700	43,300	30,367	41,844	1,211	1,100	63,278	86,245

Table 33—Number and average height of main species on milacre plots by examination, site preparation, and release treatments

Treatment and examination — Control (examinations 0–7) and Burn (examinations 0–7); each examination has No. and Feet columns.

Species[a]	Release	C0 No.	C0 Feet	C1 No.	C1 Feet	C2 No.	C2 Feet	C3 No.	C3 Feet	C4 No.	C4 Feet	C5 No.	C5 Feet	C6 No.	C6 Feet	C7 No.	C7 Feet	B0 No.	B0 Feet	B1 No.	B1 Feet	B2 No.	B2 Feet	B3 No.	B3 Feet	B4 No.	B4 Feet	B5 No.	B5 Feet	B6 No.	B6 Feet	B7 No.	B7 Feet
Trees:																																	
PSME	0					15	1.1	22	2.7	26	3.6	33	6.7	25	8.6	21	11.4	2	2.2			30	1.1	36	3.1	42	4.3	51	6.7	39	8.8	33	11.0
PSME	1					16	1.1	20	2.5	35	3.3	43	5.7	39	10.5	33	15.7					22	1.4	18	2.7	31	3.7	44	6.7	25	10.0	30	11.4
ALRU	0	1	0.5			1	3.0	9	5.0	18	7.3	18	12.4	10	13.3	9	26.4	3	0.5	3	2.5	1	3.5	3	5.2	9	16.1	8	11.7	9	17.6	8	23.2
ALRU	1	2	3.1			3	6.1	4	8.4	5	13.4	7	10.0	10	13.6	11	19.0					3	4.1	7	9.6	7	14.4	12	14.7	8	17.7	14	14.4
TSHE	0					4	0.9	3	1.1	2	1.7	4	2.3	4	2.4	5	3.2					3	0.7	3	1.5	6	2.25	5	7.5	6	8.2	6	9.3
TSHE	1					4	0.9	5	1.6	5	2.7	5	4.8	5	10.1	5	12.5					6	0.9	5	1.9	7	2.4	7	5.2	5	6.2	4	7.9
PRSP	0									2	1.7	2	1.7			2	5.4									6	1.3	18	2.0	10	2.9	5	6.8
PRSP	1									5	2.7	5	1.8	3	1.7	4	1.7							5	1.9	5	1.7	10	2.3	5	3.7	5	3.6
Woody shrubs:																																	
RUSP	0	34	2.6	18	1.5	46	2.6	51	3.6	53	3.3	64	3.8	64	4.6	59	5.0	43	1.8	5	2.3	54	1.3	49	2.2	60	2.3	67	2.5	63	4.5	66	4.3
RUSP	1	31	2.3	17	1.5	57	2.4	51	3.2	42	2.7	54	2.6	55	3.5	49	3.5	54	3.0	13	2.0	56	1.4	51	2.7	53	2.5	57	2.4	52	3.4	50	4.6
RUPA	0	9	0.8	1	0.6	12	0.7	36	1.7	33	2.5	43	2.4	45	3.0	35	3.4	3	1.2			25	0.8	38	1.2	42	1.8	56	2.0	56	3.3	45	3.4
RUPA	1	3	1.1			22	1.1	32	1.4	29	1.5	39	1.7	44	2.5	43	3.3	7	0.7			26	0.9	29	1.3	32	1.2	48	1.7	44	2.5	40	3.0
RUVI	0	9		5		24		36		38		47		45		43		8				10		13		13		34		29		32	
RUVI	1	13		18		26		31		41		51		53		56		4				9		20		22		32		36		38	
GASH	0	10	0.9	8	0.8	10	0.8	21	1.2	21	1.2	25	1.4	29	2.0	28	2.7	15	0.9			10	0.8	13	0.7	14	0.9	18	0.8	19	1.5	19	1.9
GASH	1	11	0.9	8	0.6	8	0.5	15	1.3	20	0.9	29	1.0	33	1.2	31	1.5	14	1.2			15	0.5	17	0.8	18	0.8	17	1.0	19	1.6	21	1.8
ACCI	0	18	1.7	6	1.0	26	2.7	26	4.5	25	5.1	30	4.7	24	7.8	25	8.3	13	1.6	1	3.2	5	1.7	6	2.1	5	2.6	10	2.4	8	4.2	6	5.3
ACCI	1	17	0.9	7	0.9	20	2.0	22	3.8	20	4.0	21	3.2	21	4.4	20	5.2	14	1.7	4	1.1	12	1.3	4	1.5	5	2.0	5	1.2	7	2.1	5	1.6
SASP	0	1	0.5			8	2.6	6	3.2	6	3.8	2	5.6	5	4.5	4	6.7	10	2.0	2	1.2	19	1.8	19	2.8	18	3.6	20	3.1	15	3.2	9	3.7
SASP	1	4	0.9	2	1.7	8	1.9	7	4.2	12	2.4	7	3.7	8	6.4	4	8.3	16	2.2			23	2.5	16	3.6	26	3.3	19	2.9	20	4.4	14	6.5
VAPA	0	5	2.2	1	0.4	7	2.9	16	2.6	16	2.6	10	3.4	11	3.6	10	4.0	3	3.2			7	0.9	8	1.8	18	2.2	6	1.9	8	2.2	6	2.7
VAPA	1	3	2.0	2	0.8	7	1.4	14	1.5	16	1.4	14	2.5	14	4.2	16	4.0	6	2.1			7	1.0	1	1.8	18	1.0	7	1.8	8	2.3	6	1.7
BESP	0	4	0.5			6	1.3	3	1.1	5	1.2	7	1.2	7	1.6	7	1.1	4	0.5			1	0.4	1	0.6	2	1.2	4	1.1	3	1.8	3	1.9
BESP	1	5	0.8			5	1.2	4	1.1	5	1.0	7	1.3	7	1.8	7	1.3	3	0.9			4	0.4	3	0.7	5	0.9	5	1.3	6	1.4	2	1.4
VAOV	0	5	1.1	4	1.2					11	1.9	11	1.9	15	1.6	12	3.6	2	0.7			1	0.3					3	3.2	5	1.3	3	3.1
VAOV	1			5	1.2					8		8	1.5	10	2.9	6	1.8											2	3.1	3	1.5	1	4.7
Ferns:																																	
POMU	0	51	2.3	24	1.8	56	2.5	65	2.5	64	2.5	67	2.6	72	3.0	68	1.1	55	2.2	12	2.2	55	1.5	57	2.0	60	1.9	65	2.1	65	2.3	63	2.5
POMU	1	40	2.1	13	1.7	48	2.0	52	2.48	55	2.4	56	2.4	66	2.6	64	2.7	51	2.0	13	1.7	34	1.5	40	2.1	45	2.0	51	2.0	56	2.2	61	2.2
PTAQ	0	10	3.0	11	2.3	25	2.6	32	2.7	34	3.2	35	3.8	36	4.2	30	5.0	6	3.2			12	1.8	15	2.9	17	2.8	17	2.9	25	3.2	17	4.2
PTAQ	1	15	2.7	20	2.0	29	2.7	28	2.8	26	2.3	28	3.3	23	3.0	23	3.6	5	2.7			12	2.3	19	2.8	17	2.6	17	2.3	18	2.9	11	3.5

Table 33—Number and average height of main species on milacre plots by examination, site preparation, and release treatments (continued)

Species[a]	Release	Spray: 0 No.	Feet	1 No.	Feet	2 No.	Feet	3 No.	Feet	4 No.	Feet	5 No.	Feet	6 No.	Feet	7 No.	Feet	Spray and burn: 0 No.	Feet	1 No.	Feet	2 No.	Feet	3 No.	Feet	4 No.	Feet	5 No.	Feet	6 No.	Feet	7 No.	Feet
Trees:																																	
PSME	0					13	1.3	19	3.8	30	3.9	38	6.6	27	7.7	33	12.1					22	1.5	25	3.3	28	4.8	47	6.5	33	10.2	29	12.5
PSME	1					14	1.4	19	3.0	37	3.5	45	6.0	33	9.6	30	13.8					14	1.2	22	3.1	29	3.9	34	7.6	27	12.1	26	12.3
ALRU	0			1	8.0			3	3.0	5	4.5	11	21.1	11	14.3	12	18.4					5	0.3	8	1.1	12	3.0	17	4.8	17	12.7	17	15.6
ALRU	1							1	3.4	3	3.1	6	6.9	2	9.5	4	15.7	1	0.5					8	1.5	10	2.4	13	5.2	15	10.4	14	19.9
TSHE	0					7	0.9	7	1.3	10	2.8	12	5.4	9	8.1	11	9.1					7	0.8	10	2.1	11	2.4	22	6.0	13	9.4	12	12.2
TSHE	1							6	2.2	7	3.8	13	4.3	10	8.4	9	9.8					4	0.9	8	1.3	13	2.2	15	3.8	11	5.9	12	6.3
PRSP	0									2	0.8	1	1.4	2	1.8	1	1.8									13	1.6	14	2.1	12	3.1	5	5.7
PRSP	1									1	1.2	2	1.7	3	1.8	4	1.3									3	1.0	14	1.7	5	3.4	8	4.9
Woody shrubs:																																	
RUSP	0	31	2.6	16	2.8	39	2.6	50	2.9	50	2.7	53	2.9	52	3.5	55	3.7	46	3.4	1	0.2	46	0.7	38	2.0	47	2.0	56	2.1	51	2.8	54	3.6
RUSP	1	36	2.2	20	1.9	46	2.1	51	3.3	42	2.3	52	3.1	52	4.0	57	4.6	37	2.0			34	0.9	38	2.1	35	1.7	50	1.6	47	3.2	41	3.5
RUPA	0					4	0.6	23	0.6	27	1.0	32	1.5	34	2.5	29	3.5					24	0.3	39	0.8	40	1.3	53	1.4	48	3.0	41	2.4
RUPA	1					2	0.9	27	1.3	24	1.1	31	1.8	38	2.5	36	3.0					25	0.9	31	0.9	34	0.6	48	1.2	46	2.3	46	2.3
RUVI	0	13		7		16		26		38		52		57		49		1				4		8		17		30		44		37	
RUVI	1	12		1		4		11		24		36		54		48		6				13		16		23		38		53		55	
GASH	0	8	1.1	15	0.5	20	0.7	28	0.8	28	0.9	35	1.1	39	1.6	41	1.8	6	1.8			9	0.6	8	0.6	7	0.8	11	0.7	12	1.5	13	1.6
GASH	1	16	0.9	3	0.6	3	0.4	13	1.3	13	1.0	14	1.2	16	1.4	16	1.6	12	0.9			17	0.5	13	0.6	16	0.6	18	0.8	24	1.1	25	1.4
ACCI	0	16	3.7	7	1.2	12	1.7	11	2.0	13	2.4	15	3.5	12	4.7	12	4.2	11	5.7	2	0.4	5	0.5	1	1.7	2	1.5	4	1.4	2	2.3	1	1.3
ACCI	1	8	1.8	1	0.5	11	1.9	17	2.0	18	2.1	18	2.9	18	3.9	16	5.1	8	1.2			7	1.5	8	1.5	6	3.8	10	1.3	7	1.3	7	2.0
SASP	0	3	2.4	3	4.7	9	2.6	6	3.8	11	3.9	10	4.7	7	2.9	3	3.8	3	1.7			18	0.3	21	1.3	22	1.5	17	1.3	16	1.9	19	1.6
SASP	1	4	2.2	2	0.6	9	0.8	6	3.5	4	2.7	7	3.8	4	4.3	2	5.5	3	2.1			17	0.6	21	1.7	27	1.2	23	1.2	18	3.3	17	1.7
VAPA	0	2	3.2	2	1.2	3	1.4	11	2.2	11	2.8	8	3.5	8	2.4	5	4.1	6	7.4					3	1.6	11	1.6	8	1.8	10	2.4	9	2.0
VAPA	1	1	6.5	1	3.0	7	2.6	7	2.0	10	2.3	4	2.7	3	4.7	6	2.9	4	2.7			4	0.8	4	1.7	11	1.1	6	2.0	9	2.0	6	3.1
BESP	0																	4	0.7			4	0.4	4	0.8	4	1.0	6	1.2	7	1.9	8	1.9
BESP	1	1	0.9	2	0.8	4	1.0	3	0.7	5	0.9	6	1.3	4	1.3	4	1.4	2	1.2			1	0.3			3	1.0	4	0.6	1	1.1	4	1.0
VAOV	0	1	1.0	2	0.7	2	0.7	6	3.9	6	2.6	5	3.9	6	4.0	5	5.7	5	1.9	3	1.8	1	1.4					4	2.3	3	1.3	2	1.8
VAOV	1	3	3.8	2	3.4	2	1.8					3	5.1	4	1.1	2	0.5					4	2.1										
Ferns:																																	
POMU	0	41	1.7	19	1.9	43	1.9	52	2.4	54	2.4	59	2.2	58	2.7	58	2.7	49	2.1	3	1.0	44	1.2	49	1.7	49	1.7	50	1.9	60	2.2	65	2.0
POMU	1	49	1.9	30	1.8	66	2.2	67	2.5	70	2.4	73	2.3	74	2.8	74	3.0	54	2.0			40	1.1	41	1.9	53	1.8	54	1.7	62	1.8	71	1.8
PTAQ	0	17	2.1	22	2.2	35	2.2	39	3.1	38	3.0	35	3.3	30	3.4	27	4.5	4	2.6	2	0.8	8	1.3	14	2.3	16	2.5	19	2.9	21	4.7	15	4.5
PTAQ	1	17	2.3	29	2.1	29	2.3	34	3.1	29	2.7	30	3.0	29	3.6	21	3.1	5	2.7			10	1.3	22	2.5	19	1.9	20	2.1	20	3.7	17	2.2

[a] Species are listed from most abundant downward in each group.

the numbers still slightly exceeded those in the no-release segment. Site preparation by spraying did not reduce stem counts in the first and second examinations, but later release spraying reduced the stem count which ended up 6,022 less than without release at year 10. In the spray-and-burn treatment, site preparation greatly reduced the initial numbers which were reasonably equal initially; then the release spray reduced the stem count by 9,422, yet the stem count in the release segment exceeded that in the no-release segment by 11,477 stems at year 10.

Salmonberry was the most abundant woody shrub and very competitive in height, averaging 4.13 ft by year 10 (tables 31 and 33). Salmonberry was present initially in all site preparation and release treatments, was substantially reduced during site preparation (first examination) even in the control, and also reduced in average height in six of eight instances. Release spraying generally reduced both stem count and average height, but recovery effects varied:

| Examination | Spraying effects on salmonberry | | | | | |
| | 3 | | 4 | | 7 | |
Site preparation	No release	Release	No release	Release	No release	Release
	Stem count					
Control	51	51	53	42	59	49
Burn	49	51	60	53	66	50
Spray	50	51	50	42	55	57
Spray and burn	38	38	47	35	54	41
	Average height in meters					
Control	3.6	3.2	3.3	2.7	5.0	3.5
Burn	2.2	2.7	2.3	2.5	4.3	4.6
Spray	2.9	3.3	2.7	2.3	3.7	4.6
Spray and burn	2.0	2.1	2.0	1.7	3.6	3.5

Average height of salmonberry at 10 years reached a maximum of 5.0 ft in the no-release areas of the control treatment, and 4.6 ft in release areas of the burn and the spray treatments. Although well represented initially, spray-and-burn site preparation greatly reduced subsequent stem numbers and average height of salmonberry with effects still evident in year 10.

Thimbleberry was the second most prominent woody shrub. Stem counts for thimbleberry were about 120 less than for salmonberry in the third, fourth, and seventh examinations and its average height was over 1 m shorter. Before site preparation, thimbleberry was not present in two of the four treatments, but soon afterwards it developed well in both release and no-release areas of all treatments (table 33). Release spraying appears to have had variable but minor effects on stem counts and some reductions in average height. As with salmonberry, average height of thimbleberry at the 10th year was lowest in the spray-and-burn treatment.

Trailing blackberry, the third most numerous woody shrub, is a vine whose height was not measured. The height above ground at which it might be found depends on whatever it grows upward on. Trailing blackberry was present before site preparation in all treatments and increased afterwards. Stem counts were not reduced by release spraying; in fact, at the 10th year, stem counts were equal to or higher in release areas than in no-release areas.

The relatively short evergreen shrub, salal, doubled its average height from the fourth to the seventh examination to 1.77 ft (table 31). In the control treatment with no release, it averaged 2.7 ft tall, but in all other treatments it averaged less than 2.0 ft (table 33). Release spraying did not affect stem count but reduced average height of salal in the control and the spray site preparation treatments. Again, the shortest 10th year height was in the release segments of spray-and-burn areas.

Vine maple did not thrive after site preparation. In the control without release an initial stem count of 18 increased to 30 at the fifth examination but reduced to 25 by the seventh examination, with a 10th-year average height of 8.3 ft. In five of eight site treatment-release combinations, vine maples were fewer in number at the 10th year than initially and heights averaged from 1.5 to 5.3 ft. Its development in the spray-and-burn treatment was notably lower than elsewhere. In several treatments, release spraying appears to have had a delayed effect on vine maple height growth.

Response of elder to site preparation and release seemed to differ from most other species. At the 10th year, stem counts were still low and so were most heights. Release spraying strongly reduced elder heights except in the control. Tenth-year heights were variable; in two instances they were less than initially, in three cases heights appeared to increase normally whereas the other three were intermediate. Again, average heights were much lower in the spray-and-burn treatment than elsewhere. Elder is often heavily browsed, which may account for low numbers and more than usual height variability.

Red huckleberry was present initially in low numbers and showed gains in all treatments at 10 years. Average height was reduced after release spraying in all treatments except for site preparation by spraying. Unlike several other species, red huckleberry development in the spray-and-burn treatment was reasonably similar to development in the other treatments.

Oregongrape and evergreen huckleberry were initially represented by low numbers in all treatments. Stem counts of Oregongrape show several gains; average heights were greater after release spraying in all site preparation treatments except the control. Although present early on in several treatments, evergreen huckleberry was consistently present only from the fifth examination onward. It averaged tallest for both release and no-release segments in areas sprayed for site preparation.

Five species of fern were tallied on milacres, but only two, sword-fern and bracken-fern, were abundant. The two were present in quantity before site preparation and increased over the decade. In number per acre, fern fronds often equaled or even exceeded woody shrub stems per acre (table 32).

In all site preparation treatments, sword-fern fronds greatly outnumbered bracken-fern fronds both initially and in the 10th year (table 33). With few exceptions, site preparation temporarily reduced the number of fronds and the average height of both species. As with other species, reductions resulting from site preparation were greater in spray-and-burn than in other treatments. Release spraying reduced the average height of both species, but sword-fern gained in number of fronds. Stem counts and average heights at the 10th year were generally lower in release areas than in no-release areas. Decreased numbers of bracken-fern fronds from the sixth to the seventh examination may indicate the onset of crowding and overtopping.

Discussion and Application

Since this study was started, major shifts in conservation endeavors, forest management objectives, and reforestation practices have occurred. Current endeavors are often focused on trying any method but clearcutting and broadcast burning to attain forest renewal and sustainability objectives. The author believes this study contributes substantially to the science of silviculture and quantitatively reinforces accepted reforestation practices that were compared and are still in use today.

The reported results amply demonstrate that the key objective of this study has been achieved. Quantitative data show that various combinations of seedling protection, site preparation, stock type, and release differently influence tree and vegetation development during the first decade. The foregoing pages presented the key findings surrounded by many supporting details. A brief synopsis, including range of treatment averages, seems useful to help focus the ensuing discussion:

1. Tree response to treatments:

Treatment	Survival	Height	Diameter
	Percent	*Centimeters*	
Untubed vs. tubed	50.5–82.2	498.8–520.4	7.2–7.7
Significance	P < 0.001	P < 0.001	P < 0.001
Control vs. site preparation	58.5–73.1	471.4–543.4	6.8–8.0
Significance	P = 0.066	P = 0.195	P=0.293
Small vs. large Douglas-fir stock	63.7–74.6	509.0–581.5	7.4–8.8
Significance	P < 0.001	P < 0.001	P < 0.001
No release vs. release	65.5–66.9	494.6–529.2	7.2–7.8
Significance	P = 0.026	P < 0.001	P < 0.001

2. At 10 years, tree survival, height and diameter all averaged highest in areas prepared by preburn spraying followed by broadcast burning (tables 7, 14, and 21).

3. Two-thirds of all tree mortality was to the result of stem clipping; most occurred in the first 3 years (tables 10 and 11).

4. Large planting stock averaged higher survival, height, and diameter growth than medium or small stock (tables 8, 15, 22, and 34).

5. Even after the best site preparation, tree height of every stock type benefited from release spraying (table 37).

6. Line transect, biomass, and milacre data all show that woody shrub cover was reduced by site preparation and release, averaging lowest for the decade in spray-and-burn areas (fig. 23; tables 30 and 32).

In seeking guidance from this study, everyone needs to be aware that none of the study results reflect the maximum gain possible. Every site preparation–release combination average is based on:

1. Untubed and tubed trees—half of each initially

2. Two species with different growth characteristics—initial ratio, five Douglas-firs and two western hemlocks

3. Five different Douglas-fir stock types with the best two perhaps contributing nearly half to Douglas-fir averages

Despite these leveling effects, significant differences in stand development were demonstrated among the reforestation techniques tested. Study results merit discussion from two viewpoints—additions to silvicultural science and practical application.

Statistical Comparisons

The statistical basis of study results deserves particular attention. This study was planned as a split-split-split-plot structure on a randomized complete block design. As in all experiments, it is desirable to minimize all variability (background noise) except for those factors being compared. In large field experiments, there are many sources that contribute uncontrolled variability. The more variability, the less chance that observed differences and trends will prove significant in statistical tests.

Many sources of uncontrollable or partially controllable variability existed in this study. Within and among six large, widely distributed study areas are such variable components as topography, soil, climate, and amount and composition of residual vegetation. Despite the best efforts, the site preparation and release methods applied were only similar, not identical, which might yield variable effects. As a practical necessity, different sources and sizes of planting stock had to be used and crews with different skill levels did the planting and tubing. Then there are wildlife effects, particularly foraging pressures by differing populations of mountain beaver, deer, elk, and other animals.

Despite all of the inherent variability, highly significant differences shown by statistical tests provide credence that results really differed among the levels of each factor tested. Differences in tree size and vegetative composition by year 10 are the product of the combined effects of the four factors tested—site preparation, stock type, protection, and release.

Seedling Protection

In some coastal clearcuts, protecting young seedlings from foraging animals, particularly mountain beavers, transcends the importance of all other manageable site factors. The full beneficial effects of site preparation, planting stock size and quality, and release cannot be realized if seedling numbers are decimated in the early years. Both direct and indirect methods have been used to reduce the damage likely from mountain beavers.

In this study, protecting individual seedlings with plastic mesh tubes was the chosen method. Tubing became an accepted practice after several variations of plastic mesh had been compared (Campbell 1969, Campbell and Evans 1975, Crouch 1980). Mortality of unprotected seedlings in this study averaged 49 percent (range 25 to 67 percent) by the 10th year, whereas mortality of protected seedlings averaged 18 percent (table 6). Over half of this mortality was attributed directly to clipping by mountain beavers. Most likely, a portion of the clipped unknown category might also be chargeable to mountain beavers. High levels of clipping mortality by mountain beavers have also been reported in other studies (Borrecco and Anderson 1980, Hartwell and Johnson 1983, Stein 1995).

Information on mountain beavers was thoroughly summarized by Cafferata (1992). Mountain beavers are stout burrowing rodents found in moist forest conditions westward of the Cascade Mountains, especially in the Coast Ranges. They forage near their burrows on the variety of vegetation available including conifers (Crouch 1968, Martin 1971). Their damaging effects on planted seedlings, saplings, and young trees were observed and reported many years ago (Couch 1925, Krygier 1958, Munger 1943); their damage to freshly planted seedlings became forcefully evident as planting of coastal clearcuts became routine.

In this study, tubing increased average seedling survival at 10 years by 32 percent, height by 21.6 cm, and diameter by 0.5 cm. These are clear gains in development of conifer stands, but several shortcomings should also be recognized. First of all, tubing was not 100-percent effective in preventing mortality and seedling damage by mountain beavers. About 11 percent of mortality attributed directly to mountain beavers occurred to tubed seedlings. Some clipping of tubed seedlings resulted from inadequate tube installation and tube tipping or knockdown by elk and deer, but much of it was from clipping or undermining during beaver burrowing activity. Foraging damage attributed to mountain beavers also reduced the 10-year growth of live Douglas-firs—average height 253.7 cm for 99 beaver-browsed trees, less than half the species average for undamaged trees, 556,7 cm (table 17). Height impairment was even greater for 293 beaver-damaged western hemlocks, only 32.5 percent as tall as undamaged hemlocks. Finally, there is the threat of further damage as the conifer stands close and understory forage shades out. Bark chewing already observed on Douglas-firs and western hemlocks may indicate that this progression has started with damage likely to continue in the young stands as has been observed elsewhere (Borrecco and Anderson 1980, Cafferata 1992, Neal and Borrecco 1981).

Studies continue on ways to protect planted seedlings from mountain beaver foraging. Where protected seedlings were exposed to captive mountain beavers in field pens, 11 of 20 barrier products proved effective (Runde and others 2008). In another study, mountain beaver population dynamics were determined from preharvest to seedling planting, and also the foraging effects after chemical site preparation (Arjo 2010). Prevention of mountain beaver damage to conifer seedlings by habitat manipulation is a desirable but elusive goal.

Although it provides effective protection, tubing itself has several drawbacks in addition to the cost of tubes and installation. For a variety of reasons—tube position, direction of shoot development, etc.—some seedlings are hampered in egressing the tube, causing reduced growth, severe deformation, and even a few deaths.

In this study, death of 79 seedlings and injury to 922 live seedlings was attributed to tube restrictions (tables 11 and 17). Finally, what effects do intact durable tubes have on sapling growth? The mesh tubes did not disintegrate as anticipated (table 12). Well-positioned mesh tubes stretch as tree stems enlarge, but the mesh is strong enough to cause a compression pattern on the exterior basal bark. Does this pressure interfere enough to impinge on liquid movement in the cambium and hence limit growth?

Tubing provided a physical barrier to protect individual seedlings. There are other ways to protect seedlings from mountain beavers including chemicals, habitat manipulation, and direct population control. When tubing is the protective choice, several modifications might prove helpful. Foremost is using a shorter tube. A shorter tube would be easier to install, keep upright, and provide less of an object for deer and elk to knock down, or to trash with antlers. Seedlings need protection from basal clipping by mountain beavers or hares, which usually results in death. A few inches difference in tube length is not likely to deter mountain beavers if they choose to climb. A few inches less tube may help seedling egress, but also hastens exposure of new growth to browsing. Seedlings can usually withstand repeated browsing if their lower stem and side shoots are protected. There seem to be good reasons for testing tube length and other modifications to discover the most appropriate tube and anchorage configurations.

Size of Nursery Stock

By the mid-1970s, limited evidence from several field trials indicated that large nursery stock could yield higher survival and growth than small stock (Edgren 1977, Smith and Walters 1965, Walters and Kozak 1965, Zaerr and Lavender 1976). Wildlife damage might be reduced by use of extra-large stock (Hartwell 1973). Greater flexibility in nursery practices for production of both bare-root and container stock brought questions about stock type to the forefront. The need to compare responses of several stock types after different site preparation treatments became self-evident.

Since then, more results have been reported for stock comparisons that varied widely in scope and geographic location. Most field tests indicated that larger stock performed better than smaller stock (Arnott 1981, Arnott and Pendl 1994, Edgren 1977, Helgerson and others 1992, Howard and Newton 1984, Iverson and Newton 1980, Newton and others 1993, van den Driessche 1992) but sometimes an intermediate size did best or there were no important differences (Arnott and Burdett 1988,

Hobbs and others 1989). Stock comparisons ranged from use of a single seed source with very carefully described production procedures to stock comparisons from unspecified seed sources planted on many sites.

Stock comparisons made in the Coastal Reforestation study differ uniquely in concept from comparisons made in other studies. They represent a broad sampling of the stock produced and planted at the time in large reforestation programs. On each site, the seven stock types used were from seed sources judged appropriate for that site but not all were grown in the same production facility (table 35). At each site, the 2+0 bare-root Douglas-fir stock types were from the same seed source and nursery because the large, medium, and small 2+0 stock was sorted out of the same bundles. On three sites, 2+0 and 2+1 Douglas-fir stocks were also from the same seed source but not from the same nurseries. Two bare-root and container western hemlock stocks were from the same seed source, but of course production methods differed.

Each of the seven stock types planted on one site were tested in a variety of conditions—two protection, four site preparation and two release options. In essence, each stock was tested in 16 replications on one site. In terms of stock comparisons, each site could be considered a separate study with its own mix of stock types.

Differences owing to average initial size of Douglas-fir seedlings are still evident 10 years later. The 2+1 transplant and large 2+0 stock types were similar in all initial size characteristics measured and clearly averaged larger initially than the other three Douglas-fir stock types (tables 4 and 5). Ten years later, they averaged significantly higher than the other three types in survival, height, and stem diameter (tables 34 and 37). Medium size 2+0 Douglas-fir stock still held a strong mid-position at 10 years. Small 2+0 bare-root and container Douglas-firs averaged notably lower results than the other stock types. Though there are some minor shifts among averages, the ranking of types remained remarkably consistent over 10 years.

The 2+0 Douglas-fir size comparisons made in this study can be viewed from an entirely different perspective. Different response by size of seedling within a bundle clearly demonstrates different potential among seedlings ready for planting. Although damaged seedlings and those that did not meet sorting standards had been removed, the range of sizes and growth potential within a sorted stock was still highly variable. How much of this physical size and physiological variability was induced by nursery practices and how much was controlled by genetic factors transmitted within the individual seed? Better understanding of the genetic component is necessary before nursery stock is too rigidly sorted for size.

Table 34—Average initial height and rank of stock types and 10th-year status

Species and stock type	Initial shoot length		10th-year status					
			Survival		Height		Diameter at breast height	
	Centimeters	Rank	Percent	Rank	Centimeters	Rank	Centimeters	Rank
Douglas-fir:								
Transplant 2+1	37.0	2	74.6	1	558.9	2	8.7	2
Large 2+0	39.1	1	73.6	2	581.5	1	8.8	1
Medium 2+0	28.6	3	70.4	3	543.5	3	8.1	3
Small 2+0	18.9	5	65.8	4	518.2	4	7.6	4
Container	19.7	4	63.7	5	509.0	5	7.4	5
Western hemlock:								
Bare root	26.6	1	59.1	1	409.8	2	5.0	2
Container	20.1	2	56.3	2	423.7	1	5.3	1

Pinto and others (2011) have produced a most insightful article pointing out shortcomings of past stock type trials and how to improve future trials. It seems useful to evaluate the design and practices used in the Coastal Reforestation study with criteria they advocate. All criteria they listed appear to have been met in comparing 2+0 Douglas-fir sizes sorted from the same bundles except repeated tests of the same array. Their criteria do not mention comparing stock types in different conditions, a necessary step to demonstrate their broad usefulness. The authors place heavy emphasis on knowing precisely how the stock was produced. This is good information to gather when making definitive trials, but was beyond the scope possible in this study. It is important to note that use of the same seed source and nursery techniques may not produce the same bare-root stock in successive years owing to seasonal variation in weather. To a lesser extent, weather may also cause variation in container production. What balance is needed between gathering precise production information versus replicating tests that include variations in production methods?

Rightfully, Pinto and others (2011) place heavy emphasis on comparing stock types produced from the same seed source. A follow-up cautionary note seems appropriate. Seed lots having the same source designation may still differ physically and genetically. In the Pacific Northwest, Douglas-fir seed collected from natural stands is labeled by breeding zone and elevation. Studies have shown that clinal variation exists within breeding zones; differences are evident between slopes and locations within the same elevation band (Campbell 1979, Silen and Mandel 1983). Also, seed crops vary from year to year and so do collection efforts. Thus, though labeled the same, the seed lot collected one year may come from a different within-zone location the next year. The same concern may apply to a lesser degree for seed produced in seed orchards. Confronted with the unknown variation inherent in a seed lot, it seems prudent to use a broadly based, well-mixed lot or even more than one lot in comparing stock types.

Site Preparation

Seedling survival, height, and diameter all averaged lowest in the control and highest in the spray-and-burn treatment. Response variability among sites was sufficient, however, so that statistical tests only indicate trends, not definitive differences—$P = 0.066$, 0.195, and 0.293 for seedling survival, height, and diameter, respectively. When the three measures of seedling response were aggregated, all three site preparation treatments produced much more tree volume than the control (fig. 1).

Response to site preparation departed most from the general trend on the Bay's Wolfe site. Seedling survival in the burn treatment was 1.6 percent lower than in the control, and seedling height averaged much lower in both the burn and the spray-and-burn treatments—control 475.3 vs. 436.6 and 445.2 cm. Seedling diameters also averaged lower—control 6.8 cm vs. 6.0 in the burn treatment and a remarkably low 4.7 cm in the spray-and-burn treatment (tables 7, 14, and 21). Injury to live seedlings does not provide an answer. Seedlings damaged from all causes ranked fourth at Bay's Wolfe, 462, compared to a high of 972 at Pitchfork and a low of 152 at Poposchultz (table 17).

Less tree survival and growth in the spray-and-burn and burn treatments than in the control at Bay's Wolfe appear attributable to development of much more woody cover there than elsewhere. In the burn treatment, salmonberry and thimble-berry cover combined totaled 86 percent at the third examination and increased to 197 percent by the 10th year compared to the control with 50 percent and 154 percent (app. table 38). In the spray-and-burn treatment, red alder cover increased rapidly from the fifth examination onward to 200 percent cover in the 10th year. Red alder was next highest in the burn treatment, 88 percent. Site preparation by burning plus release spraying failed to keep woody shrubs in check in the burn treatment. In the spray-and-burn area, reduction of woody shrub cover to very low levels made possible later alder establishment from the nearby seed sources. On Bay's Wolfe, vegetative cover had an extra year to develop because slash burning could not be done the first year the site was available.

Site preparation by broadcast burning has long been used to reduce slash and the residual vegetation that hinders or prevents establishment of tree seedlings. The multiple beneficial and adverse effects of slash burning were summed up years ago by Isaac (1963). More recently the accumulated information on the multiple effects of natural and controlled burning was published in a large book (Walstad and others 1990). The evolution of site preparation techniques in the Pacific Northwest has been described by Newton and Stein (2007).

Though site preparation by broadcast burning or herbicide spraying are established and widely used reforestation practices, quantitative side-by-side comparisons of these methods in coastal forests are uncommon. The results of this complex study adds to the information provided by several other comparisons, including long term revegetation on burned and unburned plots (Morris 1970); tree and vegetation competition relationships measured in Nelder plots (Cole and Newton 1987); Douglas-fir growth after different weed control regimes (Newton and Preest 1988); or spot spraying versus paper mulching (Tung and others 1986); Douglas-fir response to burn and no burn effects in a retrospective study within a salal-dominated ecosystem (Vihnanek and Ballard 1988); and Douglas-fir and vegetative responses after six site preparation treatments in coastal Oregon (Stein 1995). Hooven and Black (1978) determined the effects of spray and burn vs. no burn on the vegetation and wildlife community in a brush field west of Corvallis, Oregon. Borrecco and others (1979) determined vegetation and mammal responses after applying herbicides to reduce vegetative competition. All the studies cited above report improved survival or growth of Douglas-fir after temporary reduction and changed composition of the vegetation. But only the study comparing six site preparation methods has a design similar enough to allow direct comparisons. In that study, broadcast burning without any preburn treatment produced the best results. All three slash burning treatments tested in that study reduced woody cover to about 2 percent; then it increased to 94 percent or more by the 10th year (tree cover included).

In contrast, woody shrub cover in this study varied from 2.5 to 15.9 percent immediately after site preparation and averaged less than 71 percent in any treatment by the 10th year (trees included). The spray-and-burn treatment reduced woody shrub cover the most, from 28.0 to 2.5 percent, and it only reached 30.7 percent at 10 years with release or 33.6 percent without release. Adding tree and woody shrub cover together, in 10 years the woody component in this study averaged 70.9, 67.4, 64.4, and 66.1 percent for the control, burn, spray, and spray-and-burn treatments, respectively (combined release and no release data). Despite the markedly different increases in woody cover in the two studies, the beneficial effects of site preparation by broadcast burning are amply demonstrated (fig. 25).

Figure 25—Sprayed and broadcast-burned area at Pitchfork in (A) February 1976 and (B) 10 years later.

The primary purpose for applying an herbicide before broadcast burning, commonly called "brown and burn," is to gain a cleaner burn when much live vegetation is already present. Usually the chemical applied only desiccates the leaves, but an herbicide that reduces resprouting might be more helpful. In the 1995 study, slash burning alone reduced woody cover to very low levels; in this study it did not. Hence the spray-and-burn treatment yielded better results.

Nearly complete vegetation control is now favored when maximum survival and growth of a conifer stand is the management objective. This involves keeping the newly planted seedlings free from both annual and woody competition for about 2 years. Results of several studies demonstrated the desirability of complete vegetation control. Growth of unprotected, large 2+1 Douglas-firs was more rapid after spraying competing vegetation than for protected trees despite browsing by deer (Gourley and others 1990). In another study, the best growth of 2+0 Douglas-fir seedlings occurred when competing vegetation was fully controlled with herbicides during the year trees were planted (Newton and Preest 1988). The rapid expansion of herbicide technology has made achievement of weed-free plantations possible and is summed up by this statement, "By 1990, herbicides and technology were available for selective removal of all major weed species in forest plantations" (Newton and Stein 2007). Improvements in herbicide technology are now updated annually in the *Pacific Northwest Weed Management Handbook*; the forestry section was most recently updated by Newton and others (2012).

Chemical and manual weed control alternatives have been tested in several long-term studies (McDonald and others 1994, McDonald and Fiddler 1999, Stein 1999). The results provide some useful site preparation or release alternatives, particularly when use of herbicides is restricted. In general, manual methods are labor intensive and costly, but they provide several effective means of reducing shrub competition with trees.

Release

A release treatment is desirable when vegetative competition threatens to overtop the desired crop of tree seedlings. It is an optional treatment, applied only when previous site preparation treatments appear not to have adequately prevented competition around crop trees.

At least 10 studies in coastal forests have compared methods of releasing Douglas-fir from competing vegetation. Where tested, keeping the Douglas-firs free of all competition for 5 years or more yielded the best results (Harrington and others 1995, O'Dea and others 1994). Fortunately, less intensive manual, chemical, and combination release methods have improved Douglas-fir growth, but not all tests reported gains.

Glyphosate was one of the chemical treatments compared in three studies. After five years, 2+1 Douglas-firs kept weed-free with glyphosate for 2 years had twice as much biomass as unweeded controls (Gourley and others 1990). In a six-treatment comparison, neither glyphosate nor three other single application treatments resulted in significant differences from the control when Douglas-firs reached 10 years of age. Apparently, the vegetative competition did not become severe enough for these release treatments to be beneficial (Harrington and others 1995). In a six-year study, a single application of glyphosate doubled the stem volume relative to the control, but was less effective than five other treatments (Stein 1999).

In the Coastal study, only two release treatments were compared: none, and aerial spraying of glyphosate in the fall. The release spraying reduced the cover of woody vegetation and its span of recovery varied. The cover reduction was sufficient to improve significantly the survival, height, and diameter of the planted seedlings. In terms of relative volume, release increased volume over the control by 28 percent (fig. 1).

Gains in conifer growth realized in this study by release spraying most likely are not the maximum growth possible. At least two compromises were necessary to serve the factorial design. Release spraying was applied at the same time on all four site preparation treatments per site. Because vegetative competition was reduced more by one site preparation treatment than another, trees in some treatments needed release immediately, later, or sometimes not at all. Thus, tree size gain resulting from release might be lowest after the most effective site preparation. A similar compromise might prevail owing to vegetative differences between study sites. Sites were sprayed in the third year of vegetation development, but density of cover and thus timing of release spraying might not have been optimal on all sites. The release results in this study indicate what is possible and practical; the averages reflect spraying in different years and by different field crews.

Choosing Treatment Combinations

Two key factors govern the choice of reforestation techniques to use on a given site—management objectives for the site and the specific conditions existing on the area. Is the objective to maximize conifer development on the area or is a less stringent objective sufficient—perhaps even a mixed stand of conifers and hardwoods? Prospective vegetative competition, animal damage, and other factors differ greatly depending on the kind of stand being harvested. Harvesting a closed stand of relatively young trees may leave little slash, vegetative understory or mountain beaver presence compared to conditions found after harvesting a mixed, older stand of conifers and hardwoods with intermingled brush-filled openings.

Key decisions regarding needed reforestation efforts should be made before the existing stand is harvested. Will broadcast burning of slash be necessary or what other means can be used to reduce fire hazard and ensure sufficient access for planting? What level of vegetative competition is already established in the stand and how evident are mountain beaver activities? Is the area steep enough to limit yarding method, subsequent access, and choice of reforestation techniques? Can harvesting be completed quickly or will competing vegetation, especially shrubs, have a growing season or more to develop? Answers to these questions and others can quickly make evident the logical mix of reforestation practices needed to achieve the desired future stand.

Some level of site preparation, type of planting stock, and degree of tree protection is still needed today as in the past to promptly reforest coastal clearcuts after harvest. A natural tendency would be to use the most complete site preparation, largest stock, and best protection method, but that approach might often be more intensive and costly than necessary. The varying management objectives and site conditions require careful selection among treatment options, which today are much more numerous than the practices common when this study was started.

Despite smoke management and other restrictions, site preparation by broadcast burning is still a viable but more costly choice today. Machine piling of slash, even on steep slopes, has become an attractive alternative that allows more flexibility within an area than is possible with broadcast burning. Piled slash can be burned later under safer weather conditions, or left unburned, although such piles might provide a haven for small animals that damage young seedlings. Another option is to burn slash concentrations only at landings, if slash cover elsewhere in the unit is moderate and does not impose access that is too formidable for tree planting.

As demonstrated by study results, preburn spraying fosters cleaner burns and reduced shrub competition. A preburn spray is advisable when residual and new vegetation on a harvested site already includes substantial live woody cover. Hopefully, the subsequent slash burn provides better access and most importantly, a long-lasting reduction in woody shrub cover. Much shrub cover can be eliminated during machine piling of slash, but some preplanting vegetation control may still be desirable. With methods available today, spraying might be done by ground rather than by aerial methods and applied only where needed on the site. Hand spraying prior to harvest is advocated in some circumstances (Newton and others 2009).

Spraying understory before harvest might also disperse any mountain beavers present. Reduced food supply would force animals to seek forage elsewhere. Currently, the threat of damage from mountain beaver foraging is often reduced by trapping. There usually is sufficient time between site preparation and tree planting to run trap lines for several weeks, setting traps at easily recognizable active burrows. Considering their long-term threat to young stands, reduction of the mountain beaver population may better foster stand development than use of seedling protectors.

Several studies have clearly established that large Douglas-fir planting stock outperforms smaller stock. But how large must the stock be? Results from this study indicate that large 2+0 bare-root stock is sufficient. Nearly the same in height and diameter initially, the large 2+0 bare-root stock averaged taller and larger in diameter at 10 years than did the 2+1 stock. Even the initially smaller medium 2+0 stock was not far behind the 2+1 stock in average height at 10 years. A combination stock type, plug+1, grown for several months in a container and then outplanted for a season's growth in the nursery, has become a favored choice. It combines shortened, flexible production requirements with high field performance. Plug+1 stock or very large container stock is often used where management desires to get maximum early growth. The appropriate size to use must mesh with the site preparation planned to achieve the desired stand on the given site.

Several years after successful establishment comes the question—would the stand benefit from a release treatment? Much effort has gone into defining when release is desirable (Brand 1986, Chan and Walstad 1987, Howard and Newton 1984, Wagner and Radosevich 1991). The need for release is self-evident when many trees are being overtopped. When the need for release is less evident, simple evaluation methods such as proximity of woody shrubs of equal height (Wagner and Radosevich 1991) or an overtopping index (Howard and Newton 1984) might reinforce visual impressions.

Over the years, various reforestation guidelines have been written in narrative or decision-ladder form. Such guidelines identify the decisions to be made. But they are no substitute for the experienced silviculturist or reforestation specialist familiar with local conditions who tailors the reforestation prescription after viewing conditions on the specific site.

Acknowledgments

Completion of this decade-long study was made possible by the sustained efforts and willing cooperation of many staff members of the Siuslaw National Forest and the Pacific Northwest Research Station (PNW) plus several involved contractors. The comments that follow can only highlight some of the complications involved and the key individuals who made things happen.

Ronald Stewart and William Stein prepared the study plan that, after staff review, was approved by T.A. Schlapfer, Regional Forester; Robert F. Tarrant, PNW

Station Director; and F. Dale Robertson, Forest Supervisor, Siuslaw National Forest. During early stages of field work, Ronald Stewart transferred and primary research direction became the author's responsibility.

After sharing site selection and initial field layout with PNW, the scheduling, contracting and application of site preparation treatments, tree planting and release were carried out by ranger district staffs, usually directed by the silviculturist and assistants. Advance ordering of appropriate nursery stock was a shared responsibility with staff members at forest headquarters. Silviculturists and assistants who participated extensively included Rick Alexander, Jim Warner, Kris Allen, Bryan Lynch, Tim Trotter, Ed Lohmeyer, John Mason, Jill Brinkman, Mike Frazier, John Nesbitt, John Echhardt, Sue Bolen, Charles Bolen, and Rex Wheeler. On the supervisor's staff, Howard Wessbecker and Tom Turpin were heavily involved. These individuals and others with more limited involvement deserve praise and thanks for their intensive efforts and often for personal interest and effort far beyond the usual work expended in reforesting these clearcuts.

Research staff members were responsible for plot and line layout and the collection of tree and vegetation data. Early on they were aided by district personnel in staking planting spots, and several district individuals participated in early tree examinations. I am particularly indebted to crew leaders and several repeat crew members who provided continuity in successive tree and vegetation measurements. Crew leaders present through several years included Howard Weatherly, Valerie Banner, Cat Woods, Michael Ringer, and Dan Mikowski. Valuable repeat helpers included Charles Tully, Charles Acton, Joan Caldwell, Denise Potts, Michael Carpinelli, plus several dozen other helpers of long and short duration.

Don Temple, assigned by the Siuslaw National Forest to assist in data summation, weathered much of the tedium in getting data transferred from field sheets to electronic form. He made many partial summaries of data for early reports on specific areas. In recent months, Paul Anderson, leader of the Landscape and Ecosystems Management Team, assisted and made available Valerie Banner for the final formatting of tree and vegetation data and production of summary tables and graphs. Statistical analysis methodology was initially prescribed by John Hazard, and recent consultation was provided by Patrick Cunningham. I also thank Jerry W. Blanchard, Starker Forests, Inc.; Patrick G. Cunningham, Richard E. Miller, and Andrew Youngblood, USDA Forest Service, PNW Research Station; and Stuart R. Johnston, USDA Forest Service, Siuslaw National Forest, for their review of an earlier draft of this manuscript.

My heartfelt thanks to all who helped in any way toward completion of this study. With much help, including extended efforts converting my script to electronic form by my wife Dorothy and son Randolph, I have sorted and summed the mountains of data and selected the key points to present. Any errors, either factual or of omission naturally are my responsibility. I hope study results provide you, the reader, added guidance for reforesting sites in the Coast Ranges and elsewhere.

Units of Measure

Metric units were used in measuring trees in this study but English units were used in measuring vegetative cover. Most data have been summarized and reported in the same units as measured, with equivalents also given in key statements. For reader convenience, equivalents are listed for the units of measure used:

English to Metric

1 inch	= 2.54 centimeters
1 foot	= 0.305 meter
1 yard	= 0.914 meter
1 mile	= 1.609 kilometers
1 ounce	= 28.350 grams
1 acre	= 0.405 hectare
1 pound	= 0.454 kilogram
1 gallon	= 3.785 liters
1 cubic yard	= 0.7645 cubic meter

Metric to English

1 centimeter	= 0.394 inch
1 meter	= 3.281 feet
1 meter	= 1.094 yards
1 kilometer	= 0.621 mile
1 gram	= 0.035 ounce
1 hectare	= 2.471 acres
1 kilogram	= 2.205 pounds
1 liter	= 1.057 quarts
1 cubic meter	= 1.308 cubic yards

Literature Cited

Arjo, W. 2010. The effects of forestry site preparation on mountain beaver demographics and associated damage to tree seedlings. Western Journal of Applied Forestry. 25(3): 127–135.

Arnott, J.T. 1981. Survival and growth of bullet, styroplug and bareroot seedlings on mid-elevation sites in coastal British Columbia. The Forestry Chronicle. 57(2): 65–70.

Arnott, J.T.; Burdett, A.N. 1988. Early growth of planted western hemlock in relation to stock type and controlled-release fertilizer application. Canadian Journal of Forest Research. 18: 710–717.

Arnott, J.T.; Pendl, F.T. 1994. Field performance of several tree species and stock types planted in montane forests of coastal British Columbia. Information Report BC-X-347. Victoria, BC: Canadian Forest Service, Pacific Forestry Centre. 45 p.

Borrecco, J.E.; Anderson, R.J. 1980. Mountain beaver problems in the forests of California, Oregon and Washington. In: Clark, J.P., ed. Proceedings 9th vertebrate pest conference. Davis, CA: University of California: 135–142.

Borrecco, J.E.; Black, H.C.; Hooven, E.F. 1979. Response of small mammals to herbicide-induced habitat changes. Northwest Science. 53 (2): 97–106.

Brand, D.G. 1986. A competition index for predicting vigour of planted Douglas-fir in southwestern British Columbia. Canadian Journal of Forest Research. 16: 23–29.

Cafferata, S.L. 1992. Mountain beaver. In: Black, H.C., tech. ed. Silvicultural approaches to animal damage management in Pacific Northwest forests. Gen. Tech. Rep. PNW-GTR-287. Portland, OR; U.S. Department of Agriculture, Forest Service, Pacific Northwest Research Station: 231–251.

Chan, S.S.; Walstad, J.D. 1987. Correlations between overtopping vegetation and development of Douglas-fir saplings in the Oregon Coast Range. Western Journal of Applied Forestry. 2(4): 117–119.

Campbell, D.L. 1969. Plastic fabric to protect seedlings from animal damage. In: Black, H.C., ed. Wildlife and reforestation in the Pacific Northwest. Symposium proceedings. Corvallis, OR: Oregon State University, School of Forestry: 87–88.

Campbell, D.L.; Evans, J. 1975. "Vexar" seedling protectors to reduce wildlife damage to Douglas-fir. Wildlife Leaflet 508. Washington, DC: U.S. Department of the Interior, Fish and Wildlife Service. 11 p.

Campbell, R.K. 1979. Genecology of Douglas-fir in a watershed in the Oregon Cascades. Ecology. 60(5): 1036–1050.

Cole, E.C.; Newton, M. 1987. Fifth-year responses of Douglas-fir to crowding and nonconiferous competition. Canadian Journal of Forest Research. 17: 181–186.

Couch, L.K. 1925. Rodent damage to young forests. Murrelet. 6(2): 39.

Crouch, G.L. 1968. Clipping of woody plants by mountain beaver. Journal of Mammalogy. 49(1): 151–152.

Crouch, G.L. 1980. Plastic cages to protect Douglas-fir seedlings from animal damage in western Oregon. Res. Pap. PNW 271. Portland, OR: U.S. Department of Agriculture, Forest Service, Pacific Northwest Forest and Range Experiment Station. 6 p.

Edgren, J.W. 1977. Field survival and growth of Douglas-fir by age and size of nursery stock. Res. Pap. PNW 217. Portland, OR: U.S. Department of Agriculture, Forest Service, Pacific Northwest Forest and Range Experiment Station. 6 p.

Gourley, M.; Vomocil, M.; Newton, M. 1990. Forest weeding reduces the effect of deer-browsing on Douglas fir. Forest Ecology and Management. 36: 177–185.

Harrington, T.B.; Wagner, R.G.; Radosevich, S.R.; Walstad, J.D. 1995. Interspecific competition and herbicide injury influence 10-year responses of coastal Douglas-fir and associated vegetation to release treatments. Forest Ecology and Management. 76: 55–67.

Hartwell, H.D. 1973. A comparison of large and small Douglas-fir nursery stock outplanted in potential wildlife damage areas. DNR Note No. 6. Olympia, WA: Washington Department of Natural Resources. 5 p.

Hartwell, H.D.; Johnson, L.E. 1983. Survival and height of large and small Douglas fir seedlings in relation to animal damage six years after planting. DNR Note No. 38. Olympia, WA: Washington Department of Natural Resources. 19 p.

Helgerson, O.T.; Tesch, S.D.; Hobbs, S.D.; McNabb, D.H. 1992. Effects of stocktype, shading, and species on reforestation of a droughty site in southwest Oregon. Northwest Science. 66(2): 57–61.

Hobbs, S.D.; Crawford M.S.; Yelczyn, B.A. 1989. Early development of three Douglas-fir stocktypes on a droughty skeletal soil. Western Journal of Applied Forestry. 4(1): 21–24.

Hooven, E.F.; Black, H.C. 1978. Prescribed burning aids reforestation of Oregon Coast Range brushlands. Research Paper 38. Corvallis, OR: Oregon State University, School of Forestry. 14 p.

Howard, K.M.; Newton, M. 1984. Overtopping by successional coast-range vegetation slows Douglas-fir seedlings. Journal of Forestry. 82(3): 178–180.

Isaac, L.A. 1963. Fire—a tool, not a blanket rule in Douglas-fir ecology. Proceedings: Second Annual Tall Timbers Fire Ecology Conference. Tallahassee, FL: Tall Timbers Research Station. 2: 1–17.

Iverson, R.D.; Newton, M. 1980. Large Douglas-fir seedlings perform best on Oregon coastal sites. Technical Note No. 55. Lebanon, OR: International Paper Company, Western Forest Research Center. 9 p.

Krygier, J.T. 1958. Survival and growth of thirteen tree species in coastal Oregon. Res. Pap. No. 26. Portland, OR: U.S. Department of Agriculture, Forest Service, Pacific Northwest Forest and Range Experiment Station. 20 p.

Martin, P. 1971. Movements and activities of the mountain beaver (*Aplodontia rufa*). Journal of Mammalogy. 52(4): 717–723.

McDonald, P.M.; Fiddler, G.O. 1999. Ecology and development of Douglas-fir seedlings and associated plant species in a Coast Range plantation. Res. Pap. PSW-RP-243. Albany, CA: U.S. Department of Agriculture, Forest Service, Pacific Southwest Research Station. 18 p.

McDonald, P.M.; Fiddler, G.O.; Harrison, H.R. 1994. Repeated manual release in a young plantation: effect on Douglas-fir seedlings, hardwoods, shrubs, forbs, and grasses. Res. Pap. PSW-RP-221. Albany, CA: U.S. Department of Agriculture, Forest Service, Pacific Southwest Research Station. 11 p.

Morris, W.G. 1970. Effects of slash burning in overmature stands of the Douglas-fir region. Forest Science. 16 (3): 258–270.

Munger, T.T. 1943. Vital statistics for some Douglas-fir plantations. Journal of Forestry. 41: 53–56.

Neal, F.D.; Borrecco, J.E. 1981. Distribution and relationship of mountain beaver to openings in sapling stands. Northwest Science. 55(2): 79–86.

Newton, M.; Cole, E.C.; White, D.E. 1993. Tall planting stock for enhanced growth and domination of brush in the Douglas-fir region. New Forests. 7: 107–121.

Newton, M.; Cole, E.C.; Barry, J.W. 2009. "Waving wand" broadcast hand application of herbicides: technical basis and usage. Contributions in Education and Outreach No. 2. Corvallis, OR: Oregon State University, College of Forestry. 28 p.

Newton, M.; Kelpsas, B.; Landgren, C. 2012. Forestry and hybrid poplars. In: Peachey, ed. 2012. Pacific Northwest Weed Management Handbook. Corvallis, OR: Oregon State University Extension Service: K1–K20.

Newton, M.; Preest, D.S. 1988. Growth and water relations of Douglas fir (*Pseudotsuga menziesii*) seedlings under different weed control regimes. Weed Science. 36: 653–662.

Newton, M.; Stein, W.I. 2007. Site preparation and control of competing vegetation. In: Curtis, R.O.; DeBell, D.S.; Miller, R.E.; Newton, M.; St. Clair, B.J.; Stein, W.I. Gen. Tech. Rep. PNW-GTR-696. Silvicultural research and the evolution of forest practices in the Douglas-fir Region. Portland, OR: U.S. Department of Agriculture, Forest Service, Pacific Northwest Research Station: 41–49.

O'Dea, M.; Cole, E.; Newton, M. 1994. The effects of herbaceous and shrub competition on Douglas-fir seedlings. Western Society of Weed Science. 47: 29–34.

Pinto, J.R.; Dumroese, R.K.; Davis, A.S.; Landis, T.D. 2011. Conducting seedling stocktype trials: a new approach to an old question. Journal of Forestry. 109(5): 293–299.

Runde, D.E.; Nolte, D.L.; Arjo, W.M.; Pitt, W.C. 2008. Efficacy of individual barriers to prevent damage to Douglas-fir seedlings by captive mountain beavers. Western Journal of Applied Forestry. 23(2): 99–105.

Silen, R.R.; Mandel, N.L. 1983. Clinal genetic growth variation within two Douglas-fir breeding zones. Journal of Forestry. 81(4): 216–220, 227.

Smith, J. H.G.; Walters, J. 1965. Influence of seedling size on growth, survival, and cost of growing Douglas-fir. Research note 50. Vancouver, BC: University of British Columbia. 7 p.

Stein, W.I. 1984. The coastal reforestation systems study—five-year results. 140 p. Unpublished report. On file with: Forestry Sciences Laboratory, 3200 SW Jefferson Way, Corvallis, OR 97331.

Stein, W.I. 1990. The coastal reforestation systems study: comparing alternatives. In: Hamilton, E., comp. Vegetation management: an integrated approach. Proceedings of the fourth annual vegetation management workshop. FRDA Report 109. Victoria, BC: Ministry of Forests and Lands, Research Branch: 61–62.

Stein, W.I. 1995. Ten-year development of Douglas-fir and associated vegetation after different site preparation on Coast Range clear cuts. Res. Pap. PNW-RP-473. Portland, OR: U.S. Department of Agriculture, Forest Service, Pacific Northwest Research Station. 115 p.

Stein, W.I. 1999. Six-year growth of Douglas-fir saplings after manual or herbicide release from coastal shrub competition. Res. Pap. PNW-RP-500. Portland, OR: U.S. Department of Agriculture, Forest Service, Pacific Northwest Research Station. 55 p.

Tung, C.-H.; Batdorff, J.; DeYoe, D.R. 1986. Survival and growth of Douglas-fir seedlings with spot-spraying, mulching, and root-dipping. Western Journal of Applied Forestry. 1: 108–111.

van den Driessche, R. 1992. Absolute and relative growth of Douglas-fir seedlings of different sizes. Tree Physiology. 10: 141–152.

Vihnanek, R.E.; Ballard, T.M. 1988. Slashburning effects on stocking, growth, and nutrition of young Douglas-fir plantations in salal-dominated ecosystems of eastern Vancouver Island. Canadian Journal of Forest Research. 18: 718–722.

Wagner, R.G.; Radosevich, S.R. 1991. Neighborhood predictors of interspecific competition in young Douglas-fir plantations. Canadian Journal of Forest Research. 21: 821–828.

Walstad, J.D.; Radosevich, S.R.; Sandberg, D.V. eds. 1990. Natural and prescribed fire in Pacific Northwest forests. Corvallis, OR: Oregon State University Press. 317 p.

Walters, J.; Kozak, A. 1965. Effects of seedling size on survival and growth of plantations with particular reference to Douglas-fir. Research Paper 72. Vancouver, BC: University of British Columbia. 26 p.

Zaerr, J.B.; Lavender, D.P. 1976. Size and survival of 2-0 Douglas-fir seedlings. Research Paper 32. Corvallis, OR: Oregon State University, Forest Research Laboratory. 6 p.

Appendix

Table 35—Seed origin, production nursery, and lifting date for planting stock used in the study

Species and source	Study site					
	Pitchfork	Beaver	Upperten	Randall	Poposchultz	Bay's Wolfe
Douglas-fir 2+1:						
Seed code	205-12-061-035-1.5	205-12-061-050-1.0	205-12-061-050-1.5	205-12-252-030-1.0	205-12-062-040-1.0	205-12-252-030-1.0
Nursery	Woodstock	Woodstock	Woodstock	Silver Mountain	Silver Mountain	Prendel Creek
Lifted	2/9/1976	1/15/1977	1/15/1977	2/17/1978		
Douglas-fir 2+0:						
Seed code	205-12-061-030-1.0	205-12-061-050-1.0	205-12-061-050-1.5	205-12-061-050-1.0	205-12-062-040-1.0	205-12-053-010-1.5
Nursery	Humboldt	Humboldt	Humboldt	Humboldt	Humboldt	Humboldt
Lifted	1/23/1976			1/4/1978		
Douglas-fir, container:						
Seed code	205-12-053-010-1.0	205-12-053-010-1.0-66	205-12-053-010-1.0-66	205-12-252-030-1.0	205-12-062-020-1.0	205-12-053-010-1.5
Nursery	Beaver Creek (RLP 26)	Beaver Creek (RLP 26)	Beaver Creek (RLP 26)	Dean Creek (RLS 27)	Dean Creek (RLS 27)	Dean Creek (RLS 27)
Lifted	2/2/1976			1/11/1978		
Western hemlock, bare root:						
Seed code	263-12-252-030-1.5	263-12-061-050-1.5	263-12-061-050-1.5	263-12-062-020-1.5[a]	263-12-062-020-1.5	263-12-252-030-2.0
Nursery	Humboldt	Woodstock (plug 1)	Woodstock (plug 1)	Silver Mountain (plug 1)	Silver Mountain (plug 1)	Humboldt (plug 1)
Lifted	1/26/1976			1/26/1978	1/26/1978	
Western hemlock, container:						
Seed code	263-12-252-030-1.0	263-12-053-010-1.5-66	263-12-053-010-1.5-66	263-12-252-030-1.0	263-12-062-020-1.5	263-12-053-010-1.0
Nursery	Beaver Creek (Styro-2)	Beaver Creek (RLS 27)	Beaver Creek (RLP 26)	Beaver Creek (RLS 27)	Beaver Creek (RLP 26)	Dean Creek (RLP 26)
Lifted	2/2/1976	2/10/1977	2/2/1977	1/26/1978	1/26/1978	

[a] Six hundred bare-root hemlock of seed code 263-12-061-050-1.5 included; lifted 2/15/78.

Table 36—Damages observed on 10-year-old trees by site, species, and stock type

Number of seedlings

Site and species stock type	No change	Clipped, unknown	Clipped, mountain beaver	Browsed	Trampled	Bark chewed	Gopher	Foliage disease	Insects, terminal bud	Insects, foliage	Unknown	Tube injury	Whipped	Porcupine	All causes
Pitchfork:	3,816	2	125	36	8	404		2	1		37	357			4,788
Douglas-fir	3,215	1	31	17	4	45		1	1		24	300			3,639
Transplant 2+1	703		2	1		12					6	53			777
Large 2-0	672		3	2		4					5	67			753
Medium 2-0	659		5	3		9					4	56			736
Small 2-0	641		8	3	1	9		1	1		4	68			736
Container	540	1	13	8	3	11					5	56			637
Western hemlock	601	1	94	19	4	359		1			13	57			1,149
Bare root	313		58	6	3	156		1			10	21			568
Container	288	1	36	13	1	203					3	36			581
Beaver:	4,153	19	36	12		13			1	3	6	102	120		4,465
Douglas-fir	3,191	4	15	7		9			1	2	6	51	81		3,367
Transplant 2+1	745	1	1	1		1					2	9	20		780
Large 2-0	710		1			2					1	5	15		734
Medium 2-0	640	1	3	1		4			1		2	15	13		680
Small 2-0	575	1	2	4						2	1	15	12		612
Container	521	1	8	1		2						7	21		561
Western hemlock	962	15	21	5		4				1		51	39		1,098
Bare root	459	7	12	3		3				1		28	17		530
Container	503	8	9	2		1						23	22		568
Upperten:	2,670		46	516		93				1	6	100			3,432
Douglas-fir	2,342		11	194		44				1	5	65			2,662
Transplant 2+1	489		2	29		7				1		14			542
Large 2-0	535		1	37		7					3	15			598
Medium 2-0	512		1	40		7						12			572
Small 2-0	412		2	45		15						10			484
Container	394		5	43		8					2	14			466
Western hemlock	328		35	322		49					1	35			770
Bare root	205		21	160		29					1	20			436
Container	123		14	162		20						15			334

Table 36—Damages observed on 10-year-old trees by site, species, and stock type (continued)

Number of seedlings

Site and species stock type	No change	Clipped, unknown	Clipped, mountain beaver	Browsed	Trampled	Bark chewed	Gopher	Foliage disease	Insects, terminal bud	Insects, foliage	Unknown	Tube injury	Whipped	Porcupine	All causes
Randall:	4,316		119	27	1	19	2	1		1	1	117	18	10	4,632
Douglas-fir	3,242		34	22	1			1			1	57	15	9	3,382
Transplant 2+1	717		10	4								15	2	5	753
Large 2-0	659		7									10	3	1	680
Medium 2-0	647		7	4	1							12	5	2	678
Small 2-0	603		4	4							1	15	5	1	633
Container	616		6	10				1				5			638
Western hemlock	1,074		85	5		19	2			1		60	3	1	1,250
Bare root	514		45	5		10	2			1		26	2	1	606
Container	560		40			9						34	1		644
Poposchiltz:	5,393	3	3	7		48		1		3	1	83	3		5,545
Douglas-fir	4,036	2		4		3		1		2	1	44	1		4,094
Transplant 2+1	841			2		1						10			854
Large 2-0	823							1		1		10			835
Medium 2-0	809					1				2	1	9	1		823
Small 2-0	764	1		2		1						11			779
Container	799											4			803
Western hemlock	1,357	1	3	3		45				1		39	2		1,451
Bare root	680	1	3	2		30				1		13	2		732
Container	677			1		15						26			719
Bay's Wolfe:	3,333	13	63	72		23		2	1	1		163	95	29	3,795
Douglas-fir	2,668	4	8	12				2	1	1		72	90	20	2,878
Transplant 2+1	540	1	1	2								18	16	6	584
Large 2-0	590		1	2				1				12	27		633
Medium 2-0	514	1	1	6					1			16	21	6	566
Small 2-0	509	1	4	1								16	10	1	542
Container	515	1	1	1				1		1		10	16	7	553
Western hemlock	665	9	55	60		23						91	5	9	917
Bare root	399	3	29	23		12						55	3	3	527
Container	266	6	26	37		11						36	2	6	390
Grand total	23,681	37	392	670	9	600	2	6	3	9	51	922	236	39	26,657

a Six hundred bare-root hemlock of seed code 263-12-061-050-1.5 included; lifted 2/15/78.

RESEARCH PAPER PNW-RP-601

Table 37—Average height of 10-year old trees by site, site preparation, stock type, and release

Treatment	Release	Stock type	Pitchfork	Beaver	Upperten	Randall	Poposchultz	Bay's Wolfe	All sites
			Centimeters						
Control:	No release	Douglas-fir transplant 2+1	567.1	375.0	441.3	616.5	581.8	508.6	526.7
		Douglas-fir large 2+0	607.9	340.7	350.2	584.9	616.0	599.0	535.8
		Douglas-fir medium 2+0	538.9	321.1	374.1	539.0	563.2	569.0	497.6
		Douglas-fir small 2+0	482.9	319.1	303.1	518.4	563.6	482.5	470.3
		Douglas-fir container	383.9	254.6	247.7	531.1	559.0	592.6	456.7
		Western hemlock bare - root	355.4	223.7	256.0	364.7	375.4	274.7	319.6
		Western hemlock container	290.1	280.6	146.5	506.4	360.2	247.0	340.4
		Average	481.7	310.8	311.7	529.2	523.8	489.6	457.8
	Release	Douglas-fir transplant 2+1	591.4	396.2	401.5	535.1	565.8	463.5	503.8
		Douglas-fir large 2+0	637.4	461.1	400.1	579.2	622.2	560.4	552.1
		Douglas-fir medium 2+0	573.0	420.8	403.2	513.6	586.0	568.4	519.6
		Douglas-fir small 2+0	510.2	351.6	402.1	568.1	566.8	475.3	492.6
		Douglas-fir container	452.4	369.7	369.1	567.9	548.1	535.2	489.5
		Western hemlock bare root	420.3	386.3	362.6	400.0	412.3	305.4	389.1
		Western hemlock container	401.8	393.4	317.2	490.5	452.8	251.8	410.1
		Average	519.5	400.1	386.8	524.5	537.6	462.4	484.4
		Control average	501.1	355.8	351.7	526.8	530.7	475.3	471.4
Burn:	No release	Douglas-fir transplant 2+1	625.3	446.4	406.5	658.6	704.7	468.1	568.3
		Douglas-fir large 2+0	620.8	435.7	429.3	645.4	804.1	511.1	591.2
		Douglas-fir medium 2+0	592.6	396.7	426.1	555.4	765.0	480.4	553.5
		Douglas-fir small 2+0	544.0	376.3	414.1	553.4	718.1	451.3	534.3
		Douglas-fir container	430.4	374.6	337.0	608.5	728.5	478.5	510.7
		Western hemlock bare root	374.1	308.5	261.6	543.5	621.5	291.9	418.7
		Western hemlock container	403.3	385.3	253.4	561.7	607.3	201.8	446.2
		Average	522.3	393.3	368.2	591.6	712.4	428.2	522.5
	Release	Douglas-fir transplant 2+1	608.2	459.6	404.8	676.2	764.0	476.4	582.1
		Douglas-fir large 2+0	613.6	437.7	387.1	709.2	860.1	566.7	609.9

104

Table 37—Average height of 10-year old trees by site, site preparation, stock type, and release (continued)

Treatment	Release	Stock type	Site						
			Pitchfork	Beaver	Upperten	Randall	Poposchultz	Bay's Wolfe	All sites
			Centimeters						
		Douglas-fir medium 2+0	566.1	383.8	329.1	612.3	808.2	442.4	548.6
		Douglas-fir small 2+0	514.7	358.7	384.8	613.8	761.3	406.5	530.2
		Douglas-fir container	422.0	346.7	319.6	656.0	763.5	473.5	523.9
		Western hemlock bare root	355.6	342.5	200.1	479.1	581.3	359.3	404.9
		Western hemlock container	371.9	352.4	199.4	579.9	646.2	296.0	448.5
		Average	504.5	390.5	330.8	619.6	746.3	442.8	528.2
		Burn average	513.6	392.1	349.1	605.4	729.3	436.6	525.3
Spray:	No release	Douglas-fir transplant 2+1	441.0	548.6	407.5	540.0	570.4	505.0	509.8
		Douglas-fir large 2+0	438.1	504.4	419.9	545.7	597.6	632.1	530.8
		Douglas-fir medium 2+0	379.6	485.3	405.2	434.0	628.0	598.8	492.9
		Douglas-fir small 2+0	311.0	424.2	368.6	482.0	546.1	597.9	459.3
		Douglas-fir container	321.2	424.3	337.3	508.3	541.8	626.4	473.1
		Western hemlock bare root	244.9	444.3	246.3	420.8	475.8	383.8	382.7
		Western hemlock container	238.1	444.2	217.1	361.5	544.6	348.2	380.4
		Average	346.9	473.0	356.0	472.3	559.2	541.0	466.0
	Release	Douglas-fir transplant 2+1	677.1	551.6	418.0	677.1	587.2	555.2	587.3
		Douglas-fir large 2+0	603.4	540.6	407.5	715.0	622.9	657.5	596.9
		Douglas-fir medium 2+0	549.3	462.6	420.4	641.7	608.8	605.1	551.4
		Douglas-fir small 2+0	536.7	442.4	395.8	642.9	583.1	575.8	534.6
		Douglas-fir container	452.8	401.4	362.0	689.3	540.5	610.1	524.0
		Western hemlock bare root	335.5	449.7	294.5	640.0	531.3	447.4	454.5
		Western hemlock container	291.5	478.8	232.2	673.2	538.7	400.6	444.3
		Average	506.1	480.1	363.0	668.6	574.4	567.9	532.8
		Spray average	431.2	476.4	359.7	573.7	567.1	554.7	500.3
Spray and burn:	No release	Douglas-fir transplant 2+1	670.1	543.9	384.8	573.6	760.8	430.2	575.6
		Douglas-fir large 2+0	645.0	502.7	439.4	591.7	824.7	442.5	586.2
		Douglas-fir medium 2+0	617.3	497.4	432.7	585.7	825.7	413.0	578.7

Table 37—Average height of 10-year old trees by site, site preparation, stock type, and release (continued)

Treatment	Release	Stock type	Site						
			Pitchfork	Beaver	Upperten	Randall	Poposchultz	Bay's Wolfe	All sites
			Centimeters						
		Douglas-fir small 2+0	555.6	446.0	362.9	568.8	752.8	410.0	526.1
		Douglas-fir container	472.9	445.0	364.6	600.7	740.6	439.4	521.5
		Western hemlock bare-root	372.2	375.4	245.9	398.5	668.0	337.4	422.6
		Western hemlock container	360.3	386.7	189.0	415.9	676.3	305.6	411.2
		Average	540.3	466.8	362.6	534.5	753.2	398.4	523.6
	Release	Douglas-fir transplant 2+1	662.9	583.3	426.9	689.4	731.8	482.7	602.3
		Douglas-fir large 2+0	693.1	555.7	461.2	688.7	794.1	595.9	633.2
		Douglas-fir medium 2+0	589.3	538.9	412.8	641.1	762.0	528.8	589.4
		Douglas-fir small 2+0	597.3	487.2	383.4	662.8	714.2	518.9	574.8
		Douglas-fir container	487.4	482.7	381.9	694.5	739.9	505.8	554.5
		Western hemlock bare -oot	340.4	520.3	250.8	586.3	585.2	371.8	460.8
		Western hemlock container	368.4	560.5	238.1	633.8	601.1	344.8	492.0
		Average	547.1	535.2	389.2	657.4	708.6	485.3	563.0
		Spray and burn average	543.6	501.4	375.5	599.4	731.7	445.2	543.4
		Average of treatments	500.5	437.9	359.4	576.7	643.5	481.2	512.1

Table 38—Percentage of total cover for species found on line transects by site, examination, site preparation, and release treatments

Site species and release	Site preparation and examination																											
	Control							Burn							Spray							Spray and burn						
	0	2	3	4	5	6	7	0	2	3	4	5	6	7	0	2	3	4	5	6	7	0	2	3	4	5	6	7
Pitchfork:																												
ACCI	24.9	27.8	25.9	28.6	44.2	44.4	59.0	13.5	0.3	1.4	0.4	0.4	1.8	0.2	7.7	4.4	3.5	3.2	5.8	8.1	8.9	23.4	0.3	1.1	0.5	1.0	0.8	0.2
No release	15.4	15.6	9.4	14.1	27.6	24.8	34.2	4.4							1.8	0.3	0.6	1.3	1.7	1.2	1.5	7.2					0.4	
Release	9.4	12.3	16.5	14.5	16.6	19.6	24.8	9.1	0.3	1.4	0.4	0.4	1.8	0.2	5.9	4.1	3.0	1.9	4.1	6.9	7.4	16.2	0.3	1.1	0.5	1.0	0.5	0.2
ALRU			0.3		1.4	7.0	12.4	1.5					2.5	2.2												1.0	8.0	7.6
No release			0.3		1.4	7.0	12.4	1.5					2.5	0.7												1.0	8.0	7.6
Release										0.8				1.6														
BESP	3.6	5.6	9.4	12.9	17.8	21.5	27.5	0.9	0.3	6.6	7.4	13.8	22.8	22.3	0.1				0.5	0.5	0.3	1.4	0.2	4.0	7.8	6.6	15.6	16.1
No release	2.2	2.8	2.8	5.7	6.9	10.2	14.6	0.2	0.1	4.4	4.9	8.9	14.4	13.6	0.1				0.5	0.5	0.3	0.8	0.1	3.5	5.6	4.8	10.7	11.9
Release	1.4	2.8	6.6	7.2	11.0	11.3	12.9	0.7	0.2	2.2	2.5	4.9	8.4	8.7								0.6	0.1	0.5	2.2	1.8	4.8	4.2
CISP			1.7							12.7	0.4	0.8	3.5	0.2					0.2	0.6			0.2	4.8	0.5	0.1	4.1	1.9
No release			1.0							7.0	0.2	0.3	1.5	0.2					0.2	0.6				3.0	0.3	0.1	2.7	1.8
Release			0.7							5.8	0.2	0.6	2.0										0.2	1.8	0.2		1.4	0.1
COCO		3.6																				1.9						
No release		3.6																				0.4						
Release																						1.6						
DIFO		0.3													31.0	0.6							2.5					
No release															31.0	0.2							0.6					
Release		0.3														0.4							1.9					
DIPU		1.5	14.1	7.9	19.1	4.2	3.2				1.0	5.0	3.4	5.1		8.5	14.4	6.8	37.3	7.4	5.6		0.5	16.8	5.5	29.4	8.2	6.8
No release		0.3	8.0	7.9	11.4	1.9	1.4				0.9	2.9	0.5	0.7		6.0	9.9	4.7	18.5	2.8	2.3		0.3	6.2	4.9	8.4	4.7	3.4
Release		1.3	6.1		7.7	2.3	1.8				0.2	2.1	2.9	4.4		2.6	4.5	2.0	18.8	4.6	3.3		0.2	10.6	0.7	21.0	3.5	3.4
EPSP		3.7	8.0	1.0					1.5	4.4	0.8	0.2	0.2				4.1	0.3					3.0	8.0	1.2			
No release		0.6	3.2	0.9						0.3	0.8	0.1					2.5	0.3					0.6	4.7	1.2			
Release		3.1	4.8	0.1					1.5	4.1		0.2	0.2				1.6						2.4	3.3				
GASH	0.1	0.1	0.4	1.1	0.4	1.1	0.6								0.0	0.3		0.3	0.2	0.4	0.5							
No release	0.1	0.1	0.4	1.1	0.4	1.1	0.6								0.0	0.2			0.1	0.2	0.1							
Release															0.0	0.0			0.2	0.1	0.4							
GRSP	1.7	6.8	48.2	48.4	78.3	25.2	42.7	0.4	0.1	68.4	93.3	128.4	20.6	113.2	0.9	10.9	57.2	59.7	62.3	43.9	86.5	0.5	1.6	74.7	76.0	165.3	44.0	124.8
No release	0.8	2.7	19.2	19.3	32.0	13.0	16.2	0.2	0.1	43.2	56.6	69.2	3.7	55.6	0.5	7.0	30.5	36.8	39.1	23.4	46.7	0.3	0.6	35.9	42.1	74.1	22.2	58.4
Release	0.9	4.1	29.1	29.1	46.3	12.2	26.5	0.2		25.2	36.7	59.2	16.9	57.6	0.4	3.9	26.7	22.9	23.2	20.5	39.8	0.2	1.1	38.8	33.9	91.2	21.9	66.4
HEMI	4.8	9.0	6.6	16.0	2.3	16.4	6.6	5.7	10.6	5.2	10.2	1.7	98.7	10.1	3.8	1.7	2.5	6.0	3.9	18.0	11.2	15.8	4.0	5.8	7.5	1.4	78.8	50.0
No release	3.5	5.2	1.0	2.6	1.0	3.5	0.7	4.1	7.0	3.7	0.1	0.8	62.6	2.8	3.5	1.0	0.7	0.4	2.0	10.0	4.5	2.9	2.3	3.4	2.1	0.6	43.6	11.6
Release	1.4	3.8	5.6	13.3	1.4	12.8	5.9	1.6	3.5	1.4	10.1	0.9	36.1	7.3	0.3	0.8	1.8	5.5	1.9	8.0	6.7	13.0	1.8	2.5	5.4	0.9	35.2	38.4
HODI					0.2																							
No release					0.2																							

Table 38—Percentage of total cover for species found on line transects by site, examination, site preparation, and release treatments (continued)

Site preparation and examination

Site species and release	Control							Burn							Spray							Spray and burn						
	0	2	3	4	5	6	7	0	2	3	4	5	6	7	0	2	3	4	5	6	7	0	2	3	4	5	6	7
Pitchfork (continued):																												
MOSP	4.5				0.2			1.5							6.6	1.0			0.2	0.2		4.9	0.3					
No release	1.8				0.2			0.5							3.0	0.8			0.2	0.2		1.4	0.1					
Release	2.7							1.0							3.6	0.1						3.6	0.2					
No vegetation			24.2	30.6	9.7	12.8	5.7			28.0	50.9	15.7	15.2	5.5			11.5	19.3	7.5	7.6	8.4			31.2	68.2	5.8	20.6	5.3
No release			13.2	15.0	7.0	7.1	2.0			12.6	22.6	5.7	5.7	0.8			5.2	7.6	2.2	4.8	5.8			13.2	32.2	5.1	10.0	4.3
Release			11.0	15.6	2.8	5.6	3.7			15.4	28.3	10.0	9.5	4.7			6.3	11.7	5.3	2.8	2.6			18.0	36.0	0.7	10.6	1.0
POMU	11.4	24.4	42.5	33.5	43.6	53.5	45.7	15.7	1.7	8.9	8.0	11.0	13.3	12.7	9.1	16.5	20.7	17.2	21.5	29.9	23.1	28.9	2.5	6.7	9.2	9.2	9.5	11.5
No release	6.9	15.7	24.6	18.9	26.8	31.8	29.2	8.6	1.2	7.0	4.8	7.7	9.1	8.4	4.0	8.6	5.7	4.2	6.6	8.3	6.2	15.0	1.1	5.4	5.6	4.4	4.7	7.5
Release	4.4	8.7	17.9	14.6	16.9	21.6	16.5	7.1	0.5	1.9	3.2	3.4	4.2	4.3	5.1	8.0	15.0	13.0	14.9	21.6	16.9	14.0	1.5	1.3	3.6	4.8	4.8	4.0
PRSP					0.8	0.9	0.2					0.1									0.1					0.2	0.9	
No release					0.4	0.2	0.2					0.1														0.2	0.4	
Release					0.4	0.7															0.1						0.4	
PSME			0.4	0.4	7.6	23.9	55.0		0.1	0.2	0.5	3.4	28.8	62.9			0.2	1.0	8.9	25.6	37.4		0.3	2.1	1.6	10.2	46.3	81.7
No release					6.3	15.2	36.8				0.0	2.3	20.9	42.0				0.4	2.2	9.2	11.8		0.2	0.4	0.7	2.1	16.2	36.3
Release			0.4	0.4	1.3	8.6	18.2		0.1	0.2	0.5	1.1	7.9	20.9			0.2	0.6	6.7	16.4	25.6		0.2	1.7	1.0	8.1	30.2	45.4
PTAQ															14.8	67.4	88.0	67.2	62.7	42.2	33.0							
No release																41.6	43.0	41.1	37.0	25.0	19.3							
Release															14.8	25.8	44.9	26.0	25.8	17.2	13.7							
RHPU	0.8	2.8	4.0	9.7	12.8	30.8	34.0	1.8	1.2		1.7	1.6	1.3	1.2	0.9	1.4	3.1	2.1	0.6	1.0	2.2	0.5						
No release	0.3	2.6	1.6	7.4	12.8	26.9	29.2	0.1				0.2			0.1	0.2				0.2	0.8	0.1						
Release	0.5	0.2	2.4	2.4		3.9	4.9	1.7	1.2		1.7	1.4	1.3	1.2	0.9	1.2	3.1	2.1	0.6	0.8	1.4	0.4						
ROGY	0.7	1.0			2.2	0.8	1.9																					
No release	0.7	1.0			2.2	0.8	1.9																					
RULE		1.0							1.9							0.6							1.5					
No release		0.1							1.4							0.2							0.3					
Release		0.9							0.5							0.4							1.2					
RUPA			0.1		0.6				0.3	0.3	0.6	0.7	1.3	0.9				0.1		0.1	0.1		1.4	0.4	0.4	0.1	0.1	0.3
No release					0.6				0.3	0.3	0.1	0.7	0.7	0.9									0.2	0.4		0.1		0.3
Release			0.1								0.5		0.6					0.1		0.1	0.1		1.1		0.4		0.1	
RUSP	2.9	4.6	2.9	2.9	2.6	6.4	8.8	5.2	0.9		0.2	0.1	1.0		0.7	1.0	5.0	1.6	3.1	6.6	8.1	2.6	0.1	1.8	0.1	0.2		
No release	2.9	4.6	2.2	2.9	2.6	6.4	8.1	1.0	0.2		0.2	0.1	0.9									2.1	0.0					
Release		0.6					0.7	4.1	0.7				0.1		0.7	1.0	5.0	1.6	3.1	6.6	8.1	0.5	0.0		0.1	0.2		
RUVI	1.8	18.1	20.4	23.2	23.9	45.0	48.3	0.5	0.2	0.6	0.6	0.3	4.2	4.1	16.6	0.8	10.6	12.1	26.2	48.0	56.4	0.5		1.8	1.1	1.7	10.2	11.3
No release	1.0	12.3	12.4	17.0	15.5	27.4	27.6	0.4	0.2	0.5	0.5		1.7	2.0	14.1	0.8	8.8	9.8	19.0	29.7	33.8	0.1		0.4	0.4	0.2	1.4	3.1
Release	0.8	5.9	8.0	6.1	8.4	17.5	20.6	0.1		0.1	0.2	0.3	2.5	2.2	2.5		1.8	2.4	7.2	18.3	22.6	0.4		1.4	0.8	1.5	8.8	8.2
SASP		0.7			0.8	0.2	0.2		3.8	7.5	7.3	2.8	1.2	0.4		0.0							1.4	2.0	1.7	0.6	0.6	0.2
No release		0.4			0.8	0.2	0.2		1.1	2.9	1.8	1.5	0.2			0.0							0.1	1.1	0.7	0.2	0.3	
Release		0.3							2.7	4.6	5.5	1.3	1.0	0.4									1.3	0.9	1.1	0.6	0.3	0.2

Table 38—Percentage of total cover for species found on line transects by site, examination, site preparation, and release treatments (continued)

Site preparation and examination

Site species and release	Control							Burn							Spray							Spray and burn						
	0	2	3	4	5	6	7	0	2	3	4	5	6	7	0	2	3	4	5	6	7	0	2	3	4	5	6	7
Pitchfork (continued):																												
SESP	15.9	31.0	33.8	7.5	43.7	12.1	1.5	9.4	26.9	66.8	26.0	45.5	25.6	4.5	10.8	6.6	0.5	8.1	23.3	9.4	0.2	8.8	17.3	51.7	21.0	47.9	37.4	4.2
No release	3.0	12.3	14.9	6.4	17.2	4.2	1.3	5.6	12.7	28.3	16.6	19.4	12.3	2.3	4.8	2.4	0.5	1.9	10.0	6.6	.	2.1	8.8	29.4	10.4	23.8	15.8	1.4
Release	12.9	18.8	18.9	1.1	26.5	7.9	0.2	3.7	14.2	38.5	9.4	26.2	13.3	2.2	6.1	4.2	.	6.2	13.3	2.7	0.2	6.7	8.5	22.3	10.6	24.1	21.6	2.8
Slash	85.6	71.3	19.6	19.2	6.4	2.2	2.2	109.5	27.0	18.6	23.2	16.4	12.4	2.5	66.1	84.4	16.7	29.8	9.9	15.1	9.2	106.3	27.8	8.2	10.9	10.0	6.0	2.8
No release	56.5	49.6	15.0	9.4	4.2	0.5	1.5	48.9	11.3	6.0	10.0	7.0	4.4	2.2	29.5	41.7	9.4	14.8	3.2	8.4	5.3	63.8	18.1	3.6	5.1	5.9	2.4	0.4
Release	29.1	21.8	4.6	9.7	2.2	1.6	0.8	60.6	15.7	12.7	13.2	9.5	7.9	0.3	36.7	42.7	7.3	15.0	6.7	6.7	4.0	42.5	9.6	4.6	5.9	4.1	3.7	2.5
TSHE	.	0.4	0.9	1.4	6.7	11.2	17.4	.	.	0.6	1.3	2.2	10.6	11.8	.	0.1	.	.	.	.	0.5	.	0.0	0.4	.	1.4	9.6	22.2
No release	.	.	.	.	.	.	.	.	.	0.6	1.1	1.4	1.0	2.1	.	0.1	.	.	.	.	0.5	.	0.0	0.4	.	0.6	4.4	7.4
Release	.	0.4	0.9	1.4	6.7	11.2	17.4	.	.	.	0.2	0.8	9.6	9.7	.	.	.	.	.	.	.	.	.	.	.	0.8	5.2	14.8
VAOV	.	.	.	0.4	.	.	.	.	.	.	0.8	.	.	.	.	.	.	.	.	.	.	.	.	.	0.2	0.3	.	.
No release	.	.	.	0.4	.	.	.	.	.	.	0.8	.	.	.	.	.	.	.	.	.	.	.	.	.	.	0.3	.	.
Release	.	.	.	.	.	.	.	.	.	.	.	.	.	.	.	.	.	.	.	.	.	.	.	.	0.2	.	.	.
VAPA	1.0	2.5	.	1.5	0.2	1.4	0.8	3.6	.	.	.	.	0.6	2.3	.	.	.	.	.	0.2	.	2.2	.	.	0.1	.	0.5	0.8
No release	0.7	1.9	.	.	.	.	.	3.6	.	.	.	.	0.6	2.3	.	.	.	.	.	0.2	.	1.1	.	.	.	.	0.5	0.8
Release	0.3	0.6	.	1.5	0.2	1.4	0.8	.	.	.	.	.	.	.	.	.	.	.	.	.	.	1.1	.	.	0.1	.	.	.
Total	160	216	264	246	325	321	374	169	77	231	235	250	269	262	169	206	238	234	274	264	292	198	65	220	213	292	302	348

Table 38—Percentage of total cover for species found on line transects by site, examination, site preparation, and release treatments (continued)

Site preparation and examination

Site species and release	Control							Burn							Spray							Spray and burn						
	0	2	3	4	5	6	7	0	2	3	4	5	6	7	0	2	3	4	5	6	7	0	2	3	4	5	6	7
Beaver:																												
ABGR									0.2																			
No release									0.2																			
ACCI																												
Release																												
ALRU										1.0		0.2	5.6	14.2												1.0	5.4	11.2
No release						1.3	3.1					0.2	5.6	3.4												1.0	3.6	7.4
Release						1.3	3.1			1.0		2.3	5.6	10.7													1.8	3.8
EPSP			11.6	0.8	9.3					5.8	5.4	7.1	0.8	0.6			18.4	3.7	9.2					2.4	6.0	6.8	0.2	0.6
No release			5.3	0.7	3.9					5.1	4.6	2.1	0.8	0.6			5.9	3.0	2.6					1.1	5.6	2.6	0.2	
Release			6.2	0.1	5.4					0.6	0.8	5.0					12.5	0.8	6.6					1.3	0.4	4.2		0.6
GASH	2.7	12.3	32.8	56.0	70.3	97.7	106.5	32.0	20.5	57.2	99.7	106.5	142.2	165.2	10.2	5.8	19.0	53.6	85.8	116.7	129.3	7.6	8.7	23.0	36.4	56.1	87.0	98.2
No release	1.4	9.9	26.8	36.5	47.6	58.1	62.5	16.8	8.8	32.4	54.6	62.1	78.5	91.1	3.6	2.9	9.3	25.4	40.0	54.3	63.2	3.4	3.0	8.0	10.1	21.2	35.1	35.6
Release	1.3	2.4	6.0	19.6	22.8	39.6	44.0	15.2	11.7	24.9	45.2	44.4	63.6	74.1	6.6	2.9	9.7	28.2	45.8	62.4	66.2	4.2	5.7	15.0	26.3	34.9	51.9	62.6
GRSP		0.7		0.2	0.4					3.8	2.5					1.0	1.7	2.3	1.2					8.8	7.4	2.8	0.6	
No release		0.7								3.8	2.5					1.0	0.8	0.8	0.3					5.6	5.5	1.2		
Release				0.2	0.4												0.9	1.4	0.9					3.3	1.9	1.6	0.6	
HEMI				0.4	3.8	3.4	0.9	0.8	0.8	5.6		20.2	14.4	0.2				0.5	8.9	9.6	6.4			1.3	0.4	9.0	8.2	3.4
No release				0.2	2.2	1.7	0.5		0.4	5.2		12.4	8.8	0.2					3.2	2.4	0.6			0.3	0.4	2.6	0.9	0.6
Release				0.2	1.5	1.7	0.4	0.8	0.4	0.4		7.8	5.6					0.5	5.7	7.2	5.8			1.0		6.4	7.3	3.4
LOSP							0.7							0.9							0.8							0.2
No release							0.7							0.5														0.2
Release														0.4														
MEFE				0.8		0.3	1.5														0.8							0.2
No release				0.8		0.3	1.5																				0.1	0.1
Release																												0.1
MOSP				0.4		0.4		0.8	6.1							6.8	0.6	0.3		0.3		0.3	3.0	0.3				
No release				0.4		0.4		0.7	3.4							4.9	0.4	0.3					2.1					
Release								0.1	2.7							1.9	0.2			0.3		0.3	0.9	0.3				
No vegetation			27.5	25.9	7.8	3.5	5.1			20.2	11.9	6.1	0.7	0.1			30.7	25.9	3.8	5.0	1.8			45.8	49.9	23.0	8.7	7.3
No release			12.4	4.4	1.6	1.3	3.3			14.4	4.6	1.2					18.0	15.4	1.7	1.4	1.0			23.4	17.4	7.5	0.5	
Release			15.1	21.5	6.2	2.2	1.8			5.8	7.3	5.0	0.7	0.1			12.7	10.4	2.1	3.6	0.8			22.4	32.4	15.5	8.2	7.3
PISI																											0.6	2.6
No release							0.5																					0.5
Release																											0.6	2.1
POMU	15.3	25.4	30.9	40.2	39.6	48.7	57.4	5.2	4.8	5.9	8.5	12.6	10.4	14.4	5.7	13.1	16.2	16.0	21.0	32.7	31.5	6.2	0.6	3.4	5.6	6.6	8.6	7.3
No release	6.4	11.8	19.2	19.7	16.0	19.7	22.6	1.7	4.8	5.9	8.5	12.2	10.4	13.7	2.5	4.4	6.2	6.5	9.1	19.0	16.8	2.3	0.3	1.3	1.8	4.2	3.8	4.6
Release	8.9	13.6	11.7	20.5	23.6	29.0	34.8	3.5				0.4		0.7	3.3	8.7	10.0	9.5	12.0	13.7	14.7	3.9	0.3	2.1	3.8	2.3	4.8	2.7
PRSP												0.4		0.6												0.2	0.3	0.3
No release												0.2															0.3	
Release												0.2		0.6												0.2	0.3	0.3

Table 38—Percentage of total cover for species found on line transects by site, examination, site preparation, and release treatments (continued)

Beaver (continued):

Site species and release	Control 0	2	3	4	5	6	7	Burn 0	2	3	4	5	6	7	Spray 0	2	3	4	5	6	7	Spray and burn 0	2	3	4	5	6	7
PSME	.	0.3	0.0	0.7	3.0	10.5	19.2	.	0.3	0.4	2.5	7.0	15.0	28.9	.	.	1.3	3.1	7.4	18.9	35.5	.	.	1.2	0.5	10.2	28.0	55.5
No release	.	0.3	.	.	0.3	0.4	4.2	.	.	0.4	2.5	5.6	11.4	19.4	.	.	0.9	1.8	4.4	7.6	16.7	.	.	1.2	0.5	7.9	23.1	39.5
Release	.	.	0.0	0.7	2.7	10.1	15.0	.	0.3	.	.	1.4	3.7	9.4	.	.	0.4	1.3	2.9	11.3	18.8	.	.	.	.	2.4	4.9	16.0
PTAQ	.	0.7	1.2	3.3	8.9	6.3	6.4	1.0	23.3	31.1	26.9	23.7	20.2	23.7	1.0	.	0.6	1.4	0.8	.	.	2.0	2.1	14.5	9.2	18.1	25.0	9.6
No release	.	0.7	1.2	3.3	8.9	6.1	6.4	.	3.9	7.0	11.6	14.6	12.4	18.2	0.1	0.2	0.6	1.4	0.8	.	.	.	0.4	2.9	7.6	12.5	13.4	7.1
Release	.	.	.	.	.	0.2	.	1.0	19.4	24.0	15.3	9.2	7.8	5.6	0.9	.	.	.	.	.	.	2.0	1.7	11.6	1.6	5.6	11.6	2.6
RHPU	.	.	.	.	.	.	.	0.2	.	.	1.6	.	.	.	0.1	.	.	.	.	.	.	.	.	.	.	.	.	.
No release	.	.	.	.	.	.	.	0.2	.	.	1.6	.	.	.	0.1	.	.	.	.	.	.	.	.	.	.	.	.	.
RIBR	.	.	.	.	.	.	.	.	.	.	.	.	.	.	.	.	.	.	0.3	.	.	.	.	.	.	.	.	.
No release	.	.	.	.	.	.	.	.	.	.	.	.	.	.	.	.	.	.	0.3	.	.	.	.	.	.	.	.	.
RUPA	.	2.0	2.0	1.0	3.4	4.2	8.6	.	0.5	2.8	5.0	14.1	14.8	23.8	.	.	0.7	1.6	6.4	8.0	4.2	.	.	0.9	2.8	8.7	9.1	9.6
No release	.	1.5	1.5	1.0	2.8	1.7	6.7	.	0.5	2.0	3.8	8.0	8.0	14.2	.	.	0.4	0.6	2.8	3.6	2.3	.	.	0.7	2.4	7.5	5.4	5.6
Release	.	.	0.5	.	0.6	2.5	1.9	.	.	0.8	1.2	6.0	6.8	9.6	.	.	0.3	1.0	3.6	4.4	1.9	.	.	0.2	0.4	1.2	3.7	4.0
RUSP	47.5	72.0	125.1	104.2	123.5	110.0	88.4	70.7	55.3	95.0	100.6	98.6	90.8	97.3	19.6	31.0	103.7	106.0	121.2	99.2	83.8	58.6	30.6	79.2	71.9	83.4	88.6	93.4
No release	23.6	29.7	53.4	56.2	49.6	40.4	29.7	36.0	18.1	33.6	41.8	36.6	29.9	31.4	17.4	20.9	53.1	62.5	64.3	56.4	55.5	29.6	12.6	43.2	50.1	55.6	63.4	65.0
Release	23.9	42.2	71.7	48.0	73.9	69.6	58.7	34.6	37.2	61.4	58.9	62.0	61.0	65.9	2.3	10.1	50.6	43.5	56.8	42.8	28.3	29.0	18.1	36.1	21.8	27.8	25.2	28.4
RUVI	.	.	0.6	0.6	.	0.2	0.0	.	0.6	1.7	2.5	5.1	2.8	1.6	.	.	.	.	0.6	0.1	0.8	.	.	.	2.0	2.5	2.1	2.2
No release	.	.	0.6	0.6	.	0.2	0.0	.	0.6	1.0	1.1	2.8	0.4	1.4	.	.	.	.	0.4	0.1	0.4	.	.	.	0.1	0.4	.	.
Release	.	.	.	0.2	.	.	.	.	.	0.8	1.4	2.3	2.4	0.3	.	.	.	.	0.2	.	0.4	.	.	.	1.9	2.1	2.1	2.2
SASP	.	.	.	.	0.5	0.2	0.6	.	.	.	.	.	.	.	.	.	0.8	0.8	.	.	0.8	.	.	.	.	.	.	.
Release	.	.	.	.	0.5	0.2	0.6	.	.	.	.	.	.	.	.	.	0.8	0.8	.	.	0.8	.	.	.	.	.	.	.
SESP	.	27.2	0.3	6.5	.	0.2	0.6	.	63.3	1.2	7.1	0.2	.	.	.	19.6	2.4	16.1	.	0.4	4.0	.	25.5	8.5	7.2	.	.	.
No release	.	18.8	1.0	1.0	.	0.2	0.6	.	43.0	1.2	0.7	0.2	.	.	.	11.2	1.4	2.0	.	0.4	.	.	15.1	5.6	1.0	.	.	.
Release	.	8.4	0.3	5.5	.	.	0.6	.	20.3	.	6.4	.	.	.	.	8.3	1.0	14.0	.	0.4	4.0	.	10.4	3.0	6.1	.	.	.
Slash	86.2	77.6	12.1	13.5	5.3	2.7	2.9	108.0	39.6	23.5	10.6	3.8	2.6	1.6	143.0	129.8	32.1	26.4	20.0	4.7	3.8	62.8	54.5	26.6	20.2	19.4	9.8	2.4
No release	38.5	39.6	6.6	3.3	3.1	1.6	2.6	30.8	18.9	16.5	8.0	2.4	2.6	1.6	58.6	70.0	13.4	12.5	10.3	3.3	1.2	35.0	24.9	16.4	12.2	7.6	5.3	.
Release	47.7	38.1	5.5	10.2	2.2	1.1	0.3	77.2	20.8	7.0	2.6	1.5	.	.	84.4	59.9	18.7	14.0	9.8	1.4	2.6	27.8	29.6	10.2	8.0	11.8	4.5	2.4
TSHE	.	.	.	.	.	.	.	.	.	0.2	1.0	2.7	4.3	11.4	.	.	1.4	2.7	8.4	10.0	24.6	.	.	0.3	0.6	2.8	15.4	28.6
No release	.	.	.	.	.	.	.	.	.	0.2	0.2	0.2	1.4	3.2	.	.	1.4	2.1	5.8	7.0	14.1	.	.	0.3	0.6	2.8	9.1	15.2
Release	.	.	.	.	.	.	.	.	.	.	0.8	2.5	2.9	8.2	.	.	.	0.6	2.5	3.0	10.5	.	.	.	.	.	6.4	13.4
VAOV	.	.	0.8	1.8	.	.	.	.	.	2.0	.	.	.	.	.	.	2.7	1.6	2.5	2.5	2.8	.	.	1.3	0.4	.	0.2	.
No release	.	.	.	0.2	.	.	.	.	.	.	.	.	.	.	.	.	0.3	0.2	.	0.3	.	.	.	0.1	.	.	.	.
Release	.	.	0.8	1.6	.	.	.	.	.	2.0	.	.	.	.	.	.	2.4	1.4	2.5	2.5	2.8	.	.	1.2	0.4	.	0.2	.
VAPA	2.4	4.5	2.8	2.4	4.2	4.0	9.1	1.5	2.4	2.5	18.4	6.6	7.8	10.9	3.6	0.1	.	.	0.8	2.0	3.1	11.7	2.8	0.4	6.1	1.1	2.3	1.2
No release	1.8	0.4	2.1	1.2	1.3	1.4	2.6	.	2.4	2.5	16.1	6.4	7.8	10.9	2.4	0.1	.	.	0.4	2.0	3.1	8.2	2.8	0.4	0.4	0.4	0.4	0.4
Release	0.7	4.1	0.6	1.2	2.9	2.6	6.5	1.5	.	.	2.4	0.2	.	.	1.2	.	.	.	0.3	.	1.1	3.5	2.8	.	5.7	0.9	1.9	0.9
Total	154	221	248	259	280	293	312	220	218	260	304	317	333	397	183	207	232	262	298	310	333	149	128	219	226	252	300	334

Table 38—Percentage of total cover for species found on line transects by site, examination, site preparation, and release treatments (continued)

Site preparation and examination

Site species and release	Control							Burn							Spray							Spray and burn						
	0	2	3	4	5	6	7	0	2	3	4	5	6	7	0	2	3	4	5	6	7	0	2	3	4	5	6	7
Upperten:																												
ACCI	16.6	10.9	13.9	16.1	7.7	14.1	15.2	15.8	1.0	1.3	0.3	2.2	1.2	1.8	14.7	4.6	7.1	3.6	9.0	10.7	11.9	7.1	2.1	.	0.9	0.1	.	0.1
No release	4.6	5.8	13.1	13.6	6.3	14.0	14.3	7.1	1.0	0.8	0.3	2.2	1.2	1.8	13.5	2.3	1.8	0.8	2.1	1.8	2.1	4.5	1.6	.	0.5	.	.	.
Release	12.0	5.1	0.8	2.5	1.4	.	1.0	8.7	.	0.6	.	.	.	.	1.2	2.3	5.3	2.8	6.9	8.9	9.8	2.6	0.5	.	0.4	0.1	.	0.1
ALRU	0.3	.	.	.	6.0	9.6	12.5	.	.	.	.	.	.	.	.	.	.	.	8.5	12.4	13.5	.	.	.	.	.	.	.
No release	0.3	.	.	.	6.0	9.0	10.4	.	.	.	.	.	.	.	.	.	.	.	7.5	7.4	7.5	.	.	.	.	.	.	.
Release	.	.	.	.	.	0.6	2.1	.	.	.	.	.	.	.	.	.	.	.	1.0	5.0	6.0	.	.	.	.	.	.	.
BESP	0.4	.	.	.	.	.	.	0.1	.	.	.	.	.	.	.	.	.	.	.	.	.	.	.	.	.	.	.	.
No release	0.4	.	.	.	.	.	.	0.1	.	.	.	.	.	.	.	.	.	.	.	.	.	.	.	.	.	.	.	.
Release	.	.	.	.	.	.	.	.	0.1	1.0	0.6	2.6	2.2	2.9	.	.	.	.	.	.	.	.	.	.	.	.	.	.
CISP	.	.	.	0.5	0.1	.	.	.	.	5.9	4.0	1.1	0.8	1.5	.	.	.	0.6	0.3	0.4	0.3	.	.	1.0	0.1	1.4	7.6	0.8
No release	.	.	.	.	0.1	.	.	.	.	2.2	2.6	0.6	0.7	1.2	.	.	.	0.6	0.3	0.4	0.3	.	.	0.8	.	0.2	4.7	0.3
Release	.	.	.	0.5	.	.	.	.	.	3.8	1.3	0.5	0.1	0.3	.	.	.	.	.	.	.	.	.	0.3	0.1	1.2	3.0	0.4
COCO	6.9	2.9	9.3	10.8	16.0	23.0	27.0	.	1.2	.	.	.	.	.	1.0	1.1	1.2	.	2.6	4.6	4.8	.	1.3	.	1.2	0.4	.	.
No release	.	2.7	6.8	8.3	8.7	8.8	11.0	.	1.2	.	.	.	.	.	1.0	.	.	.	.	.	.	.	.	.	.	.	.	.
Release	6.9	0.2	2.4	2.5	7.3	14.2	16.0	.	.	.	.	.	.	.	.	1.1	1.2	.	2.6	4.6	4.8	.	1.3	.	1.2	0.4	.	.
DIFO	.	.	.	.	.	.	.	.	.	.	.	.	.	.	.	.	.	.	.	.	.	.	.	.	.	.	.	.
No release	0.6	.	.	.	.	.	0.2	.	.	.	.	.	.	.	.	.	.	.	.	.	.	.	.	.	.	.	.	.
Release	0.6	.	.	.	.	.	0.2	.	.	.	.	.	.	.	.	.	.	.	.	.	.	.	.	.	.	.	.	.
DIPU	.	.	0.6	1.2	6.2	11.7	12.1	.	.	1.0	3.4	11.7	4.0	9.6	.	.	.	0.7	16.2	17.2	17.0	.	.	1.5	2.0	7.3	8.4	12.8
No release	.	.	0.6	1.2	3.4	3.3	0.4	.	.	1.0	3.4	10.1	3.2	7.4	.	.	.	0.7	6.8	5.3	7.2	.	.	1.2	2.0	4.2	4.8	8.3
Release	.	.	.	.	2.9	8.4	11.7	.	.	.	.	1.6	0.7	2.2	.	.	.	.	9.4	11.9	9.8	.	.	0.2	.	3.2	3.6	4.5
EPSP	.	2.9	19.0	4.8	1.3	0.2	.	.	13.4	47.5	29.0	2.4	0.2	0.4	.	1.0	28.7	17.7	16.3	0.8	.	.	13.6	67.6	14.8	7.2	23.5	0.2
No release	.	1.8	9.0	4.6	.	.	.	.	9.9	37.3	26.8	2.4	0.2	0.4	.	0.6	17.8	17.2	7.4	0.8	.	.	9.5	42.4	13.2	4.0	15.2	0.2
Release	.	1.0	10.0	0.2	1.3	.	0.2	.	3.5	10.2	2.2	0.1	.	.	.	0.4	10.9	0.5	8.9	.	.	.	4.1	25.2	1.6	3.2	8.2	.
GASH	2.0	.	.	.	.	.	0.5	2.0	0.2	2.2	1.3	2.2	2.6	3.2	.	.	.	0.4	0.6	0.2	0.1	.	0.1	.	0.3	1.2	1.4	0.4
No release	2.0	.	.	.	.	0.2	0.3	2.0	.	.	.	.	.	.	.	.	.	.	0.6	0.2	0.1	.	.	.	.	.	.	.
Release	.	.	.	.	.	0.2	0.2	.	0.2	2.2	1.3	2.2	2.6	3.2	.	.	.	0.4	.	.	.	.	0.1	.	0.3	1.2	1.4	0.4
GRSP	2.4	2.6	5.1	6.0	30.5	45.4	11.5	.	0.7	11.2	53.2	62.8	112.5	30.1	16.8	23.4	30.7	31.1	25.9	52.8	16.0	0.7	.	35.1	56.3	94.8	136.9	30.9
No release	2.4	2.2	4.2	2.9	9.7	13.4	3.8	.	.	3.0	20.6	30.4	55.3	25.4	12.0	20.8	24.3	17.9	11.7	31.3	7.6	.	.	9.6	27.0	49.7	74.8	15.3
Release	.	0.4	0.9	3.1	20.8	32.0	7.7	.	0.7	8.2	32.6	32.5	57.2	4.8	4.7	2.5	6.4	13.2	14.2	21.5	8.4	0.7	.	25.5	29.3	45.1	62.1	15.6
HEMI	6.1	1.8	.	6.6	2.3	12.3	12.6	0.3	5.0	21.8	19.0	17.6	37.7	74.4	21.4	5.2	1.8	12.5	21.6	30.3	30.1	2.5	.	12.6	21.1	34.4	28.5	93.8
No release	5.2	1.8	.	0.3	1.8	6.2	1.7	.	3.2	6.6	.	11.6	14.5	29.4	5.2	4.9	1.4	9.1	18.8	25.6	25.3	2.4	.	7.6	13.0	19.0	12.0	40.8
Release	1.0	.	.	6.3	0.6	6.2	10.9	0.3	1.8	15.2	6.1	5.9	23.2	45.0	16.2	0.2	0.4	3.4	2.8	4.6	4.8	0.1	.	5.0	8.1	15.4	16.5	53.0
HODI	.	.	.	.	.	.	.	.	.	.	.	.	.	0.8	.	.	.	.	.	.	.	.	.	.	.	.	.	.
Release	.	.	.	.	.	.	.	.	.	.	.	.	.	0.8	.	.	.	.	.	.	.	.	.	.	.	.	.	.
LOSP	.	.	.	.	.	.	.	.	.	.	.	5.5	.	17.6	.	.	.	.	.	.	.	.	.	.	.	.	.	3.9
No release	.	.	.	.	.	.	.	.	.	.	.	2.0	.	2.5	.	.	.	.	.	.	.	.	.	.	.	.	.	3.7
Release	.	.	.	.	.	.	.	.	.	.	.	3.6	.	15.1	.	.	.	.	.	.	.	.	.	.	.	.	.	0.2
LUSP	.	.	.	.	.	.	.	.	.	.	.	3.3	.	0.6	.	.	.	.	.	.	.	.	.	.	.	.	.	.
No release	.	.	.	.	.	.	.	.	.	.	.	2.6	.	0.6	.	.	.	.	.	.	.	.	.	.	.	.	.	.
Release	.	.	.	.	.	.	.	.	.	.	.	0.7	.	.	.	.	.	.	.	.	.	.	.	.	.	.	.	.

Table 38—Percentage of total cover for species found on line transects by site, examination, site preparation, and release treatments (continued)

Site preparation and examination

Site species and release	Control							Burn							Spray							Spray and burn						
	0	2	3	4	5	6	7	0	2	3	4	5	6	7	0	2	3	4	5	6	7	0	2	3	4	5	6	7
Upperten (continued):																												
MOSP																		0.3					1.2	0.4				
No release									2.8						0.1						0.1		1.0	0.4				
Release									2.8						0.1						0.1		0.2					
No vegetation			19.8	36.6	7.9	3.7	3.2			70.8	54.4	25.0	3.3	3.6			24.0	31.3	13.6	4.7	7.5			48.0	54.5	7.6	0.2	7.6
No release			5.2	8.4	2.4	0.2	0.4			25.4	23.9	8.7		0.7			5.6	11.2	6.2	3.4	4.6			22.6	25.5	1.5	0.2	3.3
Release			14.6	28.2	5.5	3.5	2.8			45.4	30.5	16.3	3.3	3.0			18.4	20.0	7.4	1.3	2.9			25.4	29.0	6.0		4.3
POMU	52.4	26.0	30.2	31.9	40.2	55.9	52.7	9.7	9.9	17.0	21.6	25.0	43.9	48.9	27.7	44.6	47.8	55.4	54.7	82.6	78.3	29.8	11.8	14.4	23.5	23.1	36.8	34.5
No release	30.0	17.4	17.3	14.8	21.4	35.0	36.9	7.2	5.1	11.4	11.6	17.2	31.4	34.4	12.8	19.4	18.8	20.9	20.8	31.2	32.4	12.8	5.8	7.8	12.3	12.1	15.6	18.6
Release	22.3	8.6	12.9	17.1	18.8	20.9	15.8	2.6	4.8	5.6	10.0	7.8	12.5	14.6	14.8	25.1	29.0	34.5	33.9	51.5	45.9	17.0	5.9	6.6	11.2	11.0	21.3	15.8
PRSP																												
No release					0.6								0.2	0.3														
Release					0.6								0.2	0.3														
PSME		0.3	0.3	0.4	1.8	5.1	9.2		0.2	0.4		4.7	22.9	46.1			0.4		4.8	14.8	26.7		0.5	0.9	1.3	2.3	10.6	30.6
No release		0.1			0.9	2.8	3.3			0.2		1.4	8.3	18.7		0.3			0.2	1.5	4.1		0.4	0.5	0.3	0.5	6.5	17.4
Release		0.2	0.3	0.4	0.8	2.3	5.9		0.2	0.2		3.4	14.6	27.4		0.3	0.4	1.5	4.6	13.3	22.6		0.1	0.4	1.0	1.8	4.1	13.2
PTAQ	3.7	24.6	18.4	23.4	15.3	24.7	12.5		2.4	3.6	3.4	10.0	25.2	19.6		0.2	0.7	0.4	3.4		1.4		1.2	4.5	1.7	6.6	10.4	10.9
No release	3.7	18.3	12.3	20.3	11.2	16.8	7.7		0.0							0.2	0.7	0.4	3.4		1.4							
Release		6.3	6.1	3.1	4.1	7.9	4.8		2.4	3.6	3.4	10.0	25.2	19.6									1.2	4.5	1.7	6.6	10.4	10.9
RHPU												0.4																
No release				0.1								0.4																
Release				0.1		0.2	1.1																					
ROGY								0.1																				
No release								0.1																				
Release																												
RUPA	0.1	1.6	4.2	0.8	6.9	8.8	11.4	0.1	1.2	4.9	3.8	5.5	8.5	10.6	0.1					3.8	8.0		0.1	1.7	0.6	0.6	1.6	0.4
No release	0.1		1.8	0.3	6.2	5.8	6.9	0.1	0.6	2.0	2.6	4.7	7.1	8.2	0.1					1.0	5.1			0.2		0.3	0.4	0.3
Release		1.6	2.4	0.5	0.7	3.0	4.5		0.6	2.8	1.2	0.8	1.4	2.4					0.2	2.8	2.9		0.1	1.5	0.6	0.4	1.1	0.2
RUSP	74.0	74.5	78.7	51.1	110.3	128.1	140.4	12.6	2.4	4.3	5.2	10.6	11.8	25.6	33.9	27.1	43.6	37.1	60.7	77.2	89.4	38.6	2.6	5.8	5.4	11.4	19.0	30.6
No release	22.8	29.4	33.0	44.7	71.9	84.0	92.4	5.4	2.2	2.9	4.5	9.3	10.4	23.3	19.0	15.0	25.7	34.5	43.5	47.7	54.8	18.0	1.0	3.7	5.3	10.0	16.2	23.4
Release	51.2	45.1	45.6	6.4	38.4	44.2	48.0	7.2	0.2	1.4	0.6	1.3	1.5	2.3	14.8	12.1	17.9	2.6	17.2	29.5	34.5	20.6	1.6	2.1	0.1	1.3	2.9	7.2
RUVI	9.5	42.5	9.6	15.2	13.9	16.8	10.2		2.0	6.3	12.0	18.6	24.1	25.6					2.0	9.6	13.2		1.8	1.7	7.0	17.4	34.5	30.9
No release	6.7	27.2	5.3	11.4	5.5	5.7	2.7		0.2	0.4	0.8	6.3	9.7	10.7					0.2	3.3	5.6		0.4	0.1	0.5	5.8	15.2	12.5
Release	2.7	15.4	4.3	3.8	8.4	11.1	7.5		1.9	5.9	11.2	12.2	14.4	14.9					1.8	6.4	7.6		1.3	1.6	6.5	11.6	19.3	18.4
SASP									0.6		0.8	0.4	0.8	0.4									0.3					
No release		0.5			0.1	0.8			0.2		0.3	0.4	0.4										0.1					
Release		0.5			0.1	0.8			0.4		0.5		0.4	0.4									0.2					
SESP	8.2	3.6	0.6	26.1	0.2	0.1	0.2		12.6	1.2	12.4	2.6	18.0	1.1	1.9	11.7	4.8	11.5	1.2	1.3	1.1		49.2	7.4	18.7	1.2	15.4	1.1
No release	7.1	2.9		1.1					9.6	0.7	3.3	0.4	16.9	0.7	1.9	8.1	1.3		1.2	1.3	1.0		23.4	5.2	2.3	0.3	9.3	0.9
Release	1.1	0.7	0.6	25.0	0.2	0.1	0.2		3.0	0.5	9.1	2.2	1.1	0.4		3.7	3.5	11.3			0.1		25.8	2.2	16.4	0.9	6.1	0.2
Slash	54.2	58.3	18.4	30.8	20.5	7.2	4.9	113.2	28.9	18.6	20.7	16.8	9.8	3.5	46.6	87.7	20.6	46.0	23.7	9.8	8.0	108.8	40.8	21.1	37.8	27.2	9.1	9.6
No release	36.9	29.5	9.7	11.0	5.6	0.7	0.4	55.5	17.2	11.2	13.0	8.9	4.1	0.9	22.1	39.6	7.3	14.6	8.4	3.3	1.2	62.0	24.3	11.6	22.8	15.4	3.4	4.2
Release	17.3	28.8	8.8	19.8	15.0	6.5	4.5	57.8	11.7	7.3	7.6	7.9	5.6	2.6	24.6	48.1	13.4	31.4	15.3	6.5	6.8	46.8	16.4	9.5	15.0	11.8	5.7	5.4

113

Table 38—Percentage of total cover for species found on line transects by site, examination, site preparation, and release treatments (continued)

Site preparation and examination

Site species and release	Control							Burn							Spray							Spray and burn						
	0	2	3	4	5	6	7	0	2	3	4	5	6	7	0	2	3	4	5	6	7	0	2	3	4	5	6	7
Upper ten (continued):																												
TSHE		0.1				0.3	0.2			0.3	0.2	0.7	0.8	0.7				0.2			2.0							
No release										0.3	0.2	0.5	0.6	0.5														
Release		0.1				0.3	0.2					0.2	0.2	0.2				0.2			2.0							
VAOV																0.2	0.7											
Release																0.2	0.7											
VAPA	1.0	1.5		0.1							5.1			0.9				1.4	0.6	0.8	1.0	2.8			0.4			
No release		0.2																			0.1	1.2						
Release	1.0	1.3		0.1							5.1			0.9				1.4	0.6	0.8	0.9	1.6			0.4			
Total	236	255	228	262	288	368	338	154	85	219	250	232	330	330	163	207	212	252	266	334	330	188	130	224	248	244	344	299

114

Table 38—Percentage of total cover for species found on line transects by site, examination, site preparation, and release treatments (continued)

	Site preparation and examination																																
	Control								Burn								Spray								Spray and burn							
Site species and release	0	1	2	3	4	5	6	7	0	1	2	3	4	5	6	7	0	1	2	3	4	5	6	7	0	1	2	3	4	5	6	7
Randall:																																
ACCI	.	.	.	.	.	.	.	.	2.8	.	0.6	0.3	0.4	0.3	0.7	0.9	.	0.5	1.1	1.0	0.3	1.2	1.6	1.4	68.7	5.4	9.1	5.7	5.9	12.9	14.9	15.7
No release	.	.	.	.	.	.	.	.	1.4	.	0.6	0.3	0.3	0.3	0.6	0.8	.	0.5	1.1	1.0	0.3	1.2	1.6	1.4	68.7	5.4	1.3	1.5	1.0	1.7	2.0	3.8
Release	.	.	.	.	.	.	.	.	1.4	.	.	.	0.2	.	0.2	0.1	.	.	.	.	.	.	.	.	.	.	7.8	4.2	4.9	11.2	12.9	11.9
ADPE	.	.	.	.	.	.	.	.	.	.	.	.	.	.	.	.	.	.	.	.	.	.	.	.	.	.	.	.	.	.	.	.
No release	.	.	.	.	.	.	.	.	.	.	.	.	.	.	.	.	.	.	.	.	.	.	.	.	.	.	.	.	.	.	0.5	0.5
Release	.	.	.	.	.	.	.	.	.	.	.	.	.	.	.	.	.	.	.	.	.	.	.	.	.	.	.	.	.	.	0.5	0.5
ALRU	.	.	0.1	6.0	16.0	32.0	53.4	76.3	3.8	3.2	2.4	2.4	1.1	22.0	49.3	95.7	.	.	.	0.5	1.6	9.7	32.0	78.7	.	.	.	0.2	.	0.4	4.8	14.5
No release	.	.	.	3.4	10.6	16.1	26.2	40.0	0.4	.	.	0.3	1.1	17.7	32.9	66.2	.	.	.	.	0.7	6.6	18.6	44.6	.	.	.	0.2	.	0.4	4.8	14.5
Release	.	.	0.1	2.7	5.4	15.9	27.2	36.3	3.4	3.2	2.4	2.0	.	4.3	16.4	29.5	.	.	.	0.5	0.9	3.1	13.5	34.1	.	.	0.2	.	.	.	.	.
ATFI	.	.	.	.	.	.	.	.	.	.	.	.	.	.	.	.	.	.	.	.	.	.	.	.	.	.	.	.	.	.	.	0.3
Release	.	.	.	.	.	.	.	.	.	.	.	.	.	.	.	.	.	.	.	.	.	.	.	.	.	.	.	.	.	.	.	0.3
BESP	.	.	.	.	.	.	.	.	.	.	.	.	.	.	.	.	.	.	.	0.8	1.5	1.0	2.8	5.1	.	.	.	.	.	.	.	0.2
No release	.	.	0.6	.	.	.	.	.	.	.	.	.	.	.	.	.	.	.	.	0.8	1.5	1.0	2.6	4.8	.	.	.	.	.	.	.	0.2
Release	.	.	0.6	.	.	.	.	.	.	.	.	.	.	.	.	.	.	.	.	.	.	.	0.2	0.3	.	.	.	.	.	.	.	.
CISP	.	.	.	.	0.2	2.3	.	1.0	.	.	.	2.9	2.6	4.5	1.6	1.5	.	.	.	.	.	.	0.6	1.5	.	.	.	.	.	1.9	.	.
No release	.	.	.	.	.	0.2	0.2	0.4	.	.	.	1.4	1.0	3.1	.	2.6	.	.	.	.	.	.	0.6	.	.	.	.	.	.	.	0.3	.
Release	.	.	.	.	0.2	2.1	0.2	0.5	.	.	.	1.6	1.6	1.4	.	1.5	.	.	.	.	.	.	.	1.5	.	.	.	.	.	.	1.6	.
COCO	.	.	.	.	.	.	.	.	0.9	.	.	.	.	.	.	.	.	.	.	.	.	.	.	.	.	.	.	.	.	.	.	.
Release	.	.	.	.	.	.	.	.	0.9	.	.	.	.	.	.	.	.	.	.	.	.	.	.	.	.	.	.	.	.	.	.	.
DIFO	.	.	.	.	.	.	0.6	1.0	1.3	.	0.1	.	.	.	0.7	4.4	.	.	6.1	0.9	.	.	.	.	.	.	.	.	.	0.2	0.2	3.6
No release	.	.	.	.	.	.	0.6	0.7	1.3	.	0.1	.	.	.	0.5	2.6	.	.	0.3	0.5	.	.	.	.	.	.	.	.	.	0.2	0.2	1.1
Release	.	.	.	.	.	.	.	0.4	.	.	.	.	.	.	0.2	1.8	.	.	5.8	0.4	.	.	.	.	.	.	.	.	.	.	0.2	2.4
DIPU	.	.	4.3	7.5	6.4	20.8	6.9	23.8	.	.	11.8	17.6	6.4	32.2	14.3	17.9	.	.	.	1.8	1.2	24.5	14.4	18.0	.	.	.	7.6	10.5	48.5	17.2	12.2
No release	.	.	2.0	3.2	5.5	6.1	3.5	17.7	.	.	0.4	7.2	5.4	8.5	2.6	1.8	.	.	.	0.1	0.3	2.8	3.7	4.3	.	.	.	5.5	7.2	14.6	5.4	4.5
Release	.	.	2.3	4.3	0.9	14.7	3.4	6.1	.	.	11.5	10.4	1.0	23.8	11.7	16.1	.	.	.	1.7	0.9	21.8	10.7	13.8	.	.	.	2.1	3.3	33.9	11.8	7.8
EPSP	.	.	0.6	.	.	0.4	0.2	.	.	.	2.2	0.8	0.7	1.7	.	.	.	.	.	0.2	0.7	.	.	.	.	.	11.3	0.8	3.8	1.2	0.9	.
No release	.	.	0.6	.	.	.	0.2	.	.	.	2.1	0.7	0.2	0.2	.	.	.	.	0.6	0.2	0.3	.	.	.	.	.	6.7	0.8	2.7	1.1	0.2	.
Release	.	.	.	.	.	0.4	0.2	.	.	.	0.2	0.1	0.6	1.5	.	.	.	.	0.6	0.2	0.4	.	.	.	.	.	4.6	.	1.1	0.2	0.7	.
GASH	.	.	.	.	0.2	.	.	.	.	.	.	.	.	.	.	.	2.0	5.6	2.1	5.4	9.0	9.5	24.5	27.0	.	.	.	.	.	.	.	.
No release	.	.	.	.	.	.	.	.	.	.	.	.	.	.	.	.	2.0	5.6	1.6	5.0	9.0	9.2	24.5	25.3	.	.	.	.	.	.	.	.
Release	.	.	.	.	0.2	.	.	.	.	.	.	.	.	.	.	.	.	0.1	0.4	0.4	.	0.3	.	1.7	.	.	.	.	.	.	.	.
GRSP	29.4	22.6	76.2	31.7	21.0	11.6	15.4	29.4	8.5	4.12	30.2	107.8	88.7	87.4	51.3	34.8	20.6	27.8	76.8	51.2	37.9	23.2	24.4	5.9	9.9	0.6	19.2	109.4	91.9	40.8	62.8	47.8
No release	14.7	9.9	33.3	12.3	12.6	6.9	10.3	19.0	4.8	.	4.3	69.2	53.8	38.2	13.7	2.7	17.2	22.0	48.8	33.6	24.0	20.1	12.7	4.0	.	0.6	18.2	75.2	57.6	20.8	25.5	20.5
Release	14.7	12.7	42.9	19.4	8.4	4.7	5.1	10.4	3.8	4.12	25.9	38.6	34.9	49.3	37.6	32.0	3.4	5.8	28.0	17.6	13.9	3.1	11.7	1.9	9.9	0.6	1.1	34.2	34.3	20.0	37.3	27.3
HEMI	3.2	4.1	7.6	7.5	12.6	31.6	56.3	33.2	8.5	1.6	9.9	10.6	25.0	33.6	33.0	24.4	0.7	4.4	5.9	19.8	15.2	27.8	49.7	71.4	.	0.5	14.2	28.0	23.6	35.2	85.5	67.2
No release	2.7	3.0	4.6	0.7	2.8	8.7	12.2	19.8	5.6	.	7.5	8.2	11.3	18.8	22.7	11.2	.	.	0.2	1.8	5.9	7.2	18.7	15.7	.	.	5.2	7.8	8.1	19.4	52.0	40.6
Release	0.5	1.1	3.0	6.8	9.8	23.0	44.0	13.3	3.0	1.6	2.4	2.4	13.7	14.8	10.3	13.2	0.7	4.4	5.7	18.1	9.3	20.6	31.0	55.7	.	0.5	9.0	20.2	15.5	15.8	33.5	26.6
HODI	.	.	.	.	.	.	.	.	0.4	0.44	.	1.8	.	.	.	0.2	.	.	.	.	.	.	0.2	0.2	.	.	.	.	.	0.7	2.2	2.3
No release	.	.	.	.	.	.	.	.	.	.	.	.	.	.	.	.	.	.	.	.	.	.	0.2	0.2	.	.	.	.	.	0.7	2.2	2.3
Release	.	.	.	.	.	.	.	.	0.4	0.44	.	1.8	.	0.3	.	0.2	.	.	.	.	.	0.3	.	.	.	.	.	.	0.1	.	.	.

115

Table 38—Percentage of total cover for species found on line transects by site, examination, site preparation, and release treatments (continued)

Site preparation and examination

Site species and release	Control								Burn								Spray								Spray and burn							
	0	1	2	3	4	5	6	7	0	1	2	3	4	5	6	7	0	1	2	3	4	5	6	7	0	1	2	3	4	5	6	7
Randall (continued):																																
LOSP	15.6							15.3								0.4								2.6								2.9
No release	12.9							0.4								0.4								2.6								2.9
Release	2.7							14.9																								
MOSP		9.8	20.6					1.2	53.8	1.76	10.7		0.2				0.1				0.1		0.5	0.6	0.8		13.6	0.4				
No release		7.8	18.1				0.2	2.0	21.2		7.8												0.5	0.5	0.6		3.8	0.4				
Release		1.9	2.4				1.0	0.7	32.6	1.76	3.0		0.2				0.1				0.1			0.6	0.2		9.8					
No vegetation			17.1	14.2	17.6	4.8	0.6	3.4			25.6	10.4	8.8	3.5	2.6	0.1			18.6	20.2	26.3	21.5	2.6	3.7			40.0	11.8	12.0	15.9	2.9	2.3
No release			12.3	2.7	0.6	0.5	0.2	1.2			12.8	5.6	1.1	2.0	0.4				8.4	6.1	6.4	14.8	1.0	1.9			26.3	7.4	4.0	10.4	1.4	0.8
Release			4.8	11.5	17.0	4.3	0.4	2.2			12.8	4.7	7.7	1.4	2.2	0.1			10.1	14.1	19.9	6.7	1.6	1.8			13.8	4.4	8.0	5.4	1.6	1.6
POMU	7.6	4.9	0.8	2.2	7.4	9.0	6.8	17.1	14.3	1.68	7.6	9.7	20.3	20.7	30.7	49.7	11.4	12.4	14.6	23.0	31.2	27.2	39.0	55.1	23.5	1.7	12.0	16.7	20.6	27.9	33.7	50.6
No release	7.6	4.9	0.8	2.2	7.4	8.4	5.6	15.1	13.3		6.1	8.2	19.2	19.3	25.6	33.3	3.1	5.2	4.8	5.0	6.8	4.6	3.6	10.6	8.9		10.6	15.0	18.3	22.4	26.9	34.2
Release						0.6	1.2	2.0	1.0	1.68	1.5	1.5	1.1	5.0	5.0	16.4	8.3	7.2	9.8	17.9	24.4	22.6	35.4	44.6	14.6	1.7	1.4	1.8	2.2	2.5	6.8	16.3
PRSP					0.2	0.5	0.2						0.6	0.7	0.4	1.5													1.1	1.6	2.8	2.7
No release					0.2		0.2						0.4	0.7	0.4	1.5													0.4	0.7	1.1	0.3
Release						0.5							0.1																0.7	0.9	1.8	2.4
PSME			0.1		3.4	6.1	15.7	32.5			0.5	1.4	3.1	9.6	54.6	92.6				0.6	2.3	5.7	25.7	60.8			0.1	2.0	5.9	18.2	63.5	101
No release					1.7	3.0	7.8	13.0			0.5	1.4	2.6	8.4	34.6	45.5				0.3	1.9	4.0	14.8	26.7				1.4	3.1	4.4	24.2	40.0
Release			0.1		1.6	3.1	7.9	19.5					0.5	1.2	20.0	47.1				0.2	0.4	1.7	10.9	34.1			0.1	0.6	2.8	13.8	39.2	60.6
PTAQ	83.7	47.8	86.4	144.0	131.4	121.1	93.4	73.9	5.7		11.6	22.9	13.2	14.1	12.4	9.3	51.7	50.2	76.2	128.6	103.2	80.0	92.4	63.3	4.1		1.2	5.5	1.8	3.2	6.3	4.6
No release	37.0	21.3	44.2	83.6	84.2	75.7	48.1	36.2	5.7		11.6	22.8	12.7	14.1	12.2	9.3	40.4	36.4	48.9	79.6	72.4	46.7	59.4	40.2	4.1		1.2	5.2	1.8	3.2	6.3	4.2
Release	46.7	26.5	42.2	60.4	47.2	45.4	45.3	37.7				0.1	0.4		0.2		11.3	13.8	27.4	49.0	30.8	33.3	33.0	23.2				0.3				0.3
RISA																															0.3	1.2
Release																															0.3	1.2
ROGY					0.6	0.8	3.0	1.4																								
No release					0.6	0.8	3.0	1.4																								
RULE																																
No release															1.7	1.7														0.2		
Release																														0.2		
RUPA			3.0	15.0	15.8	25.6	34.4	32.1	0.5		0.8	4.3	8.7	18.4	35.5	46.8	0.5			5.0	6.9	12.5	32.3	40.9			0.2	9.8	15.2	22.2	60.4	83.9
No release			2.0	7.6	11.9	9.6	15.7	13.1				2.2	8.0	16.3	31.0	28.5				2.8	4.4	5.6	15.4	19.6			0.2	4.4	11.4	14.4	35.3	55.2
Release			1.0	7.4	3.9	16.1	18.6	19.0	0.5		0.8	2.1	0.7	2.1	4.5	18.3	0.5			2.1	2.5	7.0	16.9	21.3			0.1	5.4	3.8	7.8	25.1	28.7
RUSP	0.5	0.3			0.8	1.0	3.2	2.8	24.9	13.2	26.4	48.8	26.0	37.9	61.3	68.9		0.1		0.5		0.4	1.8	0.8			5.7	20.8	16.2	7.2	26.3	50.6
No release		0.3			0.8	1.0	3.1	2.3	1.6		2.0	6.8	5.2	11.0	16.7	20.7						0.2	0.8	0.2			0.1	0.4	1.2	2.2	6.3	15.6
Release	0.5						0.1	0.5	23.3	13.2	24.3	42.0	20.8	26.9	44.6	48.2		0.1		0.5		0.2	1.0	0.5			5.6	20.4	15.0	4.9	20.0	34.9
RUVI	3.5	4.4	14.3	29.5	28.2	48.4	60.2	70.9	0.1		4.0	4.2	5.4	6.4	13.8	17.1			0.3	1.0	4.4	5.3	13.7	26.7				0.5	0.6	3.5	12.8	16.8
No release	0.3	0.5	4.8	16.0	14.9	22.1	25.2	29.6	0.1		0.8	3.9	4.9	4.7	12.0	13.0				1.0	3.8	3.8	11.0	17.1				0.2	0.5	1.8	3.9	6.2
Release	3.2	3.9	9.5	13.5	13.3	26.3	35.0	41.2			3.2	0.3	0.6	1.7	1.8	4.2			0.3		0.6	1.6	2.7	9.6				0.4	0.5	1.7	8.9	10.6
SASP	8.5							15.6	8.5	3.24	1.8	8.4	5.3	8.2	27.4	15.6					0.4		1.1				0.2	2.9	1.1	0.4	1.8	3.9
No release	2.9							4.0	2.9			1.1	1.6	2.1	6.2	4.0												0.5		0.2	1.0	3.3
Release	5.6							11.6	5.6	3.24	1.8	7.3	3.7	6.2	21.2	11.6					0.4		1.1				0.2	2.4	1.1	0.2	0.8	0.6

Table 38—Percentage of total cover for species found on line transects by site, examination, site preparation, and release treatments (continued)

Site species and release	Control 0	1	2	3	4	5	6	7	Burn 0	1	2	3	4	5	6	7	Spray 0	1	2	3	4	5	6	7	Spray and burn 0	1	2	3	4	5	6	7
Randall (continued):																																
SESP	8.4	10.8	10.9	.	0.4	.	.	1.0	10.0	8.2	62.4	0.6	10.4	12.7	7.5	4.6	.	.	2.4	0.2	0.9	.	0.8	0.1	2.9	1.2	56.0	2.0	15.8	17.1	12.4	0.2
No release	3.5	2.4	9.3	.	0.1	.	.	0.7	2.5	.	47.0	0.6	3.6	11.1	1.5	0.6	.	.	.	0.0	0.2	.	0.8	0.1	.	.	17.2	1.6	3.2	8.4	4.6	0.2
Release	4.9	8.4	1.6	.	0.3	.	.	0.3	7.5	8.2	15.3	.	6.8	1.6	6.0	4.0	.	.	2.4	0.2	0.7	.	.	.	2.9	1.2	38.7	0.4	12.6	8.7	7.8	.
Slash	49.5	67.3	17.7	14.2	15.1	18.2	4.1	2.6	62.0	38.19	9.6	12.8	11.2	12.5	3.3	.	25.8	50.7	4.9	2.5	5.2	7.4	4.6	.	53.2	34.3	9.5	12.6	10.1	24.4	1.1	1.8
No release	36.9	36.8	10.5	3.5	2.2	9.6	1.6	2.6	39.7	17.25	2.2	3.0	1.9	2.4	0.8	.	10.5	22.0	1.6	0.6	0.3	1.8	.	.	21.9	17.1	5.2	4.7	3.8	5.5	0.3	0.2
Release	12.6	30.5	7.2	10.7	12.9	8.6	2.5	.	22.3	20.94	7.4	9.8	9.3	10.1	2.6	.	15.3	28.6	3.2	1.9	4.8	5.6	4.6	.	31.3	17.2	4.3	7.9	6.3	18.9	0.8	1.6
SYAL	.	.	.	.	.	.	.	0.3																								
No release	.	.	.	.	.	.	.	0.3																								
TSHE	.	.	0.2	0.2	1.1	1.4	3.5	19.1	.	.	.	.	.	.	.	0.2	.	.	.	.	0.6	6.6	21.4	36.6	.	.	.	.	.	.	.	7.7
No release	.	.	.	.	0.3	0.8	1.8	11.0									.	.	.	.	0.2	0.3	1.0	1.5	.	.	.	.	.	.	2.0	0.5
Release	.	.	0.2	.	0.8	0.6	1.7	8.2	.	.	.	.	.	.	.	0.2	.	.	.	.	0.5	6.3	20.4	35.1	.	.	.	.	.	.	2.0	7.2
VAOV																									.	.	.	.	.	0.1	.	.
No release																									.	.	.	.	.	0.1	.	.
VAPA	.	.	.	0.3	0.8	0.6	0.3	0.2	0.2	.	.	.	.	.	.	0.4	.	0.1	.	0.3	0.4	0.6	2.1	0.6	.	.	0.2	0.2	0.6	0.8	.	1.4
No release	.	.	.	0.3	0.8	0.6	0.3	.	0.2	.	.	.	.	.	.	.	.	0.1	.	0.3	0.4	0.4	0.4	0.4	.	.	0.2	0.2	0.6	0.8	.	1.4
Release	.	.	.	0.3	.	.	.	0.2	.	.	.	.	.	.	.	0.4	.	.	.	.	.	0.2	1.7	0.3								
Total	201	172	260	272	279	336	360	440	206	76	218	268	238	327	402	488	112	152	213	263	249	265	388	499	163	44	194	240	237	284	417	496

Header spanning all treatment groups: Site preparation and examination

Table 38—Percentage of total cover for species found on line transects by site, examination, site preparation, and release treatments (continued)

Site preparation and examination

Site species and release	Control								Burn								Spray								Spray and burn							
	0	1	2	3	4	5	6	7	0	1	2	3	4	5	6	7	0	1	2	3	4	5	6	7	0	1	2	3	4	5	6	7
Poposchultz:																																
ACCI	3.6	3.0	6.0	11.3	13.4	11.5	12.1	16.3	5.2			2.1	1.8	2.1	2.7	2.8									3.4		1.6	1.8	1.3	1.2	1.5	1.3
No release	2.1	0.8	2.3	2.3	5.4	5.2	6.3	8.1	1.0			2.1	1.8	2.1	2.7	2.8									1.0							
Release	1.5	2.2	3.7	9.0	8.0	6.3	5.8	8.2	4.2																2.4		1.6	1.8	1.3	1.2	1.5	1.3
ACMA															3.6	4.9																
Release															3.6	4.9																
ALRU	0.8	6.5			1.1	13.7	34.4	42.6		6.5	19.0	20.0	20.0	20.0	20.0	2.2														0.9	2.9	6.4
No release	0.8				0.5	10.6	25.9	26.4		6.5	19.0	20.0	20.0	20.0	20.0	2.2														0.9	2.9	6.4
Release		6.5			0.6	3.1	8.6	16.2																								
BAPI					0.1	0.5	1.1	2.0						2.5	2.8	1.9					0.3	1.0	1.2	0.1								2.9
No release														2.5	2.8	1.9								0.1								2.9
Release					0.1	0.5	1.1	2.0													0.3	1.0	1.2									
CISP			0.6	0.4	0.3							0.6	1.0	1.4	0.8	1.0															0.0	0.2
No release			0.6									0.6	0.5	0.8	0.8	0.6															0.0	0.2
Release				0.4	0.3								0.5	0.6		0.4																
DIFO											0.2																					
Release											0.2																					
DIPU				1.8		2.2	0.6	2.6				2.4	2.7	4.3	0.9	2.5				2.6	0.8	9.2	4.0	14.0				2.1	1.1	6.4	2.4	5.5
No release				1.7		0.6	0.3	0.2				0.8	2.7	4.3		0.6				2.6	0.6	6.2	1.4	7.9				0.1	0.6	1.3	0.9	3.5
Release				0.1		1.6	0.3	2.4				1.7			0.9	1.9					0.2	2.9	2.5	6.1				2.0	0.5	5.1	1.5	2.0
EPSP	32.6	20.7	64.8	1.8	0.1	0.2	0.2	2.6		0.1	66.4	18.2		0.3			1.1	1.0	23.8	0.9		0.6			1.1		95.0	10.6	0.2	0.6		
No release	13.8	7.0	31.3	1.7	0.1	0.2	0.3	0.2			31.2	3.4		0.3				1.0	11.3			0.6					39.1	0.9	0.1	0.6		
Release	18.8	13.7	33.5	0.1	0.1	0.2	0.3	2.4		0.1	35.2	14.8					1.1		12.5	0.9					1.1		55.9	9.7	0.1			
GASH	18.6	13.8	12.1	64.8	75.6	90.7	116	102	0.9	1.4	0.2	0.9	2.1	3.9	8.9	17.6	0.9	1.4		3.0	3.7	18.7	31.6	45.0	0.2			0.6	0.8	4.9	13.1	27.2
No release	11.2	8.6	8.3	44.2	46.0	54.3	64.5	66.2	0.2	0.3	0.2	0.9	2.1	3.9	8.4	17.2	0.2	0.3		3.0	2.7	17.0	26.8	36.3	0.2			0.6	0.8	4.9	0.5	1.5
Release	7.4	5.3	3.8	20.6	29.6	36.4	51.1	35.8	0.7	1.1					0.5	0.4	0.7	1.1			1.0	1.7	4.8	8.7							12.6	25.8
GRSP	19.4	6.7	19.0		14.2	3.4	3.8	0.4		6.7	39.6	165.6	170.7	65.5	168.0	54.2	0.7	1.1	8.3	31.9	30.2	23.1	41.3	9.6	0.7	1.1	1.7	136.3	144.8	41.4	126.4	39.0
No release	2.0		8.2		10.0	0.3	0.1	0.1			14.2	88.4	83.1	38.3	84.0	26.8	0.0	0.3	0.2	4.2	9.6	10.6	23.3	8.5	0.0	0.3	1.7	88.8	84.8	23.6	75.0	11.9
Release	17.3	6.7	10.8		4.2	3.0	3.7	0.4		6.7	25.4	77.2	87.6	27.2	84.0	27.5	0.7	0.8	8.1	27.8	20.6	12.5	18.0	1.1	0.7	0.8		47.5	60.0	17.8	51.4	27.1
HEMI	1.0		4.2	17.5	14.1	31.4	24.9	7.7				9.6	17.8	71.9	27.3	18.2	0.7			0.1	2.7	12.3	10.3	8.8	0.7			0.2	16.2	107	43.0	12.1
No release			2.1	10.0	4.4	12.3	9.2	1.6				5.2	7.4	35.1	15.3	9.4	0.3			0.1	2.0	5.6	5.7	4.8	0.3				7.3	50.4	21.8	3.8
Release	1.0		2.1	7.5	9.8	19.0	15.7	6.1				4.4	10.4	36.8	12.0	8.8	0.4				0.7	6.7	4.6	4.0	0.4			0.2	8.9	57.0	21.2	8.3
HODI				0.1		0.8	0.6	1.2																								
No release							0.2	0.4																								
Release				0.1		0.8	0.4	0.8																								
LIDE				0.3																												
Release				0.3																												
LOSP							1.0	4.4																0.9							2.0	1.2
No release							0.8	0.5																0.8							1.6	0.7
Release							0.2	3.9																0.1							0.4	0.5
MEFE				0.1																												
No release				0.1																												

Table 38—Percentage of total cover for species found on line transects by site, examination, site preparation, and release treatments (continued)

Poposchultz (continued):

Site species and release	Control 0	1	2	3	4	5	6	7	Burn 0	1	2	3	4	5	6	7	Spray 0	1	2	3	4	5	6	7	Spray and burn 0	1	2	3	4	5	6	7
MOSP	·	·	·	·	·	·	·	·	45.3		2.8						14.1	0.4							48.9		0.8					
No release	·	·	·	·	·	·	·	·	30.8		1.6						14.1	0.4							35.9		0.8					
Release	·	·	·	·	·	·	·	·	14.5		1.2						14.1								13.0							
No vegetation			27.2	13.6	5.2	2.2	1.8	2.2			38.4	2.8	1.8	1.5		0.7			19.0	12.1	9.7	8.6	1.1				65.5	5.4	4.0	0.4	0.9	0.4
No release			15.0	6.8	2.0	1.3	1.0	1.3			24.4	1.5	1.8	1.2		0.7			12.6	8.4	9.3	8.4	1.1				41.5	1.3	0.4	0.4		0.2
Release			12.2	6.8	3.2	0.9	0.8	0.9			14.0	1.3		0.3					6.4	3.7	0.4	0.2					24.0	4.2	3.6		0.9	0.1
POMU	18.2	11.5	13.0	22.5	31.2	31.1	26.9	42.4	16.1	15.8	1.6	4.9	4.4	7.2	15.4	23.2	10.0	15.8	11.4	22.1	26.4	30.5	39.4	54.2	11.1		2.8	2.2	0.6	1.6	7.4	16.3
No release	11.0	8.5	7.1	14.8	18.9	19.6	15.6	25.4	7.0	9.1	1.0	2.2	2.0	1.9	2.6	5.8	1.4	9.1	6.0	12.1	10.2	12.4	15.9	24.2	5.0		1.2	0.4	0.6	0.6	3.4	8.0
Release	7.2	3.0	5.8	7.7	12.3	11.5	11.3	17.0	9.0	6.7	0.6	2.7	2.3	5.4	12.8	17.4	8.6	6.7	5.4	10.0	16.1	18.1	23.5	30.0	6.1		1.6	1.9	0.4	1.0	4.0	8.3
PRSP																																
No release								0.1				0.8	0.2	0.8	1.0	0.2													0.1	0.2	0.3	
Release								0.1				0.8	0.2	0.5	1.0	0.2													0.1	0.2	0.3	
PSME			0.3	1.3	2.7	8.5	22.4	41.9				1.0	1.8	25.0	90.4	148				3.4	2.5	13.9	30.2	60.4				0.7	5.7	17.7	87.3	128
No release			0.3	1.0	1.9	5.6	12.2	13.7				1.0	1.8	13.8	38.4	82.1				0.5	1.8	7.2	14.2	30.9				0.2	4.5	13.2	52.8	66.7
Release				0.3	0.8	2.9	10.2	28.2						11.1	52.0	66.4				2.9	0.7	6.7	16.0	29.5				0.5	1.2	4.5	34.4	61.7
PTAQ	5.0	9.8	15.6	38.2	30.0	18.6	18.3	5.7	0.2			1.2	1.1	3.1	11.8	9.8	6.7	13.1	17.8	61.6	38.6	19.8	8.5	1.1	6.2		11.1	26.7	26.0	16.5	15.3	5.3
No release	3.5	5.2	9.0	28.5	22.2	14.3	15.9		0.2			0.8	0.5	2.3	9.9	7.8	4.9	10.3	14.0	37.4	26.5	10.6	5.4	1.1			2.4	7.6	11.7	13.7	9.2	3.5
Release	1.5	4.6	6.5	9.6	7.8	4.4	2.4	5.7	0.1			0.3	0.6	0.8	1.8	2.0	1.8	2.8	3.8	24.3	12.1	9.2	3.0		6.2		8.7	19.1	14.2	2.8	6.1	1.8
RHMA				0.9	1.7	2.2	2.2	3.5															1.1	2.4								
Release				0.9	1.7	2.2	2.2	3.5															1.1	2.4								
RHPU				1.3		2.0	0.3	9.4	5.8													0.2										
No release								1.3	2.7																							
Release				1.3	0.3	2.0	0.3	8.2	3.2													0.2										
RIBR						0.3	0.2																									
No release						0.3	0.2																									
RULA								1.1							0.5																	
No release								1.1							0.5																	
RULE									0.1	0.3																						
No release									0.1	0.3																						
RUPA			0.9	6.1	6.8	8.2	14.6	12.3	0.2			1.8	1.8	3.4	8.7	7.4						0.7	0.5	2.0				1.3	0.5	1.6	2.4	2.8
No release				3.4	5.0	2.7	5.2	5.2				0.2	0.5	1.9	4.8	5.3								0.3				0.7	0.3	1.0	2.2	2.5
Release			0.9	2.8	1.8	5.4	9.4	7.1	0.2			1.6	1.2	1.5	4.0	2.1						0.7	0.5	1.6				0.6	0.2	0.6	0.2	0.2
RUPR						1.0		2.0							6.3	1.3	0.8							12.7								
No release						0.7		0.8							5.0	1.3	0.7							9.9								
Release						0.2		1.2							1.4		0.1	0.0						2.8	0.3							
RUSP	6.5	15.8	24.1	35.3	22.5	10.7	7.6	11.8	38.9		3.2	14.3	9.6	20.5	40.6	75.2	61.6	37.2	85.0	86.8	49.2	59.1	100.6	112.7	86.9		17.9	37.4	24.2	35.3	57.6	76.5
No release	3.3	8.2	8.2	12.7	5.0	5.8	3.5	4.9	22.7		1.0	7.6	3.6	14.2	28.5	40.6	23.7	14.4	37.6	32.0	18.4	14.4	30.0	46.8	56.2		10.8	20.2	14.2	20.7	37.8	51.1
Release	3.2	7.5	16.0	22.6	13.2	4.9	4.0	6.9	16.2		2.2	6.7	6.0	6.4	12.1	34.7	37.9	22.8	47.4	54.8	30.9	44.8	70.6	65.9	30.7		7.1	17.2	10.0	14.6	19.8	25.4
RUVI	19.1	12.1	5.6	35.9	23.4	26.0	34.7	44.0	1.4	0.3	0.7	4.0	4.2	14.8	33.2	35.8	0.8		2.2	10.8	14.1	36.1	68.5	65.4			4.5	11.6	13.8	11.8	44.1	51.8
No release	5.1	2.5	1.8	14.2	9.8	8.1	14.3	17.2	1.3		0.4	1.5	3.4	7.5	17.6	20.8	0.7	0.1	0.6	6.3	8.8	21.1	46.8	37.7			1.1	1.0	3.7	3.1	10.2	11.6
Release	14.0	9.6	3.9	21.6	13.6	17.9	20.4	26.8	0.2	0.3	0.4	2.6	0.8	7.2	15.6	15.0	0.1	0.0	1.6	4.4	5.3	15.0	21.7	27.7	0.3		3.4	10.6	10.1	8.8	33.8	40.2

Table 38—Percentage of total cover for species found on line transects by site, examination, site preparation, and release treatments (continued)

Site species and release	Control								Burn								Spray								Spray and burn							
	0	1	2	3	4	5	6	7	0	1	2	3	4	5	6	7	0	1	2	3	4	5	6	7	0	1	2	3	4	5	6	7
Poposchultz (continued):																																
SASP	.	0.6	0.2	0.2	.	1.0	0.1	0.4	0.7	.	.	0.1	0.2	.	0.8	3.1	2.5	5.0	5.6	11.0	11.8	12.4	8.5	15.9	3.2	.	3.5	4.1	3.2	2.0	2.8	5.6
No release	.	.	.	.	.	.	0.1	.	0.6	.	.	.	.	.	.	.	.	2.6	3.3	7.8	7.9	4.2	3.4	5.3	1.5	.	3.5	4.1	3.2	2.0	2.8	5.6
Release	.	0.6	0.2	0.2	.	1.0	.	0.4	0.1	.	.	0.1	0.2	.	0.8	3.1	2.5	2.4	2.4	3.2	3.8	8.1	5.1	10.6	1.7	.	.	.	.	.	.	.
SESP	7.7	1.3	.	3.2	11.4	7.3	.	.	55.9	.	8.2	6.1	20.4	41.9	.	9.8	10.2	1.2	5.5	14.6	54.2	37.4	.	1.4	5.9	.	0.2	13.6	28.5	19.4	0.3	6.8
No release	7.7	0.3	.	0.5	1.8	1.1	.	.	33.5	.	7.8	3.7	9.8	9.5	.	4.6	9.5	1.2	3.1	5.9	23.3	14.8	.	0.6	3.5	.	0.2	6.4	17.1	8.0	.	3.9
Release	.	1.0	.	2.7	9.6	6.2	.	.	22.3	.	0.3	2.4	10.6	32.4	.	5.2	0.7	.	2.4	8.8	30.9	22.7	.	0.8	2.4	.	.	7.2	11.4	11.5	0.3	2.9
Slash	40.6	40.1	24.0	17.1	13.4	17.3	3.6	0.9	116	40.9	17.5	26.4	16.7	25.8	10.6	.	76.6	60.3	22.5	17.6	20.5	22.0	0.7	0.4	129.3	33.5	15.2	18.1	17.7	17.5	3.9	0.3
No release	19.5	19.9	13.5	9.8	6.0	10.1	1.2	.	62.1	13.6	5.5	9.4	7.0	10.0	2.0	.	36.6	23.4	12.0	13.2	11.3	15.2	0.7	0.4	66.1	.	6.2	5.5	6.7	8.0	1.0	0.3
Release	21.1	20.2	10.6	7.3	7.4	7.2	2.4	0.9	54.2	27.4	12.0	16.9	9.7	15.8	8.6	.	40.0	36.9	10.5	4.4	9.2	6.8	.	.	63.2	33.5	9.0	12.6	11.0	9.5	2.8	.
TSHE	.	.	.	.	.	.	1.8	5.4	.	.	.	.	.	.	.	10.0	.	.	0.2	1.6	4.8	13.7	31.4	62.6	.	.	.	1.2	2.7	7.7	16.9	22.4
No release	.	.	.	.	.	.	.	.	.	.	.	.	.	.	.	.	.	.	0.2	0.3	1.1	3.1	10.6	25.9	.	.	.	0.9	2.0	7.7	16.7	22.4
Release	.	.	.	.	.	.	1.8	5.4	.	.	.	.	.	.	.	10.0	.	.	.	1.3	3.7	10.6	20.8	36.7	.	.	.	0.3	0.6	.	0.2	.
VAOV	3.0	4.3	1.0	.	15.3	19.8	26.2	35.4	1.0	.	.	.	.	0.8	2.4	5.1	3.0	1.4	0.6	3.3	6.4	4.7	6.5	13.8	6.8	.	1.8	.	.	2.2	3.6	10.2
No release	1.1	1.6	0.8	.	5.7	6.8	8.7	16.0	1.0	.	.	.	.	0.8	2.4	5.1	1.3	0.4	0.6	3.3	2.6	1.0	4.0	8.4	.	.	0.2	.	.	1.0	1.3	3.9
Release	1.9	2.7	0.2	.	9.6	13.0	17.5	19.4	.	.	.	.	.	.	.	.	1.7	1.0	.	.	3.8	3.7	2.5	5.4	6.8	.	1.6	.	.	1.1	2.3	6.2
VAPA	0.6	.	.	14.8	6.5	5.4	9.8	11.8	0.4	.	.	0.9	0.7	.	.	.	0.5	0.2	.	2.3	2.1	2.2	1.3	1.9	.	.	.	2.7	3.2	0.7	1.7	3.0
No release	.	.	.	6.0	3.0	3.3	7.0	9.0	.	.	.	0.9	0.7	.	.	.	0.5	0.2	.	0.5	2.1	2.2	1.3	1.8	.	.	.	0.8	0.8	.	.	.
Release	0.6	.	.	8.8	3.6	2.1	2.8	2.9	0.4	.	.	.	.	.	.	.	.	.	.	1.8	.	.	.	0.1	.	.	.	1.8	2.4	0.7	1.7	3.0
Total	157	133	200	306	289	316	365	410	322	54	204	284	279	317	457	439	187	138	202	286	278	326	387	485	305	34	223	278	295	298	436	425

120

Table 38—Percentage of total cover for species found on line transects by site, examination, site preparation, and release treatments (continued)

Site preparation and examination

Site species and release	Control 0	1	2	3	4	5	6	7	Burn 0	1	2	3	4	5	6	7	Spray 0	1	2	3	4	5	6	7	Spray and burn 0	1	2	3	4	5	6	7
Bay's Wolfe:																																
ACCI	18.8	11.6	31.1	30.4	25.6	22.4	33.6	38.8		4.7	2.9	2.4	2.8	5.2	10.2	11.8	11.3	8.4	20.9	21.5	23.6	12.6	27.8	31.8	3.1			1.1	1.2	1.8	4.1	2.4
No release	2.0	1.8	4.6	3.6	4.9	5.8	10.6	26.1		4.2	0.7	1.4	1.4	4.2	5.4	2.2	10.0	6.8	13.0	10.8	15.6	9.5	19.9	26.3	3.1			1.1	1.2	1.8	4.1	2.4
Release	16.8	9.8	26.4	26.8	20.7	16.6	23.0	12.7		0.5	2.2	0.9	1.4	1.0	4.7	9.6	1.3	1.6	7.9	10.7	8.0	3.1	7.9	5.5								
AFTI																																
Release																															0.2	0.2
ALRU				2.0	3.6	12.1	46.1	66.2			1.2	11.8	19.6	41.4	80.5	87.7	2.1			0.7	0.2	1.3	19.1	35.3	0.4		0.5	10.3	16.6	94.4	184.8	200.0
No release				1.4	2.4	9.2	27.2	22.3			1.2	6.0	11.1	20.9	33.8	32.6	2.1			0.7	0.2	0.8	17.8	24.6				1.6	8.4	43.2	88.0	100.0
Release				0.6	1.2	3.0	18.9	43.9				5.7	8.4	20.4	46.8	55.1					0.5	0.5	1.3	10.7			0.5	8.8	8.2	51.2	96.8	100.0
BESP																																
No release								0.6												0.8	1.5	2.0	0.8	2.0								
Release								0.6												0.8	1.5	2.0	0.8	1.8								
CISP	1.3	1.2		5.4	4.6	6.5	3.2												1.3	0.7			0.3					3.4	2.5	0.5		
No release						0.1													0.7	0.7			0.3					1.2	0.6	0.1		
Release	1.3	1.2		5.4	4.6	6.4	3.2												0.6									2.2	1.9	0.4		
COCO																							2.2	2.7				0.2				
No release																																
Release																							2.2	2.7				0.2				
DIFO								0.7										2.1						0.2								2.8
No release																		2.1														
Release								0.7										2.1						0.2								2.8
DIPU						0.2	0.3	2.0												1.4	0.5	2.4	5.0	15.7					0.2		0.4	
No release						0.2										0.1				1.4	0.5	1.2	1.8	9.8							0.1	
Release							0.3	2.0						0.2	0.7	0.3						1.2	3.2	5.9					0.2		0.3	
EPSP	0.8	11.4	1.2	8.4	6.0	1.3	0.4		0.5	7.8	2.2	7.4	7.3	2.4			0.9	10.2	2.2	6.4	7.2	0.4	1.8				0.4	2.3	8.8			
No release	0.8	4.8	1.0	6.2	2.4	0.7	0.1			2.8	0.2	1.9	2.6	1.8			0.9	6.4	1.4	4.1	1.8		0.3				0.2	0.5	0.8			
Release		6.7	0.1	2.2	3.6	0.6	0.3		0.5	4.9	2.0	5.4	4.7	0.6				3.8	0.8	2.3	5.4	0.4	1.5				0.1	1.8	8.0			
GASH								2.0																								
No release								0.1																								
Release								1.9																								
GRSP	15.6	24.9	44.6	50.2	54.2	15.3	38.2	20.6	12.6	35.7	45.4	38.1	34.2	15.8	7.5	5.2	10.8	22.9	41.5	36.0	27.6	27.9	54.4	36.8		0.2	4.2	32.6	78.0	24.7	6.0	1.5
No release	8.1	19.4	31.6	33.4	30.8	10.8	14.3	19.0	8.9	15.6	25.4	10.7	6.4	0.6	0.2	0.2	2.6	14.0	35.2	28.2	15.2	13.1	21.1	9.9			1.3	11.8	42.0	12.8	2.2	1.5
Release	7.5	5.6	13.0	16.8	23.5	4.5	23.9	1.6	3.7	20.1	20.0	27.4	27.8	15.1	7.3	5.0	8.2	8.9	6.4	7.8	12.4	14.8	33.3	26.9		0.2	3.0	20.9	36.0	11.9	3.9	
HEMI	51.3	12.0	85.2	36.8	37.3	34.3	41.0	57.4	34.5	6.2	55.5	43.0	32.0	35.7	31.4	25.8	21.4	13.6	54.4	36.2	32.1	27.0	48.1	51.0			12.2	17.0	28.5	26.2	17.2	25.6
No release	34.0	7.3	44.5	17.7	17.1	19.5	21.1	18.9	29.3	1.8	34.7	31.6	18.8	17.1	17.1	13.0	15.9	13.6	32.7	18.0	15.2	17.4	19.7	21.0			2.3	8.4	12.7	13.6	13.5	10.5
Release	17.3	4.8	40.8	19.1	20.2	14.8	19.9	38.5	5.2	4.3	24.0	8.3	13.2	18.6	14.3	12.8	5.5		21.7	18.1	16.9	9.5	28.4	30.0			10.0	8.6	15.8	12.5	3.7	15.1
HODI								0.1								0.1							1.7	0.6						1.1	1.8	3.4
No release																							1.7	0.6						1.1	1.4	3.4
Release								0.1						0.3		0.1															0.3	

121

Table 38—Percentage of total cover for species found on line transects by site, examination, site preparation, and release treatments (continued)

Bay's Wolfe (continued):

Site preparation and examination

Site species and release	Control								Burn								Spray								Spray and burn							
	0	1	2	3	4	5	6	7	0	1	2	3	4	5	6	7	0	1	2	3	4	5	6	7	0	1	2	3	4	5	6	7
LOSP																																
Release																							0.2	0.2								
LUSP																				0.8								2.9				
No release				0.2																0.2								0.2				
Release				0.2																0.6								2.7				
MEFE																																
No release						0.4	0.4	0.5					1.2	0.7	0.9	1.3						0.4						1.2				
Release							0.4	0.5					1.2	0.7	0.9	1.3						0.4						1.2				
MOSP	29.9		5.1						15.8	5.5	6.4						40.6	1.6	30.4	1.2	0.2				29.0		80.0	0.6				
No release	18.7		0.4		0.3				8.3		4.6						17.9	0.4	6.6						17.0		50.2					
Release	11.2		4.8		0.3				7.5	5.5	1.8						22.7	1.2	23.8	1.2	0.2				12.1		29.8	0.6				
No veg.	23.4	49.6	11.8	8.2	3.6	2.0	1.0		10.0	22.1	4.9	2.9	2.7		2.0		24.3	46.0	18.0	17.5	12.5	0.3	2.0		38.1	152.9	46.8	36.8	7.0			
No release	3.5	17.9	5.0	3.6	0.4	0.5			0.4	5.8	1.2		1.0		1.0		16.1	18.7	10.8	6.8	3.8	0.3	1.0		16.1	76.6	23.4	22.0	1.9			
Release	19.9	31.8	6.8	4.6	3.2	1.4	1.0		9.6	16.2	3.7	2.9	1.7		1.0		8.2	27.2	7.2	10.7	8.7		1.0		22.0	76.3	23.4	14.9	5.0			
PHMA																																
Release													0.2																			
PISI														0.4	1.3	2.4								0.2								
No release															0.1	0.4																
Release														0.4	1.2	2.0								0.2								
POMU	7.1	10.5	7.7	9.8	12.8	14.8	20.4	24.2	13.6	29.4	24.4	43.8	40.1	46.1	56.1	47.1	23.5	22.0	19.3	32.2	33.2	28.9	47.0	51.3	12.3		4.7	8.6	13.6	11.6	23.8	25.4
No release	5.8	7.2	4.9	6.8	10.3	7.5	10.8	12.6	11.5	18.7	15.5	29.2	24.8	26.5	31.3	23.8	13.9	8.4	8.1	11.4	12.0	16.5	27.4	24.7	9.9		2.6	3.0	7.7	8.4	12.4	15.7
Release	1.3	3.3	2.8	2.9	2.5	7.3	9.7	11.6	2.1	10.7	8.9	14.6	15.4	19.6	24.8	23.3	9.6	13.7	11.2	20.8	21.2	12.3	19.6	26.6	2.4		2.1	5.6	5.9	3.2	11.4	9.7
PRSP														0.3																		
Release								0.9						0.3																		
PSME				1.7	3.3	11.2	47.7	80.6			0.2	0.8	1.0	2.7	16.2	32.3		0.5	0.5	0.5		8.2	48.4	94.5			0.3	1.4	6.4	19.2	55.8	65.6
No release			0.3	0.2	0.4	4.5	16.2	53.3			0.2		0.5	0.9	2.2	10.3		0.5	0.3	0.5		5.4	21.6	44.0			0.2	0.4	0.8	4.3	21.0	26.4
Release			0.3	1.4	2.9	6.7	31.5	27.3				0.8	0.4	1.8	13.9	22.0			0.2			2.8	26.7	50.5			0.2	1.0	5.6	14.9	34.8	39.2
PTAQ			0.8	0.3	0.6			0.9								0.1				0.8	1.0						2.5	8.3	11.2	5.6	9.1	2.5
No release				0.2	0.6															0.7	1.0							3.3	4.4	1.2	2.6	1.7
Release			0.8	0.1				0.9								0.1				0.2							2.5	5.0	6.8	4.4	6.5	0.8
RHPU				0.2										0.5	0.3	3.3							0.4	3.7					0.1	0.4	1.8	4.5
No release				0.2										0.5	0.3								0.4	2.1						0.4	1.8	
Release																3.3								1.6					0.1			4.5
RIBR							0.4							0.7															0.1	0.4	1.8	4.5
No release							0.4							0.7																0.4	1.8	
Release																													0.1			4.5
RISP																0.1																
Release																0.1																

Site preparation and examination

Site species and release	C0	C1	C2	C3	C4	C5	C6	C7	B0	B1	B2	B3	B4	B5	B6	B7	S0	S1	S2	S3	S4	S5	S6	S7	SB0	SB1	SB2	SB3	SB4	SB5	SB6	SB7
Bay's Wolfe (continued):																																
RUPA		0.2	2.4	8.8	9.7	9.8	30.6	36.2	1.3		9.8	30.5	25.9	39.7	64.6	62.6		0.4	0.4	5.1	1.7	9.7	38.8	59.9			1.5	33.9	43.9	38.2	125.7	65.1
No release			1.7	5.4	6.2	6.4	20.0	13.8			3.2	12.5	15.2	12.2	20.7	18.5			0.4	3.1	1.7	4.7	23.2	32.8			0.6	16.2	28.4	27.9	78.4	51.0
Release	0.2	0.2	0.7	3.4	3.4	3.4	10.7	22.4	1.3		6.6	18.0	10.7	27.5	44.0	44.1		0.4		2.0		5.0	15.7	27.1			0.9	17.7	15.6	10.2	47.3	14.1
RUSP	30.8	20.7	47.8	67.5	50.3	75.8	107.2	118.2	50.6	11.3	76.2	92.2	89.0	99.8	144.2	134.2	13.3	17.5	33.9	56.4	29.5	45.4	79.1	74.8	3.2		3.2	0.2	0.2	0.3	1.6	8.2
No release	15.4	15.9	28.4	36.6	37.8	55.4	66.8	51.2	10.9	7.3	35.9	36.7	55.1	58.0	85.0	69.5	0.9	4.8	9.4	19.4	19.5	29.9	38.8	35.4	0.9		0.8	0.2	0.2	0.3	1.0	3.9
Release	15.4	4.8	19.4	30.8	12.5	20.4	40.4	67.0	39.7	4.0	40.3	55.5	33.8	41.7	59.3	64.7	12.4	12.8	24.5	36.9	10.0	15.5	40.3	39.4	2.3		2.4		0.1		0.6	4.3
RUVI					1.4	0.7	4.8	2.2		0.2		2.1	3.4	5.7	2.6	0.2				2.0	4.9	6.3	25.1	11.7			0.1	2.2	1.8	1.5	2.8	
No release					0.2	0.1	0.4	2.2					0.2		0.1					2.0	4.9	5.5	15.5	5.3			0.1	2.2	1.8	1.4	2.5	
Release					1.2	0.6	4.4			0.2		2.1	3.2	5.7	2.5	0.2				1.9		0.8	9.6	6.4					0.2	0.2	0.3	
SASP			4.4	8.4	6.9	2.4	10.2	13.9	9.9		8.7	8.3	10.4	7.7	18.6	31.9	0.7		2.2	7.2	5.2	1.3	1.3	1.4			6.4	24.6	14.6	2.4	9.4	19.8
No release			3.1	3.6	4.1		0.8	11.5	4.7		4.7	5.1	6.4	5.6	10.8	18.0	0.7		1.9	5.2	5.2	0.4	0.8	0.8			2.6	13.1	7.7	2.2	3.8	5.4
Release			1.2	4.7	2.8	2.4	9.4	2.4	5.2		4.0	3.2	4.1	2.2	7.8	13.9			0.3	1.9		0.8	0.5	0.6			3.8	11.5	7.0	0.3	5.6	14.4
SESP	20.4		5.0	13.6	41.6	67.5	4.2	0.5	32.9		4.6	3.3	12.0	8.8	0.3		7.6		17.3	29.4	61.6	84.6		0.6	0.8		10.5	16.1	17.1	80.2		
No release	11.5		2.2	3.7	21.2	28.3	3.4	0.5	5.2		0.8	0.3	1.8	1.8			5.5		9.0	18.1	32.6	32.2					4.8	11.2	4.6	34.6		
Release	8.9		2.9	9.9	20.4	39.2	0.8		27.7		3.8	3.0	10.1	7.0	0.3		2.1		8.3	11.4	29.0	52.4		0.6	0.8		5.7	4.9	12.5	45.6		0.6
Slash	23.1	54.8	33.0	22.0	27.0	17.5	5.7	19.8	46.0	77.9	31.7	32.2	24.2	11.7	2.3	22.2	38.3	59.2	36.8	18.8	18.1	8.8	1.4	10.3	85.4	44.9	37.1	29.9	18.8	26.0		11.9
No release	8.9	24.4	10.2	7.2	7.5	5.0	2.5	15.3	32.7	46.6	24.2	26.6	16.1	8.3	2.3	16.0	13.1	22.8	12.3	9.9	5.0	3.4	0.5	7.3	37.7	19.4	14.8	14.2	9.7	11.2		4.0
Release	14.2	30.3	22.7	14.8	19.5	12.5	3.2	4.5	13.3	31.2	7.6	5.6	8.1	3.4		6.2	25.2	36.4	24.5	8.9	13.0	5.5	0.9	3.0	47.8	25.5	22.3	15.8	9.0	14.8		7.9
TSHE			0.4	0.2	0.2	0.5	1.5	3.2				0.4	0.5	0.4	5.6	0.8			0.2	0.4	0.4		0.1	0.6							3.9	5.5
No release			0.4	0.2		0.5	1.5	0.3					0.5	0.4	2.9	0.4			0.1	0.4	0.4		0.1	0.6							0.7	2.1
Release								2.9				0.4			2.7	0.4			0.1												3.2	3.4
VAOV															0.1							0.2	0.0									
No release															0.1							0.2	0.0								0.0	
Release																																
VAPA	0.8		0.7	1.2	1.2	0.6	1.4	2.1	2.1		1.2	3.2	0.8	2.7	0.6	4.0	2.0		0.2	0.6	0.3	0.4	1.6	3.0			0.4	0.2		0.2		1.4
No release			0.6	0.5	0.8		1.4	2.0	2.1		1.2	3.2	0.8	2.7	0.6	4.0	1.7		0.2	0.6	0.1	0.4	0.4	1.3			0.4	0.2		0.2		1.4
Release	0.8		0.2	0.6	0.5	0.6		0.1									0.3				0.2		1.2	1.7								
Total	223	197	281	275	290	295	398	491	230	201	275	322	307	328	445	473	197	204	281	277	263	268	406	489	180	198	211	234	271	335	448	446

Column groups: C = Control, B = Burn, S = Spray, SB = Spray and burn; numbers 0–7 denote examinations.

www.ingramcontent.com/pod-product-compliance
Lightning Source LLC
Chambersburg PA
CBHW081218280526
45787CB00006B/2440